Compiled by
Chris Milner

Consultant editor
Nick Pigott

Design
Kelvin Clements, Tim Pipes, Justin Blackamore

Reprographics
Jonathan Schofield, Michael Baumber

Sub-editor
Nigel Devereux

Editorial Assistant
Sarah Wilkinson

Group production editor
Tim Hartley

Production manager
Craig Lamb

Publisher
Dan Savage

Commercial director
Nigel Hole

Business development director
Terry Clark

Managing director
Brian Hill

Chief executive
Ian Fisher

Published by
Mortons Media Group Ltd, Media Centre,
Morton Way, Horncastle, Lincolnshire LN9 6JR
Tel: 01507 529529
All material copyright
Mortons Media Limited, 2012.
All rights reserved.

The Railway Magazine address: as above

Printed by:
William Gibbons & Son, Wolverhampton

ISBN 978-1-906167-91-2

A *Railway Magazine* Publication

MEDIA GROUP LTD

THE RAILWAY MAGAZINE]

UP EXPRESS NEAR WELWYN GARDEN CITY, L.N.E.R.

Three-cylinder, 2-8-2 locomotive No. 2001, "   "

Contents

Above: The colour illustration
from the frontispiece of the
January 1935 issue of *The
Railway Magazine.*

Welcome to the best of

There won't be many subjects that have not been covered in *The Railway Magazine's* illustrious 115-year history from narrow gauge to broad gauge, from steam to gas turbine, from the unusual to the bizarre, it's probably been in *The RM* at some time or other.

After publishing more than 1,300 issues of *The RM*, we've embarked on a compilation of selected features that have appeared over the decades from the publication of the first issue in July 1897.

The Railway Magazine was launched by Joseph Lawrence and former railwayman Frank Cornwall, who believed that there would be an amateur enthusiast market for some of the material they were then publishing in a railway staff magazine - *The Railway Herald*. Former auctioneer George Augustus Nokes was appointed editor and wrote under the pseudonym G A Sekon. The first issue was a sellout, and Sekon quickly built the magazine's circulation to about 25,000.

The magazine also embarked on 'Illustrated Interviews' with senior railway officials, showing readers that the editor had his finger on the pulse of a burgeoning industry, where major locomotive builders were not only supplying British train companies, but also building for the rest of the world. As a result, readers were introduced to and educated about railway operations in far flung places including India, Argentina, North America and South Africa.

Being on good terms with the higher echelons of the railway industry has been one of the key aspects for the magazine's success, thus being able to report 'from the horse's mouth'. And that trait is still very much true today.

Over the years, as photography of trains increased in popularity, the pages of *The Railway Magazine* became the outlet for the work of photographers who, as a result, become very well-known names in railway enthusiast circles – cameramen such as H Gordon Tidey, W Leslie Good, Frank R Hebron, F E Mackay, O J Morris, Derek Cross, Maurice Earley and, of course, Bishop Eric Treacy. It was O J Morris who had the honour of having the first colour transparency reproduced in the December 1938 issue and that image is reprinted here.

The magazine also claims a record for the longest unbroken published series, begun in 1901 under the title British Locomotive Practice and Performance, characterised by detailed logs giving the timings of notable trips, recorded by observers with a stopwatch.

Its first writer was the New Zealand-born Charles Rous-Marten, who recorded the controversial *City of Truro*-hauled 'Ocean Mail' run, allegedly at 100mph, in 1904. Successive columnists have included former Great Eastern Railway engineer Cecil J Allen, O S Nock and Peter W Semmens.

In terms of front cover illustration, *The Railway Magazine* did, by and large, keep the same basic design for some 50 years and it wasn't until 1963 that a larger format with a colour cover was adopted.

Past issues from the turn of the century had included colour drawings or paintings as a frontispiece, but a colour photographic spread had to wait until the spring of 1975 – the rest of the publication being in black & white. That change gradually led to more colour pages for news photographs and

features, but even by the end of the 1980s, *The RM* contained no more than 16 pages of colour and it was still a few more years before every page could be in printed in colour.

For this reason, although we have remained faithful to the text, we have used a little journalistic licence to make this bookazine more attractive, and have replaced a few of the original black & white illustrations with similar colour versions of around that time. To add some variety, we have also included several new pictorial compilations based on the Panorama-style news galleries of the 1960s and 1970s.

With so many issues published, selecting material that readers will find interesting and varied has been both a challenging and rewarding task.

Just flicking through the pages has shown

The Railway Magazine

This illustration of 'Schools' class 4-4-0 No. 927 *Clifton*, about to leave Waterloo with the 12.30 to Bournemouth by O. J. Morris, was the first time a colour reproduction had been produced directly from Dufaycolour film, appearing in the December 1938 issue.

the phenomenal depth of railway history and subject matter covered, including the quirky. In many cases, one can see parallels with events today, or for example, how BR wasted time and money with ill-thought out schemes and projects that had no longevity.

Researching history can show how long major projects take to come to fruition. In 1994 the Channel Tunnel was opened, yet a 1913 issue of *The RM* shows that it was being talked about in Parliament then, a year before the First World War. Given the ongoing debate about HS2, I suspect there are a few of us wondering if we will see that scheme's fruition in our lifetime.

To our many loyal readers and subscribers, *The Railway Magazine* is viewed as an institution, a one-stop shop for all things railway. Back in 1897 pre-launch publicity for the first issue claimed that: "*The Railway Magazine* will aim at supplying the fullest, latest and most correct information on every branch of the service".

More than 115 years on, we like to think that we still provide the same service to our readers as our Victorian forefathers envisaged. Over the years, the magazine's editors have strived to make it a journal of record, and that's something that will continue.

While it's impossible to please all tastes in a publication such as this, hopefully this pot-pourri has a bit of something for everyone, and there is a possibility that additional volumes might be produced. If there are any features you would like to see reprinted in future volumes, please write to us at the address on page 3 or email us at railway@mortons.co.uk

My thanks are due to Morton's Media management for supporting the compilation idea, but particularly to design team leader Kelvin Clements and designers Tim Pipes, Justin Blackamore, Leanne Lawrence, reprographics technicians Jonathan Schofield and Mike Baumber and sub-editor Nigel Devereux, who have worked hard to turn around the pages in double-quick time. Special mention too for Sarah Wilkinson, who has done a sterling job scanning the text from the back issues, and to editor Nick Pigott for his encouragement and guidance.

I sincerely hope you enjoy this fascinating snapshot into our wonderful railway history.

Chris Milner
Horncastle, July 2012.

Wisbech station, Great Eastern Railway, showing the platform used by the Wisbech and Upwell trams.

The Wisbech and Upwell Tramway

By SCOTT DAMANT,
General Manager's Staff,
Great Eastern Railway

IF a history were written dealing with the railway enterprise as exhibited in this country during the last decade of the present century, the characteristic features of the years 1897, '98, and '99 would undoubtedly be the multiplication of schemes for the provision of light railways. For some years past it has been recognised that light railways constitute one of the most feasible means of benefiting rural districts situated away from the main lines of transit yet devised.

The chief difficulty in the way of providing light railways in the past has been the financial one. Obviously the districts where such lines would be a boon are poor, scantily populated, and devoted almost entirely to agriculture. Local landowners are, in such cases, seldom wealthy, and outside capitalists fight shy of providing the means wherewith to build a line between places they have never so much as heard of. A scheme for a light railway between Little Pudlington-in-the-Slush and Great Hogwell-in-the-Mire is of vast importance to the enlightened inhabitants of those idyllic spots; alas, it does not appeal so forcibly to the hard-headed man of means with a partiality for a

fair return in the way of interest on his investments generally.

Wherever there is a thriving manufactory. the rail has come to it or it has gone to the rail. The conveyance of the raw article to the

The Wisbech and Upwell Tramway is at best a judicious cross between the railway proper and an urban tramway

manufactory, and of the finished goods from it, pays the railway company well enough, but the rates for grain, roots, manure, and so forth, are now so universally low that the carriage of agricultural produce may be said to be probably the least remunerative of all railway goods traffic. Consequently railways

have become increasingly reluctant to extend their lines into purely rural districts, and our agriculturalists have suffered, although agriculture is, after all, still the staple industry of the country, engaging, as it does, far more of the population than any other.

In 1895 a practical step was taken towards removing the financial difficulty in the way of an extended system of light railways. The Queen's Speech that year referred to "a proposal for facilitating the construction of light railways", which it was hoped would "be found beneficial to the rural districts". A Bill was consequently introduced and passed into law in 1896, whereby it was provided that, where the council of any county, borough, or district have agreed to, advance any sum to a light railway company, the Treasury may lend the company a sum not exceeding one quarter of the total amount required, at an interest of not less than 3⅛%. Another clause in the Act provides that "where it is certified to the Treasury by the Board of Agriculture that the making of any light railway would benefit agriculture in any district, or by the Board of Trade that by the making of any such railway a necessary means of communication would

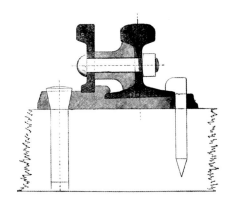

Section of the rail, guard rail, sleeper etc, of the Wisbech and Upwell Tramway.

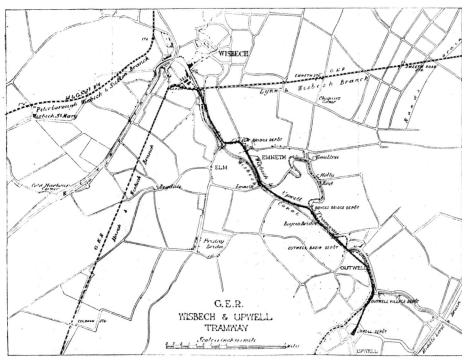

G.E.R.
WISBECH & UPWELL
TRAMWAY
Scale 1 inch to 1 mile

be established between a fishing harbour or fishing village and a market, or that such railway is necessary for the development or maintenance of some definite industry, but that owing to the exceptional circumstances of the district the railway would not be constructed without special assistance from the State, and the Treasury are satisfied that a railway company existing at the time will construct and work the railway if an advance is made by the Treasury", then the Treasury may advance a sum not exceeding one-half the total amount required for the construction of the railway.

The interest taken in, light railways has not been confined to this country, as is evidenced by the fact that at the sixth session of the International Railway Congress, to be held in Paris next year, question XXXVIII (1 of section 5) will deal with "The Influence of Light Railways on National Wealth".

As a natural outcome of the Act of 1896, schemes for the construction of light railways abound on all sides, and therefore a little information about the Wisbech and Upwell Tramway may not be devoid of interest to the readers of *The Railway Magazine*. Strictly speaking the Wisbech and Upwell Tramway be best described as a judicious cross between the railway proper and the ordinary urban tramway. Starting from Wisbech station, Great Eastern Railway, the tramway proceeds via Elm Bridge, Boyce's Bridge,

Outwell Basin, and Outwell Village to Upwell, and as it traverses an entirely agricultural district it constitutes a valuable object lesson to those interested either in the promotion or the working of light railways.

The ancient town of Wisbech, situated on the banks of the River Nene, is the commercial capital of the Cambridgeshire fen country. It is a well-built, spacious town, and under the rule of its mayor and corporation evinces considerable vitality, alike in the development of its agricultural resources and in the furtherance of its trade as a port. Since 1847 the Great Eastern, or its predecessor, the Eastern Counties Railway, has served Wisbech. The Midland, too, has been there for a good many years, and since 1889 the Great Northern has had joint access with the Midland. As far as the journey to London is concerned, the shortest route is, of course, via the Great Eastern, the distance from Wisbech to Liverpool Street Station being under 94 miles. The Midland and Great Northern companies, however, help to put the town in

touch with other parts of the country. Altogether Wisbech, although it can only boast a population of about 10,000, has little to complain of in the matter of railway conveyance.

Although the facilities for transit from Wisbech have long been all that could be desired, until a few years ago the statement that such was the case contained little but an interesting topographical fact to the inhabitants of a vast stretch of land which lay almost at its doors. If the reader will glance at a map of the Great Eastern Railway he will see the land in question situated partly in Cambridgeshire and partly in Norfolk. Surrounded as it is on all sides by the Great Eastern Railway, it has the appearance of an inverted triangle, of which the base is the line from March to Magdalen Road via Wisbech, and the apex is the city of Ely. Now, that triangular piece of land in the very heart of the Fen country has always been most admirably adapted for the growth of fruit, roots, and corn, but until some mode of transit was devised, whereby this produce could be taken expeditiously and cheaply to the rail the fertility and richness of the soil was of but little benefit to those who owned and farmed it.

During the later Sixties and early Seventies several schemes were devised for traversing this district by ordinary railway, and in 1873 a Bill was actually passed entitled The Upwell, Outwell and Wisbech Railway Act. It was, however, easier to pass an Act of Parliament than to find the money needed to build the railway. After several ineffectual efforts to 'raise the wind' the promoters formally abandoned the scheme in 1884, the Great Eastern Railway having in ▶

Elm Road station.

the meantime obtained powers to construct, and actually opened for traffic, what is known as the Wisbech and Upwell Tramway. The Act for the construction of this tram was passed in 1881, and the line was opened on August 20, 1883, as far as Outwell Basin, and as far as Upwell on September 8, 1884.

The plans for the tramway were prepared by John Wilson, then consulting engineer to the company, now engineer-in-chief, and the work was carried out under the direction of Harry Jones, now district engineer at Ipswich. The tramway runs sometimes on the main road, sometimes on the green sward alongside, and sometimes over private property, which, of course, had to be acquired. Generally speaking the landowners were quite willing to sell on reasonable terms, as they recognised that the tram would materially increase the value of their remaining property. In one case, however, the owners claimed £590 for 2 roods 15 perch of land situated about a mile and a half from Wisbech. The company contested this, and the jury at Wisbech awarded the owners £250, including compensation for severance. This verdict probably had a salutary effect on any other owners who may have been disposed to be exorbitant in their demands, and the rest of the land was purchased at a moderate figure.

The tramway is so constructed that when on the roads it complies with the Board of Trade requirements in such cases, and when off the roads it is in the nature of an ordinary light railway. The metals, 50lb to the yard, are fish-plated and laid on permanent-way chairs and sleepers, the gauge being the ordinary rail gauge of 4ft 8½in. Where the tram runs along the public highway the sleepers are covered with ballast to the level of the road, and the metals are protected by guard rails, which form a groove for the flanges

WISBECH STATION ... dep	morn.	morn.	morn.	even.	Not Sats.	even.	Sats. only.	even.	even.	...
WISBECH STATION ... dep	7 15	9 43	11 45	2 28		3 0		5 0	8 0	...
Elm Bridge	7 26	9 55	11 58	2 41		3 13		5 12	8 13	...
Boyce's Bridge	7 41	10 9	12 12	2 55		3 27		5 26	8 27	...
Outwell Basin	7 49	10 17	12 21	3 4		3 36		5 35	8 36	...
Outwell Village	7 57	10 25	12 27	3 10		3 42		5 41	8 42	...
UPWELL ... arr	8 5	10 33	12 35	3 16		3 50		5 49	8 50	...

UPWELL ... dep	morn.	morn.	even.	even.		even.		even.	even.	...
UPWELL ... dep	8 15	10·33	1 0	3 19		3 55		6 5	8 55	...
Outwell Village	8 23	10·46	1 8	3 27		4 3		6 13	9 3	...
Outwell Basin	8 31	10·54	1 16	3 35		4 11		6 21	9 11	...
Boyce's Bridge	8 40	11 4	1 23	3 43		4 19		6 31	9 18	...
Elm Bridge	8 53	11 17	1 37	3 56		4 32		6 43	9 32	...
WISBECH STATION ... arr	9 5	11 28	1 50	4 8		4 45		6 55	9 45	...

On Sunday the train does not run.

	1st Class	3rd Class
Wisbech and Outwell Village or Upwell	4d.	3d.
Elm Bridge and Upwell		
Wisbech and Boyce's Bridge or Outwell Basin	3d.	2d.
Elm Bridge and Outwell Basin, or Outwell Village		
Boyce's Bridge and Outwell Village or Upwell		
Outwell Basin and Boyce's Bridge, Outwell Village or Upwell	2d.	1d.
Outwell Village and Upwell, Wisbech and Elm Bridge, Elm Bridge and Boyce's Bridge		

of the wheels. The tramway is so laid that ample room is left for ordinary vehicular traffic, in no case approaching nearer than 8ft, and very seldom nearer than 10ft, to the crown of the road. The steepest gradient on the tramway is 1 in 32, and the sharpest curve has a radius of 120ft. Probably the most important engineering work is the wrought-iron girder bridge, of 25ft span and 25ft wide,

The dissentient minority is composed of certain small shopkeepers in the villages

which crosses the Wisbech Canal, erected in place of the old brick bridge, called the New Common Bridge, which was of 16ft span and 16ft wide. The approaches to the bridge had to be considerably reduced and the gradients rendered more easy. Bridges had also to be erected over Outwell Basin and over the River Nene at Outwell Village.

The cars start from and end their journey at the Wisbech station, alongside of an island platform, which on one side of its length is 1ft 2in high only. This is because the height of the floor of the tram from the rail level is 3ft, against 4ft 2in, which is the difference between the rail level and the flooring of an ordinary carriage. Originally waiting accommodation was only provided at the terminus at Wisbech, at the terminus at Upwell, and at Outwell. Subsequently, however, such accommodation has also been provided at the other fixed stopping places. The term 'fixed stopping places' is used because the tram stops to pick up or put down passengers at any spot en route. The waiting accommodation at Elm Road was only erected last year.

The staff at each of the depots consists of one man only, except at Upwell, where a lad is also employed. The tickets are issued by a conductor, who travels with the tram and collects the money. There are no signals whatever, the service being purely a shuttlecock one. When the tram terminated at Outwell Basin uniform fares were charged of 3d first class and 2d third class for any distance. Now, however, a graduated scale is in force (see tables at top of page).

During the year 1898 the total number of passengers carried amounted to 114,307. But, of course, it was principally as a goods line that the tramway was constructed, and in the conveyance of cattle, roots, fruit, vegetables, hay, straw, and corn to the outer world, and of coal and manufactured articles generally from the outer world, it has been of indubitable service to the inhabitants of the district it serves, and they are almost unanimous in its praise. That there are some grumblers is, of course, inevitable. In this case the dissentient minority is composed of certain small shopkeepers in the villages, who complain that since the advent of the tram many of their former customers have paid weekly visits to Wisbech, there to do their shopping. The need of the tram, however, is

Locomotive for the Wisbech and Upwell Tramway: Wheels, 3ft diameter; cylinders, 12in diameter, 15in stroke.

From *The Railway Magazine*, February 1899

proved by the large quantity of goods and coal carried over it.

Now, with regard to the rolling stook used on the tramway. The engines were designed for the purpose by T W Worsdell, then locomotive superintendent of the Great Eastern, and till latterly of the North Eastern Railway. They are not built with a view to attaining any great speed, as the tram is not permitted to proceed at a great rate than 8mph. They are designed to work from either end, with brakes so powerful that the engine and cars, when going at the full stipulated speed, can be stopped in their own length. In addition, there are automatic regulators, which will shut off steam, and thus prevent the engines going at a greater speed than 8mph. The cylinders are of 12in internal diameter, the pistons having a stroke of 15in. The wheels are of cast-steel, 3ft in diameter, and the distance between the centres is only 6ft 6in, to enable the engine to take the curves easily. The maximum steam pressure is 140lb per sq in, and by continuing the exhaust pipe into the water tank, which contains 400 gallons, the waste steam is condensed, so that very little is emitted when the engines are at work. A feature of the engines is their being cased in with wood and sheet-iron, so that none of the working parts are visible from the outside.

They are so quiet in their movements that it is very seldom that horses or other animals are frightened when passing the tramway. At each end of the engines is a cow-catcher, which extends to within four inches of the ground.

In spite of some fears expressed when the scheme was first mooted, the mishaps on the Wisbech and Upwell Tramway have been few and far between. Occasionally a young and venturesome cow has been known to dart in front of the engine, and try conclusions with it. The result, as predicted by the great originator of railways, has been "vorra bad for

Composite bogie carriage.

Nine vehicles constitute the maximum in a passenger train, 10 in a mixed train

the coo". On the occasion of the opening of the first portion of the tramway a horse attached to a Midland Railway trolly became restive, and, turning off the road, dragged the trolly through a quickset hedge into a garden. This may have been through fear of the tramway; on the other hand, it may be that the poor brute recognised that with the advent of the 'iron horse' such predatory visits as his into Great Eastern territory would cease to be as profitable to his owners as hitherto. This view is strengthened by the fact that shortly afterwards a Great Eastern trolly was met with a horse in the shafts, and another fastened behind. The animals cocked their ears and gazed inquiringly at the strange monster approaching them. On observing that it was branded with the familiar initials GER, the sagacious beasts proceeded calmly on their way. This simple little anecdote is perfectly true. Should any reader of *The Railway Magazine* presume to doubt it the writer can procure a clergyman,

an ex-mayor, and a policeman to substantiate the story. But the unbelieving inquirer must pay all expenses!

The cars are divided into two classes, which were formerly known as first and second class respectively. On January 1, 1893, the Great Eastern Railway Company abolished second class throughout their system except in the suburban and Continental services, and since that date the classes have been designated first and third. In appearance the cars are somewhat like the familiar street tramcars. The number of vehicles used varies with the time of the year and the requirements of the traffic. Nine vehicles constitute the maximum in a passenger train, 10 in a mixed train, of which four may be goods trucks. Coal trains consist of four trucks in winter and five in summer.

The results of the working are considered satisfactory to the company, especially in the matter of goods traffic. In consequence the Great Eastern obtained power in 1895 to build a tramway as a goods line only from a point near Whittlesea to Benwick. This work has now been carried out.

And now a word of warning to those interested in light railway undertakings. The Wisbech and Upwell Tramway pays the Great Eastern Railway Company not so much directly as indirectly. This is because the great bulk of the goods traffic does not commence or terminate at Wisbech, it is carried over the main line of the railway to or from that place. Were the tramway a separate undertaking solely dependent on its own earnings, with a manager, secretary, and clerical staff drawing salaries, and a. board of directors receiving fees, if asked whether it would then pay or not, the writer could only piously exclaim with the erstwhile famous Dr Byrom, "God bless us all, that's quite another thing!" ∎

New rolling stock.

Western Enterprise

THE first of a new series of diesel-hydraulic locomotives, to be known as the 'Western' class, has been undergoing trials on the Western Region of British Railways. It is numbered D1000 and named *Western Enterprise*, and is in a distinctive experimental livery described as "desert sand" colour. No. D1000 was built at Swindon Works, which has a further 34 of the class on order; also, 39 are to be produced at Crewe Works, London Midland Region, making a total of 74. They are for express passenger and freight duties.

Rated 2,700hp, the new design is some 500hp more than the most powerful diesel-

Length over buffers	68ft 0in
Weight in working order	108 tons
Fuel capacity	850 gal
Water capacity	980 gal
Maximum tractive effort (at 30% adhesion)	72,600lb
Continuous tractive effort (at 14.5mph)	45,200lb
Driving-wheel diameter	3ft 7in
Bogie wheelbase	12ft 2in

A high power-to-weight ratio has been achieved by the use of stressed-skin construction

hydraulic locomotive previously in use on the Western Region; it comes within the British Railways type 4 designation. The 'Western' class locomotive has two bogies, each with three axles, all of which are driven. It is geared to a maximum service speed of 90mph. Other principal features are as follows:

Following the introduction on the Western Region, in February, 1958, of the first main line diesel-hydraulic loco-motive, No. D600, which was built by the North British Locomotive Co Ltd, and the subsequent introduction of further types, based on the same principles of power and transmission, such as the D800 series built at Swindon and the D7000 series built by Beyer Peacock (Hymek) Limited, a more powerful type of locomotive again based on the same principles was required. No. D1000 is the first of these. The locomotives were designed and are being

constructed to the general requirements of the British Transport Commission, under the overall direction of Mr J F Harrison, chief mechanical engineer, British Railways Central staff. Mr R A Smeddle, chief mechanical & electrical engineer, Western Region, is responsible for the detailed design and construction of the locomotives at Swindon, while Mr A E Robson, chief mechanical & electrical engineer, London Midland Region, is responsible for the construction of those at Crewe.

The design is based on that of the D800 class locomotives, in so far that a high power-to-weight ratio has been achieved by the use of stressed-skin construction, while the principles of bogie construction are also similar. The bogies for the new locomotives are, however, of the three-axle type. As is also the case with the D800 class, welded construction is used almost throughout.

The underframe and superstructure are in principle constructed in the same way as for the D800 class locomotives. Two tubular members running the whole length of the locomotive from one buffer beam to the other form the basis of the underframe. To these tubes are welded deep longitudinal and

'Western Enterprise' – the name says it all. D1000 in desert sand livery leaves Shrewsbury with 1M18, a Paddington to Birkenhead service in May 1962.
PHOTO: RAIL PHOTOPRINTS/HUGH BALLANTYNE

Almost new but back at Swindon for attention, No. D1005 *Western Venturer* sits outside Swindon Works on August 12, 1962. RAIL PHOTOPRINTS/DAVE COBBE COLLECTION

transverse plate members, the resulting structure being covered on top and sides by steel plate welded to it. The superstructure consists of framing of angle and other sections covered by steel sheeting. For rigidity two bulkheads are provided which also serve to separate the cab at each end of the locomotive from the engine-room.

The bogie frames are composed of mild steel plate and are of all-welded construction.

The traction and braking forces are transmitted between bogie and underframe by means of curved manganese-steel rubbing plates. Transverse forces are transmitted by a linkage system connecting bogie to underframe, the end of the links being provided with flexible rubber bearings.

The body weight is transmitted to each bogie by means of brackets supported by large rubber blocks which in turn are carried on the buckles of two large laminated springs. From these springs the weight is transferred through coil-springs to the bogie frame, and thence by laminated springs to the top of the roller bearing casings and finally to the axle. Roller bearings of the self-aligning type are used on all axles. The bearings of the outer axle of each bogie are each contained in a casing forming an arm which is connected to the bogie frame by large pins with flexible rubber bearings. Normal-type axleboxes and horns are used for the inner axle bearings, except that

rubber pads are interposed between the horns and their manganese rubbing plates.

The two Bristol Siddeley-Maybach MD655 type 'tunnel' engines are pressure charged by single-stage exhaust gas turbo-chargers and inter-cooled. These engines have 12 cylinders divided into two banks in 'V' formation, and apart from being inter-cooled are generally similar in construction to the MD650 engines used in the D800 class locomotives. Each engine has an output of 1,350hp at 1,500rpm but is capable of being uprated to 1,440hp. The engine speed control is pneumatic and infinitely variable, and is similar to that used on the 1,700hp type 3 diesel-hydraulic locomotives built by Beyer Peacock (Hymek) Limited.

Two Voith-North British hydraulic transmissions are fitted. The primary parts of each transmission are driven through a cardan shaft and step-up gears by a diesel engine. The transmission contains three ▶

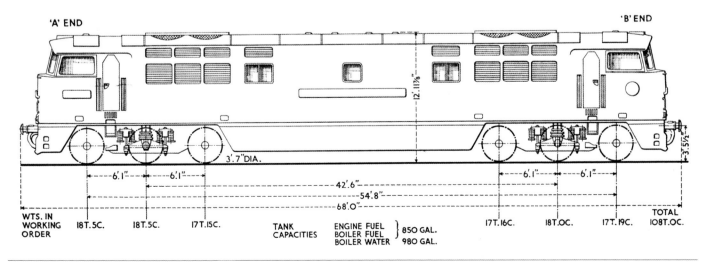

'A' END   'B' END

| WTS. IN WORKING ORDER | 18T.5C. | 18T.5C. | 17T.15C. | TANK CAPACITIES | ENGINE FUEL BOILER FUEL BOILER WATER | 850 GAL. 980 GAL. | 17T.16C. | 18T.OC. | 17T.19C. | TOTAL 108T.OC. |

An oil-fired pre-heater is provided for raising the cooling water temperature before starting

torque converters, each of which is designed for a particular range of locomotive speed, the transition from one stage to the next being effected hydraulically by draining oil from one circuit and filling the next. The changeover is completely automatic, the control system selecting that converter which will give optimum efficiency under the prevailing engine and locomotive speed conditions. The secondary parts are mounted on a common shaft and drive the output shaft through a gear train which incorporates the electro-pneumatically controlled reversing mechanism. A filling pump circulates oil through the converter in use and then through a heat exchanger where the heat is transferred to the engine cooling water.

The drive from each hydraulic transmission to the axle-mounted gearboxes is through a cardan shaft to an intermediate gearbox mounted between the two outer axles of each bogie and on the bogie frame. Cardan shafts connect this gearbox to the final drive gearboxes of the two outer axles, while the inner axle final gearbox is driven through a cardan shaft connected to the middle axle gearbox. The intermediate gearbox is water-cooled by means of an auxiliary circuit to the main cooling system.

A dynostarter is provided for each engine, and is driven through a cardan shaft incorporating a flexible coupling from an auxiliary driving flange on the transmission.

When acting as a generator the dynostarter supplies current at a constant voltage of 110 for the various auxiliaries and for charging the battery. When acting as an engine starter the current is drawn from a 48-cell lead acid battery.

The radiator, cooling fan and motor, header tank and associated pipes are supplied by a contractor as a complete unit for each engine. The fan is driven by a hydraulic motor, the oil pressure being supplied by a hydraulic pump which is driven from an auxiliary driving flange on the transmission through a cardan shaft and a flexible coupling. The pressure of oil to the motor, and hence the speed of the fan, is controlled by a thermostatic valve situated in the cooling water system. Movable shutters, automatically controlled, are provided on the outside of the radiator units. The shutters are actuated by means of hydraulic cylinders. The cooling water circuit includes the engine, lubricating oil and piston cooling oil heat exchangers, transmission oil heat exchanger and intermediate gearbox. A separate circuit is used for the engine inter-cooler, including a separate compartment of the header tank. An oil-fired preheater is provided for raising the cooling water temperature before starting.

A vacuum-controlled straight air brake system is fitted, in which the driver's vacuum brake valve applies the train brake while at

A green liveried and Crewe-built Class 52 No. D1037 *Western Empress* near Burnham with an up service for Paddington.
RAIL PHOTOPRINTS/DAVE COBBE COLLECTION

From *The Railway Magazine*, March 1962

the same time a proportional application of the locomotive air brake is made. A driver's air brake valve enables the locomotive brake only to be applied. A 'passenger goods' cock is provided in each cab which slows down the proportional brake application when placed in the 'goods' position.

A deadman's system of brake application is included, which is cancelled by depressing a pedal or the main control handle.

It can also be cancelled by means of a push-button on the co-driver's side of the cab. Compressed air is also used in the control system, for sanding and for operation of the windscreen wipers.

The Western Region system of automatic warning is fitted. In this system, if the distant signal is at 'clear' a bell sounds in the cab; if at 'caution' a siren warning is given and the brakes partially applied. If the driver acknowledges the warning by resetting the apparatus in the cab, the partial brake application is cancelled. If, for any reason, however, this is not done within a certain time the brake application is completed by the emergency automatic brake (e.a.b.) valve, the action of which cannot be cancelled by

the driver under these circumstances. Power is automatically cut off when the train pipe vacuum falls to a pre-determined value.

The e.a.b. valve, which was developed at Swindon, functions automatically when any partial brake application is made which is not initiated by the driver. It thus responds to the opening of a passenger communication valve, when it brings the train to rest in a manner similar to that initiated by an unacknowledged a.w.s. warning.

The Western Region system of automatic warning is fitted

The internal lighting can be supplied either from the battery or the dynostarter and may also be connected to an external supply of 200-250vAC through a changeover switch and step-down transformer. The train destination and tail-lights work at a pressure of 110v.

A comprehensive system of controls and warning devices is fitted. The same system of

pneumatic control for the speed of the diesel engine is used as for the 1,700hp Type 3 locomotives. Electrical control is used for practically all other equipment.

A large measure of standardisation has been achieved between the electrical control equipment and that used for the type 3 locomotives. The principal items of this equipment are housed under a desk occupying the full width of the locomotive in each cab.

The locomotive is fitted with a train-heating boiler situated in the centre compartment. Although the boiler is designed for a working pressure of 80lb per sq in, in fact steam is supplied to the train at a pressure of 60lb per sq in. The same fuel is used as for the diesel engine and is carried in common tanks.

Comprehensive fire-fighting apparatus is provided. The warning system uses fusible links, which operate a bell in each cab. The fighting apparatus consists of three 50lb cylinders containing liquid carbon dioxide, connected to spray nozzles situated in various positions. This system can be operated from any one of four pull-handle positions. In addition, three hand-type extinguishers are carried in each cab. ■

LNER Class C1 4-4-2 No. 4442 heads a Newmarket to King's Cross Pullman special back to the capital by using the goods avoiding line at Cambridge on May 14, 1936. J C BUTTON

Cambridge as a Railway Centre

By S P W CORBETT

CAMBRIDGE, owing to its geographical position, is of far less importance as an industrial centre than the sister university town. So far as its railways are concerned, Cambridge suffers from being situated on routes which lead to no place of any great size, and at the end of very lengthy branches. The Cambridge main line of the late Great Eastern Railway is the principal artery of traffic. This actually runs from south-west to north-east through the station, but for the sake of simplicity the two ends will be referred to as 'north' and 'south'.

The main block of buildings at Cambridge is the same as when the station was opened in 1845, except that the booking office has been extended into what was once the covered carriage stand. On the walls of this building, both on the approach side and at the ends, are 19 crests worked in stone. It is not known locally to whom they belong individually, but they are believed to be the crests of the landowners through whose property the Eastern Counties Railway ran. The original station

consisted of one platform as at present. Some say that there was in addition a short island platform built about 1850, which remained in existence for several years, but the officials are unable to find any documentary evidence for it. In 1899 an Act was sought to provide powers for the rebuilding of the station with an island platform, but it was strongly opposed by both university and town in Parliament, as the opposers objected to using a footbridge, so that the Act was never passed. Since then the railway has made no attempt to inconvenience or weary its patrons by footbridge or subway, though the walk now necessary from the front coach of a long down train to the exit is just as tiring as either. The university authorities also insisted that the station should be not less than a mile from Great St Mary's church, which is in the centre of the town. Queen Victoria is said to have supported this, fearing lest her son, an undergraduate at the time, might wish to go up to London more often than was good for him.

As it now stands, the station consists of a main platform 1,625ft long, and four bays, two at each end. The main platform is, of course, used as two; the platform line is connected with the through line by a scissors crossover midway, so that both halves can be used by up and down trains alike. The usual procedure for a down train is to run in on the through line and take the scissors crossing to the northern half of the platform. If it is very long, 13 coaches or more, it usually leaves the last one standing on the crossover, effectually blocking both the through line and the northern approach to the south half of the platform. Up trains reverse the process. The chief objection to this type of layout is that up and down trains have to cross each other's path at least once. The method of working is satisfactory so long as trains run in their proper course, but delay is frequently caused to those running late. It is also difficult to move empty stock without blocking one or other approach to the station.

The two bays at the London end of the station, Nos. 1 and 2, are used by the slow trains for Liverpool Street and Hitchin, by certain of the King's Cross buffet car expresses, and by the Haverhill branch trains indiscriminately, while the LMS Bletchley trains nearly always use No. 1. The two north bays, Nos. 5 and 6, are used by the LMS Kettering trains, LNE Newmarket, March, and Ely line slow trains, and the Mildenhall branch trains, but at less busy periods these also occupy the main platforms. As at all big stations, there are certain particularly lively periods. One of these is between 3.50pm and 4.20pm, when trains leave for every route radiating from Cambridge. The north end is also very busy about 10am.

As will be seen from the plan, the goods accommodation is laid out on the same large scale as the traffic with which it deals. To the south of the station there are up and down reception lines. Down trains are held there until they can be allowed to cross the main lines to gain access to the goods lines, which pass round the back of the station sidings. These reception lines, which are controlled at the south end by Trumpington signalbox, also help to relieve the congestion between the station and the junction with the line from Hitchin. The station working is controlled by two signalboxes, north and south; both are power-operated, and the rearrangement of the signalling carried out in 1926 was described in *The Railway Magazine* for March, 1927.

As far as train services are concerned, Cambridge suffers, as has been said, from its uncentral position. The service to and from London has been greatly improved by the introduction of the buffet car expresses on the King's Cross route. They have had the effect of diverting some of the traffic from Liverpool Street to King's Cross, since the latter is a more convenient station to reach from many parts of London. But much additional traffic has been created by these facilities, as is proved by the growth of the trains concerned. Originally designed for three coach trains, such is their popularity that their minimum load is normally five coaches – rarely four in midweek on certain trains – while on Saturdays it rises to 10, 11, and even 12 of the latest type of coaches, which has a disastrous effect on punctuality, seeing that timekeeping is virtually impossible with more than eight, and even with the normal load hard work has to be performed by the locomotives. At present these trains leave Cambridge at 9.25am, 12.30, 3.30, 5.25, and 10.10pm, returning from King's Cross at 9.35am, 12.40 (12.15 on Saturdays), 2.5, 8.10 and 11.40pm. They stop intermediately at Letchworth, Hitchin, and Welwyn Garden City, while the 9.25am and 10.10pm up, and the 12.15 (Saturdays only) and 2.5pm down, make an additional call at Royston. The 11.40pm stops conditionally at Royston on Thursday nights only to set down. Other fast trains leave Cambridge for King's Cross at 8.26, 10.10am, 2.4, and 6.20pm. Corresponding down trains

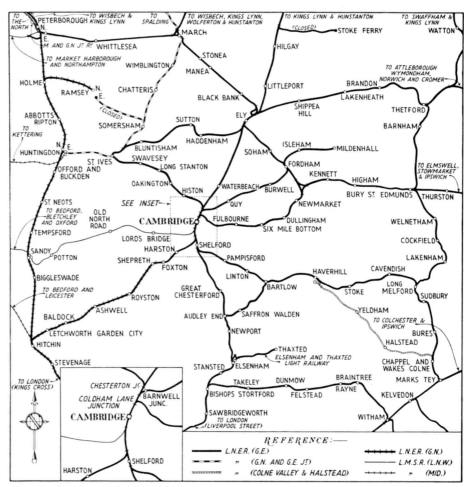

Map showing lines in the Cambridge area.

depart from King's Cross at 12.40 (Saturdays only), and 9.55pm (the latter runs through to Newmarket and Soham on Saturday nights), while the 3.0, 5.0, and 6.15pm main line trains convey portions for Cambridge, detached at Hitchin.

The Hitchin line leaves the Liverpool Street main line 2.6 miles south of Cambridge, at Shepreth Branch Junction. This name is a legacy of the old Great Eastern, which built a branch as far as Shepreth, where an end-on

As far as train services are concerned Cambridge suffers from its uncentral position

junction with the Great Northern was effected. It was a unique feature of the intermediate stations of Foxton and Harston that they were owned by the Great Eastern, and yet never served by a Great Eastern train. At the junction trains to and from the Hitchin direction have to reduce speed to 30mph. Beyond the services mentioned in the last paragraph, the only other important trains to use this route are the royal trains between King's Cross and Wolferton, Newmarket race specials, and occasional

excursions from King's Cross to Hunstanton, now composed of the latest tourist train stock. Most of these trains, when not stopping at Cambridge, take the goods lines through the station, but the royal trains run over the through passenger line next to the platform line.

The expresses on the Liverpool Street route are for the most part heavy, and convey portions for Hunstanton, Norwich and Yarmouth, and March. In proportion to the traffic carried, certain of these trains appear to be overloaded, and it is a moot point whether rearrangement of the stock workings might not allow the formations to be materially reduced, and much-needed acceleration effected. The chief departures from Cambridge for Liverpool Street are 12.59, 7.48, 9.7, 10.1, and 11.15am, and 12.58, 3.56, 4.45, and 7.7pm. Of these, the 9.7am and 12.58, 3.56, 4.45, and 7.7pm trains carry restaurant cars, while the 10.1am now conveys a buffet car from Yarmouth and the 11.15am one from Bury St Edmunds, which return on the 2.37 and 4.45pm from Liverpool Street respectively. In the down direction expresses leave Liverpool Street at 4.35, 8.30, 10.5, and 11.50am, and at 2.37, 4.15, 4.45, 5.49, 7.10, 8.22, and 10.12pm, with restaurant cars on the 8.30 and 11.50am, and 5.49 and 7.10 pm services. Cheap day tickets are issued from Cambridge to London on Wednesdays, Thursdays, and ▶

M&GN 4-4-0 No. 26 shunts at Cambridge shed on October 10, 1936. *RM* ARCHIVE

D16/3 No. 8868 stands in the north end bay of Cambridge station.

Saturdays at the cost of single fare (7s 2d), and on Thursdays and Sundays half-day tickets at the low cost of 4s from noon till 4.45pm. All tickets are interavailable to Liverpool Street and King's Cross. To provide a return as late as possible for these excursionists, a fast express leaves Liverpool Street every Thursday night at 11.50pm, calling at Bishops Stortford only, and due into Cambridge at 12.57 am. The 25.5 miles from Bishops Stortford to Cambridge, beginning with the climb to Elsenham, are allowed only 27 minutes – an average speed from start-to-stop of 56.7mph. This is considerably the fastest train on the GE route, and keeps excellent time, even though fairly heavily loaded. A train runs at the same time on Saturday nights, but calls at all stations from Broxbourne to Bishops Stortford inclusive, and arrives at 1.15am. There is in addition a good service of stopping trains.

On Sundays there is a through train from Liverpool Street to Doncaster, and vice versa, via March and Lincoln. The down train leaves Cambridge at 11.5am, and the up arrives at 6.6pm. Other fast Sunday trains are the 5.8pm from Cromer to Liverpool Street, due out of Cambridge at 8.27pm, and allowed 75 minutes for the non-stop run to Liverpool Street,

and the 8.30pm return half-day excursion from Liverpool Street, taking the same time as the up train just mentioned, and now advertised to convey ordinary passengers. In summer an additional up express runs, hooked non-stop from Norwich to Cambridge in 82 minutes. It is remarkable that a town of this importance

The fastest time for the 41¼ miles to King's Lynn, is the 64 minute allowance of the 6.8pm

should not be served on weekdays by a single non-stop train from London, even though less than 60 miles distant. There have, however, been non-stop services in the past. Before the war, for many years the 11.5am and 4.30pm expresses from Liverpool Street to York were allowed 73 minutes for the non-stop run, and the 12.20pm from St Pancras to Hunstanton and Norwich reached Cambridge non-stop in 71 minutes. In the 'radical alterations' of 1914 the best time from Liverpool Street came down to 70 minutes, but did not last for long.

We must next deal with the Newmarket, Bury St Edmunds and Ipswich line. It leaves the main line to Ely at Coldham Lane Jct, about ¾ mile north of Cambridge, and immediately traverses a very sharp curve, of such length that the branch runs for a time in a south-easterly direction, and of such sharpness as to necessitate a speed restriction of 15mph. When the branch was opened in 1851, it left the main line in the middle of the station. It was replaced by the line now in use in 1896, owing to the inconvenience of the exit across all the running lines and sidings at the station. The remains of the original embankment at the Newmarket end can still be seen about a mile from Cambridge by the old route, but 1¾ miles by the new. At Coldham Lane Jct the actual connection is made with the goods lines only, so that trains have to cross over from them to the passenger lines between there and Cambridge.

The best eastbound train leaves Cambridge at 9.6am, and takes 82 minutes for the 54½ miles to Ipswich, inclusive of stops at Newmarket, Bury St Edmunds, and Stowmarket. Another fast train leaves at 10.8am, calling at Higham, Thurston and Elmswell in addition to the former places. On Wednesdays only an express leaves Cambridge at 12.25pm for Bury St Edmunds, stopping at Newmarket only; otherwise the next train is a slow train departing at 1.32pm, calling at all stations to Bury St Edmunds, and connecting there with the York to Harwich through train. The only other fast train is the 6.9pm ex-Cambridge, the continuation of the 4.45pm ex-Liverpool Street, conveying the buffet car brought down on the latter. A rather slow connection is made at Bury St Edmunds with the 'North Country Continental' express for Harwich by the train leaving Cambridge at 6.37pm.

In the reverse direction an express corresponding to the 9.6am eastbound leaves Ipswich at 8.25am, and calls at the same places, taking one minute less. It affords an excellent service off the Continental from Parkeston Quay, which it follows 20 minutes later. A semi-fast train departs from Ipswich at 12.29pm, and a good connection is made at Bury St Edmunds by the Felixstowe to Sheffield express with that forming the 4.45pm from Cambridge to Liverpool Street. There is one fast train each way on Sundays, at 9.22am from Ipswich, returning from Cambridge at 6pm. These trains are usually made up of all assortments of ex-GE stock, but standard LNE sets are now provided on the buffet car service to and from Liverpool Street.

The services between Cambridge and Norwich, and Cambridge and King's Lynn, are for the most part slow, and beyond Ely light, the traffic being insufficient to warrant the running of faster trains. Some of the short runs are quite smartly timed, however; for example, the 2.7pm from Norwich is allowed 24 minutes for the

From *The Railway Magazine*, December 1934

20½ miles from Wymondham to Thetford, and in the opposite direction the 7.10pm from Liverpool Street, due out of Cambridge at 8.34pm, is allowed 18 minutes for the 14¾ miles from Thetford to Attleborough. This train, indeed, makes the fastest weekday run from Cambridge to Norwich in 95 minutes, with five intermediate stops, and another conditional call on Saturdays. In the up direction the 2.5pm is the fastest train, taking 104 minutes with five stops.

The fastest overall time for the 41¼ miles from Cambridge to King's Lynn is the 64 minute allowance of the 6.8pm ex-Cambridge (4.45pm ex-Liverpool St), which runs on Mondays, Fridays, and Saturdays only beyond Ely; the 4.5pm (2.37pm from Liverpool Street) takes 65 minutes; but most of the trains stop at every intermediate station from Ely to King's Lynn and take about 10 minutes more. One of the most insignificant, yet most important trains going north from Cambridge is the express at 9am to Ely, where connection is made with the northbound Continental, providing the best service from Cambridge to the Midlands via Peterborough, and the whole of the north of England and Scotland via Sheffield or York. The corresponding connection off the southbound train arrives at 7.59pm from Mondays to Fridays, and 11 minutes earlier on Saturdays. There are altogether 16 trains daily each way between Cambridge and Ely; on Sundays six down, and five up.

The other double line LNE branch from Cambridge is that leaving the main line at Chesterton Jct two miles north of Cambridge.

Former Midland Railway 2-4-0 No. 182 with a Kettering train at Cambridge.

This goes to March via Chatteris, and is used by the LMS branch trains as far as St Ives, whence they follow the LNE single line branch to Huntingdon East. The former GN & GE joint section started at St Ives. All trains from Cambridge via Chatteris stop at every intermediate station. At March connections are made with the lines to Peterborough, Lincoln, and King's Lynn via Wisbech. It may be noted here that the through carriages off the 2.37pm from Liverpool Street which formerly went to March via Ely, and to Peterborough, were diverted a few months ago to continue from March to Wisbech and King's Lynn.

On the LMS Kettering branch there are three trains each way from Tuesdays to Fridays inclusive, and four on Mondays and Saturdays. This might be a possible route to the north, if the main line connections at Kettering were not

so bad, and the journey on the branch not so long. Of the down trains, the 8.33am ex-Kettering stops at every intermediate station and arrives at Cambridge at 10.16, while the 5.18pm (which starts at 7.58pm on Saturdays) stops conditionally to set down at stations between St Ives and Cambridge. The other down trains and all the up are booked nonstop over the LNE section from St Ives to Cambridge and vice versa on a timing of 20 minutes for the 14¾ miles, inclusive of the severe service slack at Chesterton Jct. The local services from St Ives to Huntingdon East are worked, of course, by the LNER.

The Western Division of the LMSR enters Cambridge immediately outside the station at the south end. It is double track from Sandy. The connections to the north suffer on this line also from over-long-waits at Bletchley and from ▶

An unusual locomotive at Cambridge: GC Robinson B5 class 4-6-0 No. 6072 waits with a Leeds excursion formed of buffet car stock in the summer of 1934. *RM* ARCHIVE

GNR 4-4-2 locomotives Nos. 3255 and 3252 on a King's Cross train leaving Cambridge, in early 1934.
RM ARCHIVE

the closeness of the intermediate stations between there and Bedford. Thus the fastest time from Cambridge to Crewe, a distance of 157 miles, is 4½hr. The writer believes that the closing of many of the stations between Bletchley and Bedford, and all between Potton and Cambridge – or their conversion into halts – would enable fast trains to be introduced (most of the line is suited for high-speed running), whereby much of the traffic now lost to the roads might be won back. A fast morning and evening through service would then be possible each way between Cambridge and Oxford, in less than two hours, a facility much desired by the inhabitants of both universities. At present the journey takes about three hours, with a change and a long wait at Bletchley. The only through train is the 10.45am from Oxford, reaching Cambridge at 1.13pm.

The best departure from Cambridge to the north by this route is at 9.30am, which connects at Bletchley with the 10.40am from Euston to North Wales and Carlisle. Other trains leave Cambridge at 7.40 and 11.8am (connecting with the 12.5pm from Euston), 2.2, 4.42, and 6.25pm, the last-mentioned providing a service to Scotland by the 'Royal Highlander'. Down trains arrive at Cambridge at 8.41 and 11.10am (a connection leaves Birmingham at 7.30am), 1.13, 4.53, 6.4, and 8.52pm. The best service from the north is by the 8.30am from Carlisle (12.43pm from Crewe), which connects with the 4.53pm arrival at Cambridge. There is also a new Saturday night train to Bedford at 9.25pm, returning at 11.50pm. All Cambridge trains are semi-fast from Bletchley to Bedford, the smaller intermediate places being catered for by additional trains to and from Bedford only. There are two services each way on Sundays.

Finally, there are two single line branches; which have not yet been dealt with. One leaves the main Liverpool Street line about ¼ mile south of Shelford, the first station out of Cambridge, going via Haverhill and Long Melford to Marks Tey, where the Ipswich main line is joined. This line is 6¼ miles longer than the direct Colne Valley line, formerly an independent company, from Haverhill via Halstead to Chappel, the first station north of Marks Tey, but trains from Cambridge all go via Long Melford to Sudbury or through to Marks Tey. They are very slow, and the journey of 46½ miles to Marks Tey occupies slightly under two hours in one instance only. The other branch, from Cambridge to Mildenhall, starts halfway between Coldham Lane and Chesterton Jct at Barnwell Jct. This station, although situated alongside the main line, has platforms on the branch only. Thereafter the branch runs roughly parallel with the Newmarket line as far as Fordham, where it joins and crosses the Newmarket-Ely line. There are four trains each

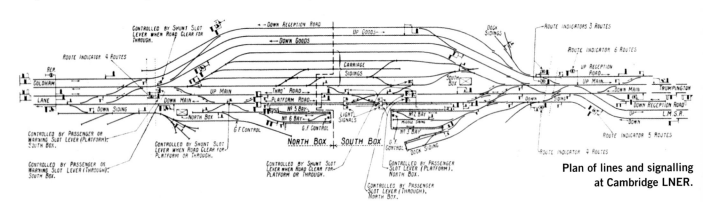

Plan of lines and signalling at Cambridge LNER.

way daily, with one extra on Saturdays. The last up evening train, however, travels from Fordham to Cambridge via Newmarket. The trains usually consist of three or four old six-wheelers, now comfortably refurnished and provided with corridor connections to permit the issue of tickets en route.

Goods traffic through Cambridge is very heavy, as there is a constant procession from March to the various East End depots in London. Many of the heavier trains use the Chatteris line between March and Cambridge, as the loops on that route are able to accommodate 90-wagon trains, whereas the Ely route loops can only take 55, and the latter carries more passenger traffic. Even at the least busy time of the year, in May and June, at least 75 freight trains pass through Cambridge every 24 hours. A considerable amount of fruit traffic is remarshalled at Cambridge for the London depots during the summer months, and also potato traffic, which lasts through most of the year. Other seasonal traffic is provided by the beginning and end of university terms, naturally largely passenger. Certain trains are divided, and through carriages on the busiest days are run on the 9am from Cambridge to Manchester, Liverpool, and York. On these occasions the Liverpool and York portions of the Continental are run separately from Ely, with the Cambridge carriages attached. The LMSR also runs a special to Bletchley.

A large variety of passenger engines can be found at Cambridge. There are five Ivatt Atlantics shedded there for working the King's Cross trains; two crews are allotted to each of four, one being kept spare, so that there is a link of eight drivers and eight firemen. This link is exactly the same as when the trains were first introduced; two men are from the old GNR,

LNER D16 No. 8882 heads a Cambridge-Newmarket train near Cherry Linton. *RM* ARCHIVE

▶ General view of Cambridge station and goods lines from Hills Road bridge.

View of the junction of the LMSR branch to Bletchley with LNER main line.

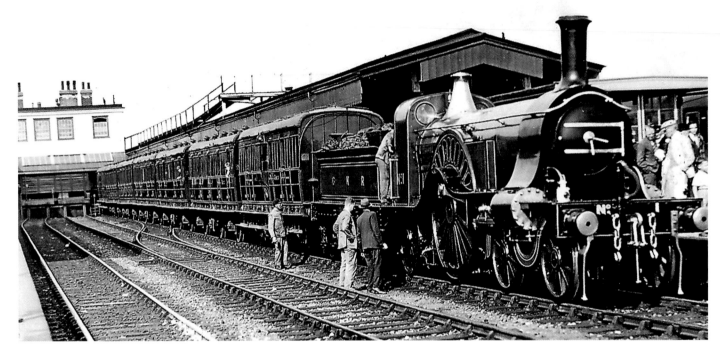

one from the GCR, and the nest from the GER. There is also a special link for the royal trains. This has three regular turns, one to King's Cross (leaving Cambridge at 2.4pm and returning on the 6.55pm from King's Cross), and two to King's Lynn, thus keeping the men acquainted with the whole road. When a big Atlantic is unavailable, a small 'Klondyke' class 4-4-2, a 'Sandringham' (B17) class 4-6-0, a GE 8500 (B12) class 4-6-0, or any variety of 'Claud Hamilton' 4-4-0 is provided. One of those fitted with a Gresley boiler has recently arrived at Cambridge, No. 8816, and the drivers speak very enthusiastically of her capabilities. The royal trains are worked by the two "Super-Clauds" Nos. 8783 and 8787, painted green, and kept spotlessly clean. They are not allowed to be driven hard, to diminish the risk of a failure when working a royal train.

'Sandringham' and GE type 4-6-0s work the majority of the expresses between Liverpool Street, Cambridge, and Norwich, both from Cambridge and Stratford sheds. The reboilered examples now appear frequently, though there are none shedded at Cambridge itself as yet.

'Claud Hamilton' class 4-4-0s work most of the Liverpool Street stopping trains, and also the 'Eastern Belle' on her Hunstanton trip, larger types being unable to work between Ely and King's Lynn. This class, indeed, is the most ubiquitous in the district, as they also work regularly to King's Lynn, and to March, Norwich and Ipswich, but on the latter route anything from GE 2-4-0s to GE 4-6-0s and GN 2-6-0s are indiscriminately used. The engine workings

north of Cambridge are sometimes very complicated. For example, a King's Lynn 'Claud Hamilton' 4-4-0 works a train to March via Wisbech, then makes a trip to Peterborough and back, after which it continues to Cambridge via Ely, and so home with an express via the main line.

In addition to the types already mentioned, ex-GN 4-4-0s and an occasional Pacific appear on the slow trains to Hitchin and King's Cross, while the latter also work the Pullman race

A considerable amount of fruit traffic is re-marshalled at Cambridge

specials to and from Newmarket for the more important meetings. The Mildenhall branch trains are normally worked by GE 2-4-2 tanks, or 2-4-0 tender engines, which are also responsible for most of the Marks Tey services. Newcomers to the shed are some of the GN type 4-4-0s cut down for working in Scotland. These have been noted on the 6.9pm from Cambridge to Bury St Edmunds, and on the Marks Tey branch. GE 0-6-0 tanks are employed for shunting in the station, while Sentinel shunters are employed in addition in the yard. At times Wisbech tram engines may be seen in the shed sidings.

For working the Kettering branch the LMS

provide ex-Midland 2-4-0 and 0-6-0 classes. Probably the run to St Ives is the last 'express' service which these veterans still work regularly. Midland engines are housed in the LNE shed at Cambridge; the Midland shed was closed a few years ago. The Western Division engines, however, have their own shed, at the south end of the station alongside the junction with the LNER; it is a sub-shed of Bletchley. Ex-LNW 'Precursor' 4-4-0 and 'Prince' 4-6-0 classes are the most frequent visitors, while 'Experiment' 4-6-0s, 'Cauliflower' 0-6-0s, 2-4-2 tanks, and Midland compound 4-4-0s appear with varying regularity. The LNE shed was reconstructed last year, and now boasts a mechanical coaling plant. There is also a good repair shop.

At the beginning of October, Mr P N Wright succeeded Mr Aungier Peacocke MBE as stationmaster at Cambridge. Mr Peacocke had occupied that position for 18 years, and had been in the service of the LNER for 49 years. The stationmaster has under him six inspectors, four yard foremen, one station foreman, 11 ticket collectors, two parcels foremen, eight parcels porters, 17 signalmen, seven relief signalmen, nine passenger and 40 goods shunters, and 23 porters, as well as a large clerical staff. In conclusion, the writer's thanks are due to Mr Peacocke; Mr Johnston, the district control officer; and to Mr Robinson, the assistant civil engineer, for their courteous assistance in providing information for this article, and also to Mr F I G Rawlins for help in the same direction. ∎

Notes and NEWS

The electric locomotive that worked the tramway to the mental hospital at Cheddleton from 1899 until the line was closed in 1954.

A Seat 135 Feet Long

A CURIOSITY in railway station equipment forms a part of Kirkby station, on the Furness main line of the LMSR between Barrow and Millom. This is a seat on the down platform which is about 135ft long, and would probably accommodate at least 100 passengers if they sat reasonably close together. It is set into the wall of the platform, and extends from the station buildings to the ramp. Why this exceptional provision should have been made for the population of Kirkby, probably in Furness Railway days, we are unable to explain.

From the January 1941 issue

Stowaways in Tender

ONE boy died and another was taken to hospital after a trip of more than 100 miles in the coal tender of the 'Shamrock' Euston to Liverpool express on January 16. The fireman discovered one of the boys when the train was about 150 miles from London. The train was stopped at Madeley signalbox, and the other boy was discovered unconscious in the tender. Both were given first aid in the signalbox by a doctor from the train, but one boy died before reaching hospital. The other was detained in hospital suffering from shock. It is believed that, when the engine was passing over a water pick-up trough at Whitmore, the boys were soaked by overflow water and stood up. The one who was fatally injured is thought to have struck his head on an overline bridge.

From the March 1958 issue

Cheddleton Hospital Tramway

WHEN the construction of the mental hospital at Cheddleton, in Staffordshire, was begun in 1895, a tramway was laid to connect the site with the North Staffordshire Railway, about half a mile distant.

The line was used for the transport of building materials, and was worked by a contractor's steam locomotive until the hospital was brought into use in August, 1899. It was then electrified, with overhead conductors, and retained by the hospital authorities to convey coal and stores. Relatives and friends of patients at the hospital were carried on visiting days, but these services ceased in about 1920.

The tramway remained in use for the conveyance of coal until early in 1954, when it was closed and dismantled. The gauge of track is said to have been slightly less than the British standard of 4ft 8½in.

From the January 1956 issue

The Ffestiniog Railway in Wartime

PASSENGER traffic on the 2ft gauge Ffestiniog Railway was suspended at the outbreak of war, and the present activities of the line are confined to the conveyance of slate from the quarries in the Blaenau Ffestiniog district. The permanent way and other works appear to be in fairly good condition, excepting the portion of the line on the Traeth Mawr embankment from Boston Lodge to Portmadoc (Harbour) station, which is a little-used section now. The Harbour station roads are employed for the storage of wagons and a few of the passenger vehicles. Beyond this station the accommodation tracks are overgrown, and the elevated water tank which supplied the locomotives is now almost destroyed. The physical connection across High Street,

Portmadoc, with the terminus of the now-defunct Welsh Highland line still remains, as does the siding serving the Harbour; the latter is also used tor the storing of wagons. Most of the passenger vehicles are housed in the carriage sheds at Boston Lodge.

Of the locomotives, the only Fairlie at present in use is No. 10 *Merddin Emrys*. The other locomotive of similar type No. 3 *Taliesin*, is partly dismantled, presumably for boiler and motion repairs, as one of the boilers and a motor bogie have been removed, and is standing in the fitting shop at Boston Lodge Works. Locomotive No. 1 *Princess* is also in frequent use, and appears to take alternate turns with the Fairlie No. 10; but both No. 5 *Welsh Pony, and No. 11* (the 0-4-0 Baldwin petrol-engined rail-

tractor), appear to be idle. An unnumbered Simplex four-wheel petrol tractor is, however, in fairly frequent use. The 0-4-0 locomotive, No. 4 *Palmerston* is employed as a stationary boiler, having been lifted off its wheels and placed in the yard at Boston Lodge to supply power to a small steam hammer. A collection of locomotive parts is also to be seen in the yard at Boston Lodge, conspicuous among which is a complete locomotive cab from the Welsh Highland 0-6-4 Fairlie locomotive *Moel Tryfan*. Another cab, presumably that belonging to the famous old Ffestiniog Railway Fairlie locomotive No. 7 *Little Wonder*, is in an adjacent siding among the remains of some older wagons and carriage underframes.

From the January/February 1945 issue

Diesel working of fast freight trains

London Midland Region diesel-electric locomotive, No. 10001, at the head of a freight train near Berkhamsted. PHOTO E D BRUTON

By F T BUDDEN

RELATIVELY short railway distances in Great Britain present a problem in diagramming main line diesel locomotives so that maximum advantage may be taken of their high availability. The London Midland Region locomotives, Nos. 10000 and 10001, already have hauled a number of well-known trains, including, as twin units, the up 'Royal Scot', returning to Glasgow on the 9.5pm from Euston. In Scotland, a single unit has headed the 'Bon Accord' (1.35pm Glasgow to Aberdeen), the 10.35am Glasgow Central to Liverpool as far as Carlisle, and the 2.2pm all stations Carlisle to Glasgow. In England, a single unit worked the 4.50pm Euston-Blackpool and the 8am Blackpool-Euston expresses for a short period.

A much more unusual duty during the winter months has been the operation of one of the fastest freight trains in Britain, the daily (except Saturdays) 2.55pm Camden to Crewe, thence Glasgow. The traffic conveyed is for Scotland and the timing calls for speeds little short of express passenger scheduling The vehicles making up the train are selected and the train is braked or piped throughout.

Maximum booked speed is 53mph, and as the train is due to pass Basford Hall Junction at 6.23pm with loads up to 45 vehicles, it will be seen that operation of this train is no easy matter. An important aspect of the working is that the locomotive was designed originally for a maximum operating speed of 90mph and the traction motor gear ratio was arranged accordingly. With the considerable running at much lower speeds, with heavy loads, involved in the duties now described, motor current values are appreciably higher than they would be with the generally higher sustained speeds applying in express passenger working.

The maximum load permitted on the down journey is 45 vehicles. For all practical purposes, 45 vehicles are equivalent to a trailing load of approximately 515 tons, and to take this up to Tring, with one 1,650hp diesel-electric unit, in the 51 minutes allowed, leaves no opportunities for easy running. The start from Camden Yard is inevitably slow, and the crossing over to the fast line means cautious running from Camden until Willesden is cleared.

Table I shows the official schedule for the down journey and the actual times recorded on a run with No. 10000 described below. On this journey, the timing and speeds of which are shown in columns 4 and 5 of the table, the load was 37 vehicles, equivalent to approximately 430 tons. The weather was indifferent, with intermittent rain squalls and a moderate side wind. This important train follows the 2.45pm down Manchester express, and as departure from Camden before time is permitted, easy running is usual before crossing over to the fast track.

When Willesden was cleared acceleration on the four miles of level was rapid. On the following 7½ miles of rising 1 in 339 the speed was maintained at 42-43mph, with main ammeter showing 1,500-1,800amp. The motor group ammeters indicated a perfect current distribution, the pointers showing exactly equal values. These meters are fitted as 'slip' indicators. At starting from Camden, with the train on a sharp curve, and with peaks of 2,500amp on the main ammeter, not the slightest sign of slip tendency was observed; this might be expected with an adhesion factor of 6.9.

An interesting feature of the operation was the excellent way in which the driver kept the train moving at an almost constant speed. Past Carpenders Park and through Watford speed was allowed to rise very little; it was 48mph at the entrance to Watford Tunnel, with a sustained 43-45 up the seven miles of 1 in 335 to Tring, current wavering through a range 1,400-1,500-1,700amp. Beyond Tring, power was eased appreciably, with speed increasing to a maximum of 60mph at the bottom of the six miles of 1 in 333 beyond Cheddington. This speed was the highest reached on the run. The mean speed Tring-Roade was 52.5mph, and running throughout almost exactly on section to section timing, but about five minutes ahead. Again, there was a mean of 51.7mph over the 19.8 miles from Blisworth to Rugby. After a cautious

TABLE I—Official Schedule of 2.55 p.m. Fast Freight, Camden-Crewe

Miles	—	Schedule	Actual	Actual speed based on mileage
		p.m.	p.m.	
0	Camden ... dep.	2.55	2.50	
1¾	Kilburn High Road pass	3.01	2.56	17.5
4¼	Willesden Junc. ,,	3.08	3.04	18.8
16¼	Watford Junc. ,,	3.26	3.20½	43.6
30½	Tring ... ,,	3.44	3.40	43.8
45½	Bletchley ,,	4.01	—	52.5 (Tring–Roade)
58½	Roade ... ,,	4.17	4.12	
61½	Blisworth ,,	4.21	4.16	45.0
79	Hillmorton ,,	4.43	4.36	52.5
81¼	Rugby ... ,,	4.46	4.39	45.0
95¾	Nuneaton ,,	5.05	4.59	42.8
108¾	Tamworth ,,	5.20	5.15	48.8
115	Lichfield ... ,,	5.28	5.23	46.9
123	Rugeley ... ,,	5.38	5.32½	50.5
128¼	Milford ... ,,	5.45	5.39¼	46.6
132¼	Stafford ... ,,	5.50	5.45¼	40.0
137½	Norton Bridge ,,	5.59	5.53	40.6
146¼	Whitmore ,,	6.12	6.05½	42.0
155	Basford Hall Junction ,,	6.23	6.16¼	48.8
155¾	Basford Hall North arr.	6.28	6.21	9.5
	Mean Speed (Official) =	43.8 m.p.h.		
	Mean speed (Actual) =	44.3 ,,		

No. 10000 hauling the 2.55pm ex-Camden freight over Bushey Troughs.

passage through Rugby, matters were taken fairly easily, the speedometer showing 45-50mph almost the whole way. The descent from Whitmore through Madeley and Betley Road was made quietly, passing Basford Hall Junction 61 minutes early.

A noticeable feature of the run was the braking. The whole distance, Camden-Crewe, was completed without a stop. No adverse signals were experienced, but permanent way slacks and the cautious passages through Rugby and Stafford meant some braking. Nowhere, save at the stop at the end of the run, was the train pipe vacuum reduced by more than three-four inches. With the ability of the locomotive to make time, the deceleration of the train at the various points, and down the bank from Whitmore, could be handled quietly. This feature must reflect favourably on vehicle maintenance and on the well-being of draw gear, not to mention the comfort of the guard!

The fuel consumed was 172.3gal, or 1.1gal per mile. The fuel per ton-mile is then 0.0025gal, or an expenditure of about 400b.t.u. – a clear indication of the high thermal efficiency of the diesel engine. Next day the down journey comprised 44 vehicles, the fuel consumption being 173.5gal, or an expenditure of 360b.t.u. per ton-mile. These figures apply to the train only. In the last case mentioned, if allowance is made for the locomotive, the b.t.u. per ton-mile comes down to about 290.

From the utilitarian viewpoint, the use of a liquid fuel has manifest advantages. On the run just described, the preparation of the locomotive before departure and shedding at Crewe were simplicity itself. A matter of minutes before the unit was due off the shed at Willesden, the engine was started. Until then, the consumption of fuel and lubricating oil was nil. A few minutes after reaching Crewe, the engine was stopped, the radiator shutters closed, lights switched off, and cab doors locked.

These are admittedly minor items and undoubtedly the diesel-electric locomotive is a complex machine and cannot be maintained adequately with the organisation which suffices for the steam locomotive. This is part of the inevitable price paid for a thermal efficiency, at the wheel treads, of 28-30%. Lubricating oil (engine) consumption was at the rate of 0.0074gal per mile, with water consumption negligible. Table II shows a section of the data applying to actual operation on the fast freight work described.

The running is segregated into sections 'Service' and 'Shed', which is useful in analysis. With the exact measuring of fuel and lubricating oil, mileage run, with the registration of the revolutions made by the diesel engine, and the precise hours of running, the London Midland operating authorities have an extremely accurate measure and record of what is being done. It is even possible to check, up to a point, the way in which the locomotive is being driven.

From Table II it will be seen that, for the down trip, the miles, engine revolutions, fuel, and time booked against 'Shed' are considerably higher than the figures for the up journey. This is explained by the fact that the locomotive is based on Willesden Shed and has to cross over to the up tracks north of Willesden and then proceed to Camden. The shed movements at Willesden and Crewe, with the running to Camden, total eight miles. This mileage is recorded on the locomotive, and is shown in the first 'journey' column in the table. The up working terminates at Willesden, which involves about three miles' booking, yard to shed.

The up journey of this turn is on normal express freight timing, with possible interruptions of direct passage. The permitted load is higher, and 55 vehicles are not uncommon. This means higher fuel consumptions and total engine revolutions, and these aspects of the working show up in the appropriate columns of the record sheets.

A close study of this operational data gives a lead to potential economies in various directions. With the locomotives rostered on similar duties for an extended period, abnormality in the records shows up readily; for example, the fuel consumed, which is measured continuously through fuel meters in the supply pipes to the engine fuel pumps and is accurate to close limits. The operational records show a remarkable consistency. On the down (fast) journeys over many thousands of miles, with train weights varying 285-515 tons, the fuel per mile varies from 0.80-1.17gal. The fuel per ton-mile varies only from 0.0021-0.0026gal. Including the weight of the locomotive, the figures become 0.00172-0.00192, a variation of only 11%.

With consistent handling of the locomotives, it seems that only one major factor should affect these figures to any appreciable extent – the weather. Stops for adverse signals have an influence, and this can be detected in some of the records. ■

TABLE II—Operating Data

—	Journey No. 1	Journey No. 2
From	Camden	Crewe B.H.S.
To	Crewe	Willesden
Depart	2.50 p.m.	5.00 a.m.
Arrive	6.20 p.m.	10.45 a.m.
No. of vehicles	39	26
Shed fuel (gal.)	9.9	6
Shed revs.	35,200	24,500
Shed miles	8	3
Time in service	3 hr. 30 min.	5 hr. 45 min.
Shed and light running time	1 hr. 20 min.	50 min.
Fuel (gal.)	179	134.5
Distance (miles)	156	152
Engine revs.	145,200	190,000

Gone... With regret – 1

Top: A two-car DMU ticks over at the all wooden station of New Holland Pier in September 1976, with a train to Barton-upon-Humber. Opened in March 1848, by the Manchester, Sheffield & Lincoln Railway, it was closed on June 14, 1981, with the pier converted to an animal feed terminal.

Left: U Class 2-6-0 No. 31791 stands at Swindon Town station on September 9, 1961, with the last train from Cheltenham. All traffic on the former Midland and South Western Junction Railway ceased in 1966.

Bottom: A Cravens two-car DMU catches the sun under the overall roof at Fraserburgh on August 31, 1964, with a local service to St Combs. Services to St Combs ended in May 1965, with services from Aberdeen to Fraserburgh ceasing three months later.

Top: A Swindon 'Inter-City' three-car DMU stands at Stranraer Town station on September 11, 1965, waiting its next duty. The station closed on March 7, 1966, with all rail services transferred to Stranraer Harbour.

Left: A Western Region three-car DMU enters Holt Junction (for Devizes branch) on March 27, 1965 with a Chippenham to Westbury service. The station closed a year after this view was taken.

Bottom: A Derby lightweight DMU waits for the 'right away' to Workington from the attractive station at Keswick on August 28, 1963. The service itself had ceased within three years.

ALL PICTURES: TRACKS NORTH

Great Western Railway 0-6-4 pannier tank crane engine No. 18 *Steropes* built in 1903, at Swindon in September, 1927. PHOTO: H C CASSERLEY

Crane engines

By H C CASSERLEY

THE withdrawal in past months of the former North London Railway locomotive from Bow, and one of the three ex-Great Eastern engines from Stratford works, indicates that the crane locomotive will soon be extinct on British Railways.

The idea of fitting a crane to an engine for shunting duties, primarily in works yards, appears to have originated with the North London Railway engine in 1872. It was not until some years later that other railways copied the idea and adapted existing engines by mounting a small crane, with a fairly short jib capable of lifting about four or five tons, usually on the bunker, although this position was varied in one or two cases in later instances.

The North London engine started life as long ago as 1858 in the form of a small 0-4-0 saddle tank constructed by Sharp, Stewart & Company for the North & South West Junction Railway for working the Acton-Hammersmith branch. It was taken over by the NLR shortly after wards, becoming at first No. 37, and later 29 and 29A in that railway's list, although latterly the number was not actually carried on the engine. In 1872 it was converted at Bow Works into a 0-4-2 saddle-tank, and the crane fitted, in which form it remained practically unaltered for a period of nearly 80 years. During that time its solitary duty was works shunter at Bow, where it remained until it was

taken to Derby for scrapping in December, 1950. This must have been the longest journey undertaken by the North London engine since it travelled south after being built in Glasgow nearly a century before. At the time of the Grouping, North London engines were at first incorporated in the LNWR stock, and the engine became No. 2896 in that railway's list, but in June, 1926, it was completely renumbered 7217 in the LMSR stock, becoming No. 27217 in February, 1935. Under the British Railways scheme it was finally renumbered No. 58865 in March, 1949, but was not repainted and retained the initials LMS on the saddle tanks to the end.

In 1891, Holden fitted one of a class of five Great Eastern Railway 0-6-0 tank engines,

The 0-6-0 crane tank engine built for the Great Northern Railway (Ireland) in 1928, at Dundalk in May, 1950. H C CASSERLEY

LMS 0-4-2 crane tank No. 2896 built in 1858 as a 0-4-0 saddle tank for the North London Railway, is seen at Bow in August, 1925.

From *The Railway Magazine*, October 1951

forerunners of the later well-known series designated between J65 and J69, with a crane for use in Stratford Works yard, and two others were similarly converted in 1894. These engines, originally built by Ruston & Proctor in 1868 as Nos. 204-206, were thenceforth known merely as B, C, and D, and remained as such until they were again given numbers under the LNER 1946 renumbering scheme, when they became 8667-8669, and subsequently British Railways 68667-68669. The third of them has recently been withdrawn from service, and it seems likely that the other two may soon follow. These were the oldest engines in service on the LNER in its last days, just as the NLR 0-4-2 was the oldest LMSR engine running: it is curious that the holders of these honorary titles on both railways should have been engines of this particular description.

The Lancashire & Yorkshire was another railway which made a similar conversion about the same time; in this case the engine was a 2-4-0 tank, one of a class of three built by Beyer, Peacock in 1873 for the East & West Junction Railway but returned to the makers, and taken over by the LYR. This particular engine, No. 518, had its crane added in 1896 and became No. 518A, but later reverted to 518. It lasted until 1921. One of the Barton Wright 0-6-2 tanks, No. 11601 (formerly LYR No. 146) also was latterly fitted with a crane, and used at Horwich works until its withdrawal in 1931.

The North Eastern Railway possessed two 0-6-0 tanks fitted with cranes, Nos. 590 and 995, originally constructed in 1888. They retained the same numbers when taken over by the LNER. No. 590 was scrapped in May 1937; the other locomotive was sold in 1933 to the Hartley Main Collieries and, renumbered 26, lasted until 1943, when it was cut up.

The LNWR built eight 0-4-2 saddle tanks fitted with cranes for shunting duties at Crewe locomotive and Wolverton carriage works, between 1892 and 1895. Originally Nos. 2132-2134, 853, 151, 187, 144, and 195, they were renumbered very shortly after construction, the first six as 3246-3249, 3251 and 3252 respectively in the running duplicate list, and the last two as Carriage Department Nos. 2 and 5, Wolverton. These latter were withdrawn in 1929, Nos. 3246, 3251/2 followed in 1932-3, but 3247-9 lasted until 1946-7. When the complete LMSR renumbering scheme was evolved these particular engines were excluded, and continued to bear their LNWR numbers right to the end, although they duplicated certain Midland Class 3 0-6-0s, so that for several years the railway possessed engines bearing the same numbers. Most of them were repainted in standard LMSR style, but No. 3249 retained its old distinctive LNWR number plate right up to the time it was

Great Western Railway 2-4-0 tank engine, originally built in 1875 for the South Devon Railway, at Swindon in September, 1927.

South Eastern Railway 0-4-0 crane tank, built by Neilsons in 1881, at Stewarts Lane in June 1946, combines the crane and chimney.

scrapped in 1947.

In 1905, H A Ivatt rebuilt one of Patrick Stirling's GNR 0-4-4 works tank locomotives, No. 533, constructed in 1876, with a crane for use in the works yard, and this engine became Doncaster Works No. 3. It was scrapped in 1928.

The Great Western Railway owned four crane locomotives; three were built with cranes and not merely conversions of older engines. The first two were Nos. 17 *Cyclops*, and 18 *Steropes*, turned out in 1903, while a third No. 16 *Hercules*, was added as late as 1922. They were 0-6-4 pannier tanks, and in effect were elongated versions of the standard 0-6-0 pannier tanks but fitted with

the crane attachment. The fourth engine was a small 2-4-0 tank, No. 1299, one of three engines originally built in 1875 for the South Devon Railway, but the date when the crane was added is not certain. Nos. 16, 18, and 1299 were a familiar sight at Swindon works for many years, while No. 17 worked mostly at Wolverhampton. The GWR, however, took a sudden dislike to them, and all four were cut up in 1936.

The South Eastern Railway was early in the field with this type of locomotive, and a diminutive 0-4-0 works tank was built for that line by Neilsons in 1881, and a second one followed in 1896. These two engines, Nos. 302 and 409, differed from all the ▶

North Eastern Railway crane engine, formerly No. 995, constructed in 1888 and sold by the LNER in 1933.

others mentioned in that the crane was attached to the front end around the chimney. Later SECR 302 and 409, they became at first A302 and A409 in the Southern Railway list, but in 1930-31 were transferred to the service list as 234S and 235S. No. 235S remained at Ashford and was scrapped in 1935. No. 234S was sent to Lancing for shunting in the carriage works, but in 1938 was transferred back to the running stock as 1302. Latterly it was at Stewarts Lane and used for shunting in a milk dock containing a very sharp curve, on which duty it lasted until July, 1949, when it was cut up without receiving the allocated British Railways number, 31302.

The final engine of this type to be built was a 0-6-0 tank, No. 31, on the Great Northern Railway (Ireland), constructed by Hawthorn, Leslie in 1928. This locomotive is distinctive in that the crane, a comparatively large structure with a maximum lift of eight tons, is mounted directly over the boiler. The jib extends well forward over the front of the engine, necessitating the provision of an intermediate wagon when the engine is engaged on ordinary shunting duties. As the jib bridges the top of the chimney, which actually appears to support it, when in its normal resting position, a cavity is provided, in effect an extension of the chimney itself, to allow for the exit of smoke and exhaust.

This completes the history of crane engines in this country so far as the main line companies were concerned. The GNR (I) and the two remaining Stratford engines are the last of the type, and it seems unlikely that any more will be built in the future.

One or two industrial concerns also own, or have owned, locomotives of this type, but although they would appear to be most useful machines for lifting and transporting weights of a few tons about works yards, crane locomotives seem to have fallen out of favour. In most, if not all, cases the cranes had been out of use during the latter years of the engines' existence. ■

One of the eight 0-4-2 saddle-tank crane engines built at Crewe between 1892 and 1895, still carrying the London & North Western Railway number plate, at the locomotive works in August, 1939.

Former Great Eastern Railway 0-6-0 tank engine No. 68667 is one of the remaining examples of crane engines on British Railways, at Stratford in March, 1949. PHOTOS: H C CASSERLEY

Lengthy Tank Engine Journeys

ONE of the longest regular tank-engine workings, in this or in any other country, is that made daily from Whitehaven through to Preston by one of the standard 2-6-4 tanks of the LMS. The train concerned leaves Whitehaven at 11.20am, usually consisting of four or five non-corridor bogie coaches, with a corridor third and a first-class brake on rear for London. From there to Carnforth, where the main line is joined, is 74½ miles, and from Carnforth on to Preston is a further 27¾ miles, making a continuous run of 101¾ miles, which occupies 3hr 14min, 11 stops included. Water is taken at Barrow, where the train is booked to stand from 12.50 to 1pm, this being roughly the midway point of the journey; here, also, a through coach is attached on rear from Barrow to Leeds, detached at Carnforth to run over the Midland Division. Between

Barrow and Carnforth, therefore, a train of seven or eight coaches, and occasionally nine, is customary, which the tank has to haul up the heavy grades past Furness Abbey and Dalton to the summit between Lindal and Ulverston. The sharpest timing of the journey is the 26 minutes allowed for the 21 miles from Lancaster—including a rising start at 1 in 100 to Preston. We have recently noted a start-to-stop time, with one of the engines concerned, of precisely 24 minutes for this length, speed gradually rising irom 61½mph, at Bay Horse, to 68mph at Brock, over a line but little easier than level; in fact, the 12 miles from Galgate to Barton were run in 10min 55sec, with a seven-coach load of about 210 tons all found, at the conclusion of this run. This was an excellent example of the capabilities of this handy and efficient type. *August 1931*

The Orient Express

A LONGSTANDING reader sends particulars of a journey by the tri-weekly 'Orient Express', as far as Vienna. The express runs from Ostend, in connection with the 2pm service from Victoria on Tuesday, Thursday and Saturday. The train at Ostend consists of two baggage cars, one diner and one or two sleeping cars. Leaving Ostend at 8.15pm. there is a stop of two minutes at Ghent and Brussels is reached at 9.42pm. Dinner is served between Ostend and Brussels. Cologne is reached at 2.38am, and here the Amsterdam-Vienna sleeping car is attached to the train. Stops are made at Wiesbaden, Frankfurt-am-Main, Würzburg, Nuremberg, Regensburg, Passau, Linz and St Polton. At Linz the composition of the train is altered. The diner is taken off, together with one of the baggage cars, and the sleeping car from Calais, which runs in

connection with the 11 o'clock service from Victoria, is attached, also two sleeping cars from Paris and a dining car from Paris. Vienna is reached at 6.3pm, central European time. The distance from Ostend to Vienna is about 827 miles and, allowing for one hour difference in time, an hour for customs at the German frontier, and half an hour for customs at Passau, together with another half an hour for making up the train at Linz, it means the net time to Vienna is about 19½ hours. The average speed between Ostend and Vienna is about 43mph. The first-class fare from London at the present time is £8 12s 11d, which works out slightly over 21d per mile, plus a rather heavy supplement for train-de-luxe and sleeping car. Altogether, the journey is a very comfortable one and, I should say, equal to pre-war. *May 1927*

Conductor-Guard Trains

THE Great Eastern Railway is developing the principle of a 'conductor-guard' working on branch trains already in use on certain light railways and light traffic sections, and generally analogous to the methods adopted where rail motor cars or motor trains are employed on other lines, as a means for operating less remunerative branches more economically. Incidentally this enables facilities to be increased and avoids any possibility that such sections or particular stations might have to be closed as not being able to pay their way.

As now introduced, modem corridor main line rolling-stock is employed, thus giving branch travellers greater comfort and permitting of steam heating during the winter months. The conductor-guard has a complete set of single and return tickets to meet standard requirements, and in order to cover instances where through tickets are ordinarily issued at a fare less than the sum of the branch fare and the continuation on the main line, provision is made whereby, although re-booking is necessary, only the difference between the branch fare originally paid and the through fare is charged. An important factor is that goods, milk and other traffic at intermediate stations can usually be operated within the ordinary eight-hour day, and beyond that period there is no need for station staff except in the signalboxes, ticket issuing and collecting being dealt with on the trains.

Special rolling-stock may eventually be introduced, but for the time being the experiment is being carefully watched. It appears to offer very wide possibilities, and we fully anticipate to find it adopted in many more sections, either regularly, or on Sundays or days when traffic is relatively light. It is at present in operation on the Bentley-Hadleigh, Cambridge-Mildenhall, Mellis-Eye, Heacham-Wells, and Thetford-Bury St Edmunds branches, and on Sundays between Epping and Ongar. *November 1921*

Southern Railway expresses

Four cylinder 'Lord Nelson' 4-6-0 No. 851 *Sir Francis Drake* leaving Salisbury for Waterloo.

Two Drummond locomotives at Vauxhall, SR 'Express' locomotive No. 711, Class T9, 4-4-0, coupled to a mixed traffic 4-4-0 with water-tube firebox and Westinghouse brake, en route from Nine Elms to Waterloo in LSWR days. PHOTO: C J HOUSEGO

From *The Railway Magazine*, November 1941

Above: Driver Payne and fireman Whelton with No. 865 *Sir John Hawkins.*

Right: 'Schools' class three-cylinder 4-4-0 locomotive No. 937 *Epsom*, arriving at Salisbury on 11am from Waterloo.

These four pictures are reproduced from two recent articles by Mr Frank E Box in *The Southern Railway Magazine* entitled With the Nine Elms Top Link to Salisbury. No. 851 emerges from Fisherton tunnel at Salisbury taking the Waterloo line.

Driver Bushnell and fireman Whelton with No. 864 *Sir Martin Frobisher.*

One of the well-known Metropolitan 4-4-4 tanks, No. 104: These engines, Nos. 103-110, were introduced from 1920 to work Aylesbury line trains, and were taken over by the LNER on November 1, 1937, in whose stock they were classified H2 and numbered 6415-6422.

English 4-4-4 tank locomotives

THE 4-4-4 wheel arrangement is not one which has found particular favour in British locomotive practice. A note from E C B Ashford recalls that only four British railways, prior to Grouping, built 4-4-4 tank engines; they were the Wirral, Midland & South Western Junction, North Eastern, and Metropolitan Railways. The Wirral was the first in the field, in 1896, with three engines of this type, built by Beyer, Peacock & Co; they had 17in x 24in inside cylinders, 5ft 2in driving wheels, 160lb pressure, and a weight in working order of 59¾ tons. A year later two 4-4-4 tanks, designed and built by Sharp, Stewart & Co, were delivered to the Midland & South Western Junction Railway, Nos. 17 and 18; these were also inside cylinder engines, with 17in x 24in cylinders, 5ft 3in driving wheels, 160lb pressure, and a weight of 59¼ tons, and carried the numbers 17 and 18. The GWR, on taking over the two M & SWJR tanks

at the time of the Grouping in 1923, re-numbered them 25 and 27, and rebuilt No. 27 with a taper boiler in 1925; No. 25 was withdrawn in 1927, and No. 27 in 1929. Of all the British 4-4-4 tanks, the, most numerous series was Sir Vincent Raven's Class D of the North Eastern Railway, which first appeared in 1913, and of which 45 examples, Nos. 1326-1330, 1499-1503, 1517-1531, and 2143-2162, were built. These very handsome locomotives had the usual Raven three-cylinder arrangement, with cylinders 16½ in x 26in, 5ft 9in driving wheels, 160lb pressure, and a weight of 84¾ tons. They were intended originally for the Darlington and Saltburn line, but their use was later extended to Tyneside. In more recent years, the 39¾ tons of adhesion weight being found insufficient, they have been rebuilt as 4-6-2 tanks, but although they were the only three-cylinder 4-4-4 tanks in existence, they are not

unique as three-cylinder 4-6-2 tanks, as there is also the same designer's series of 20 three-cylinder 4-6-2 mineral tanks. The former are now classed as A8 in the LNER locomotive list, and the latter as A7. In their rebuilt form the A8 engines carry 175lb pressure and weigh 87 tons. The last 4-4-4 design to be introduced was that of Charles Jones for the Metropolitan Railway, and built by Kerr, Stuart & Co, in 1920; these are outside cylinder engines, eight in number, and have now been incorporated in the LNER locomotive stock, and numbered 6415 to 6422 inclusive. They have 19in x 26in cylinders, 5ft 9in driving wheels, 160lb pressure, and a weight of 77 tons. Just before the end of last century, after the appearance of the Wirral and M & SWJ 4-4-4 tanks, S W Johnson prepared a 4-4-4 tank design for service on the Midland Railway, but the engines never materialised. ∎

From *The Railway Magazine*, November 1941

Top: One of the two M & SWJR 4-4-4 tank locomotives, No. 25, GWR. The Midland & South Western Junction Railway had two of these engines, Nos. 17 and 18, renumbered, when the line was absorbed by the GWR, 25 and 27.

Centre: No. 2143 of the numerous Raven 4-4-4 tanks, NER. These engines were rebuilt as 4-6-2s of Class A8, LNER.

Left: Wirral 4-4-4 tank locomotive No. 14.

Slipping and sliding

PRACTICE AND PERFORMANCE: THE LONGEST-RUNNING RAILWAY SERIES IN THE WORLD

***The Railway Magazine's* chief correspondent 'gets to grips' with the reasons behind one of the railways' most controversial and irksome problems**

By PETER SEMMENS
MA, CChem, FRSC, FCIT, MBCS

Violent forces of nature are unleashed when a locomotive gets into adhesion difficulties: In this dramatic illustration, the sparks are flying as 9F 2-10-0 No. 92013 valiantly grapples with a troublesome ballast train in the Banbury area in 1966.

WHILE many people will connect 'adhesion' with glues of one sort or another, the Concise Oxford Dictionary gives, as a fourth definition, 'the maintenance of contact between the wheels of a vehicle and the road'. Even this does not really embrace our use of the word, as it is the flanges which ensure that railway vehicles' wheels stay on the track. In the railway industry, the word means that, at the point where the wheels are in contact with the rail, the two surfaces are not moving relative to each other in the direction of travel.

Loss of adhesion can take two forms: when an axle is being driven, it is possible for the wheels to spin round more rapidly than the vehicle is travelling. Alternatively, when braking, the wheels can 'lock up' and skid along the track instead of rotating.

Neither is good news for the railway operator.

In this article, I shall describe the factors affecting adhesion and the problems it can cause with the haulage of trains, although, with modern technology, controlled loss of adhesion can these days be used advantageously under certain conditions.

Friction is generated whenever one flat surface is moved over another. Under a given set of conditions, there is a 'coefficient of friction' for every pair of materials which can

be measured in the way shown diagrammatically in the figure at the foot of this page. Weights are added to the pan on the right until movement between the two materials starts. The coefficient, usually referred to as u ('mu') is defined as the ratio of the force required to make the upper surface move (w) divided by that pressing the two of them together (W). If W equals 100 and w 25, the coefficient becomes 25/100. In the laboratory this is usually expressed in decimal form – 0.25 in the example shown – while in railway parlance it is often given as a percentage – 25% in this case.

As long as the two surfaces are flat, the actual area of the two that are in contact does not affect the force w. At first sight this seems strange, but looking at where they meet under ultra-high magnification, it can be seen that only the minute irregularities in them actually come into contact. The pressure on these is so high that some degree of plastic flow takes place to relieve them, with microscopic bonds being formed between the two faces. The cross-sectional area of these depends on the total weight being supported, so the actual area of contact between the two surfaces is determined solely by the forces pressing them together. Severing these bonds produces the

friction, the force necessary only being related to their cross-section and the nature of the two surfaces.

It is important to remember that these coefficients of friction only apply when the two surfaces are absolutely flat. If there are lumps or bumps in either, other factors come into play, increasing the force needed to make one move over the other. Even when nothing larger than grains of sand is introduced between them, friction increases greatly.

When horses were the main form of motive power, their iron-shod hooves dug into the soft surface of the unmade roads of those days, which gave them a good grip, like the heels of tug-of-war contestants.

This sort of grip is different from that existing between steel, or cast-iron, wheels and rails. During the pioneering days of steam traction, the difficulty of getting sufficient adhesion between two such surfaces was serious enough to prompt one design which was driven by what amounted to a pair of mechanical legs.

Blenkinsop was more successful when he used a rack-and-pinion drive on several locomotives built by Matthew Murray for the Middleton Railway, but the breakthrough came further north.

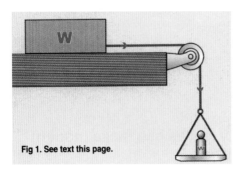

Fig 1. See text this page.

It was on Tyneside that William Hedley, the builder of *Puffing Billy*, settled the big debate with some full-size experiments. He constructed a special carriage, whose wheels were driven by gearing from crank-handles, turned by men standing on platforms attached to the vehicle. This showed that, with enough weight on the wheels, sufficient tractive effort could be transmitted from them to the cast-iron rails to make the steam locomotive a feasible form of motive power.

The coefficient of friction between two polished and dry steel surfaces is normally about 0.25, although in particularly favourable circumstances it can be considerably higher. If any lubricant gets between the two surfaces, the coefficient plummets, so any of Railtrack's flange lubricators provided to reduce the wear on curves must deliver the grease accurately to the inside of the rail head and not allow it to spread onto the running surface.

Even water, by dampening rails, can reduce adhesion and cause difficulties. In the UK the pressure between the driving wheels and the rail is usually sufficient to melt the ice crystals resulting from a light covering of snow, but not a thick layer of ice. The troubles of the 'wrong sort of snow', however, mainly result for other reasons, such as it getting blown into electrical equipment.

'Leaves on the line' cause much more of an adhesion problem. The media, as well as many of the general public, find it difficult to appreciate how a few leaves can make modern multiple-unit trains stall on banks which locomotives used to climb without any difficulty. The fallen leaves get crushed on to the rails by the first train that passes after they have landed, but it is not these themselves which cause the main problem.

Forcing the 'mush' into intimate contact with a highly-polished steel surface enables some of the decomposition products in the leaves to react chemically with the iron to produce a surface layer. Although only a few molecules thick, this material has a very low coefficient of friction, so the next train to arrive stalls. The layer is thin enough to wear off quickly if trains pass over the affected stretches, but that can only happen if they are able to cope with the conditions!

When all trains were hauled by locomotives, the available adhesion weight was high. An LNER Class V1 hauling a train on Scottish suburban branches had just over 57 tons adhesion weight. One of today's two-car Class 156s turns the scales at 70 tons, and each car can seat some 75 passengers. The maximum loaded weight of a set is about 80 tons, and only about half of this will be carried by the powered bogies. So it has a little over 40 tons adhesion weight.

A skilful driver could control the tractive effort of a steam locomotive a lot more accurately than can be done using today's

Stirling Single No. 1: Its 8ft diameter driving wheels imposed far lower 'point forces' on the rail joints of track than today's diesel and electric trains. CHRIS MILNER

diesel and electric power controllers with their limited number of operating positions. Even those steam locomotives provided with lever reverse, which only had a few notches available, still had more settings than one of today's multiple-units, quite apart from the infinitely variable throttling available using the regulator.

Some steam locomotives were provided with more easily adjustable regulators than

> ## Leaves on the line cause much more of an adhesion problem. The media, as well as many of the general public, find it difficult to appreciate how a few leaves can make modern multiple-unit trains stall on banks

others, which also helped the driver to stop any slipping. The GWR design was particularly good in this respect, as I recall from one incident when I was on a footbridge, watching one of its trains starting from a station. It moved off smartly and as the cab passed me I noted that the driver, having checked the road was clear, was getting something out of the locker on the tender, with his back to the regulator!

Things get even worse with 'Pacers'. A two-

car Class 144 weighs 48½ tons, of which little more than half will be available for adhesion, because each car has only one driven axle. With all seats occupied, the weight of a train would go up by eight tons, but even then this would only give about 28 tons adhesion weight, almost exactly half that of a V1. Being multiple units, 'Pacers' are fitted with a limited number of power notches, giving the driver little scope to match torque or tractive-effort accurately with adhesion. Today's need for higher performance requires a transmission which produces tractive efforts that are proportionately greater than those available in steam days.

Most steam locomotives were fitted with sanders which increased adhesion significantly Modern traction in this country is not, because it is impossible to prevent sand getting into underfloor equipment, swept in by the streams of air needed for combustion or cooling.

Modern technology can, nevertheless, produce better adhesion with high-powered locomotives in a different way, which can be especially valuable with freight. In text books, it is usually only quoted for the point at which the test item just begins to move, so is more correctly referred to as the 'static coefficient of friction'. As the speed at which the two surfaces move relative to each other increases, the coefficient of friction rises initially, but when the differential becomes more than a few mph, it starts to drop again, falling progressively to a much lower value. These effects are probably due to the way the micro-bonds between the two surfaces, referred to earlier, are formed and broken. With modern technology, advantage can be taken of this initial increase in friction, as will be described later.

▶

Increasing temperature also causes the coefficient of friction to fall, and this can have a profound effect on railway brakes, but that aspect of adhesion will have to be considered in another article.

To use the tractive effort produced by a locomotive's transmission it is therefore necessary to provide sufficient weight on those wheels that are doing the driving, The civil engineers stipulate the maximum axle-loads permitted for each part of the railway system, but this figure may have to be qualified by reference to the diameter of the wheels involved. The 'point-forces' on rail joints from driving wheels eight feet in diameter, such as those on Stirling's Singles, will be less than with today's diesel or electric traction, where the diameter of their wheels is often little over three feet.

Hammer blow

Other factors must be taken into account. Balancing the reciprocating weights on a steam locomotive leads to 'hammer blow' at speed. Because the LMS 'Turbomotive' did not have a reciprocating drive, it was allowed an extra ton or so of adhesion weight on each driving axle compared with the conventional 'Princesses'. Similarly 'nose-suspended' traction motors are particularly heavy on the track. (They can also worsen the ride for passengers in EMUs).

The civil engineers have other limits which restrict the weight of locomotives. These are the overall weight and the 'weight per foot run', both of which are significant when assessing the load capacity of underline structures such as bridges and viaducts, rather than the strength of the track itself. The ponderous Class 40s and 'Peaks' were examples of the need to fit carrying axles to keep within the maximum able-loading figures, and, as a

The LMS 'Turbomotive': Because it had no reciprocating drive, it was allowed an extra ton or so of adhesion weight on each driving axle compared with a conventional 'Princess Royal'. *RM* ARCHIVE

result, full use could not be made of the weight of these locomotives for adhesion purposes.

If the weight permitted on a single axle is not enough to provide sufficient tractive effort within the adhesion limits, more driving wheels will have to be provided. This is not difficult with modern technology, when powered axles can be distributed along the length of the train, but it greatly influenced the design of steam locomotives. Many of the earliest designs had single driving axles only, but, as the size and weight of locomotives increased, two or more coupled ones were adopted, each of which could support the same amount of weight. If the springing and spacing of the axles are worked out correctly, each axle can benefit from the maximum weight permitted.

There are various drawbacks with this. A locomotive with two, or more, coupled axles is never as free running as a Single. When steam-sanding equipment was developed in the late 19th century, many designers took the opportunity to revert to single driving axles. The "Spinner" epithet applied to the Midland Singles was testimony to their free running characteristics.

In addition, with more than four coupled axles it is often difficult to make the locomotive flexible enough to negotiate curves, even slowly. The BR Standard 9F 2-10-0s had flangeless wheels on the centre coupled axles for this reason, and some other designs had thinner flanges on other driving wheels.

Stability

As well as needing carrying axles to support the weight of locomotives as they became heavier, with fast-running designs, it became necessary to fit leading pony trucks or bogies for stability. At the other end of the locomotive, trailing wheels were also needed to accommodate wide fireboxes of the type pioneered by Ivatt on his large GN Atlantics. The presence of any such axles reduces the proportion of the all-up weight available for adhesion, which helps to explain why more than half the steam locomotives ever built for use on this country's railways had the 0-6-0 wheel arrangement, either in tank or tender form.

Locomotives without any rear carrying wheels are always less inclined to suffer from lack of adhesion. For example, a 4-6-0 is less likely to slip than a comparably powerful 4-6-2 with the same adhesion weight. This is because the drawbar, situated between the locomotive and its tender or at the rear of the bunker on a tank design, is several feet above rail level. As the tractive forces come into operation they try to make the front-end lift, as happens in an exaggerated form with dragsters. This transfers some of the weight off the front wheels and on to the rearmost pair. If the latter are on a driving axle it might benefit from the added adhesion weight, but anything transferred to a carrying axle results in a loss.

Adequate adhesion is most important at low or zero speeds, or two reasons. Firstly there is a significant 'sticksion' effect with a train, which requires a lot of extra tractive effort to get it moving from rest. Secondly, the highest tractive efforts are produced at low speeds, even though most modern traction is capable of producing its maximum power output over quite an extended speed range.

Only a little over half the total weight of a Class 144 unit is available for adhesion because the units have only one driven axle. Unit No. 144012 should have no problems with wheel slip on a perfect spring day as it waits at Keighley on May 18, 1987 with an all-stations service to Leeds. CHRIS MILNER COLLECTION.

Because (Power) = (Tractive Effort) x (Speed), the faster a train goes, the less tractive effort is needed to use the same power output from the prime mover (in the case of a diesel) or that available from the supply system with straight electrics. It follows from this that most problems with loss of adhesion occur at low speeds, which, with steam, often occurred before the train itself started to move. 'Runaway' slipping sometimes took place, and could damage the locomotive, the track, or both.

Colin Tether has reminded me that at one time an 'adhesion factor' used to be quoted for each steam class. This was obtained by dividing the adhesion weight (in pounds) by the nominal tractive effort (NTE). For example, No. 71000 *Duke of Gloucester* had a NTE of 35,100lbf and an adhesion weight of 66 tons (147,840lb). This gave it an adhesion factor of 4.21. The adhesion factor is the reciprocal of the coefficient of friction necessary to enable the full tractive effort of the locomotive to be exerted without slipping taking place. In this case, the figure corresponds to what we would refer to these days as 24% adhesion.

The Southern 1-Co-Co-1 diesel-electric locomotive No. 10203, with a nominal power of 2,000hp at the flywheel, produced a tractive effort of 50,000lbf up to 10½mph, and had an adhesion weight of 109.5 tons, making its corresponding adhesion factor 4.91. Its output was deliberately restricted at low speeds, being only 1,400hp at the drawbar at 10½mph, compared with an available maximum of 1,760hp from the generator for traction. If its tractive effort had not been held constant below this speed, at an output of 1,400hp the adhesion factor would have fallen to 2.00 at 5mph and 0.90 at 2mph. Adhesion figures of 50 and 110% would be necessary to achieve this – always assuming that the correspondingly higher electric currents did not burn out the windings.

Most modern motive power either uses a similar control system to prevent the production of a tractive effort that is higher than that which can be handled by the adhesion under 'normal' conditions, while, alternatively, the design of the equipment provides a built-in limit. However, if a coefficient of friction lower than that assumed at the design stage is encountered, slipping can still occur, but some forms of motive power have control systems which will automatically notch back the output when slipping occurs.

Nearly all steam locomotives were driven by reciprocating pistons which turned the wheels by means of connecting rods and cranks. This arrangement results in variations in torque as the driving wheels rotate. The maximum force from a single cylinder is obtained when its connecting rod and crank are at right-angles to each other, but this falls

Modern technology can, nevertheless, produce better adhesion with high-powered locomotives

to zero when they are in a straight line at each end of the piston stroke.

As most steam locomotives are fitted with more than a single cylinder, the tractive effort as the wheels rotate does not actually decrease to zero. Even so there can still be considerable variations in the course of each revolution of the driving wheels. At 100% cut-off and full boiler pressure, the forces on a two-cylinder design vary over a range of 40%, with four peaks and troughs per revolution. The same applies to a conventional four-cylinder design, but on a 'Lord Nelson', with its cranks at 45°/135° instead of the usual 90°, the variation drops to 7%. This is even better than the 15% obtained with a conventional three-cylinder drive.

These inherent variations prevented any steam locomotive designer from taking advantage of the initial increase in the coefficient of friction as the relative speed increases between a set of slipping wheels and the rails.

With modem forms of motive power, the torque from the traction motors at a given speed is virtually constant, and the development of high-speed electronics enables controlled slipping to be maintained at low speeds by varying the current. To take greatest advantage of this effect, the difference in speed between the slipping wheel and that along the track must be kept within a very narrow band.

Friction

If the wheels start to rotate too fast, the coefficient of friction starts to drop again. For maximum effect the relative speed has to be maintained on the narrow peak of the curve. While the output of a traction motor suffers a fall-off in torque as its speed increases, that curve is not as steep as the decrease in friction, and corrective action has to be taken if maximum tractive effort is to be maintained. This is difficult or impossible to do manually as the control systems on modem motive power, especially those required to work in multiple, are normally provided with a limited number of 'notches' on the power controller. So there is no way in which it can be juggled by the driver to keep the slipping speed within the limits needed.

To achieve the full benefits of controlled slipping, two additional sets of equipment are needed. First of all, the locomotive's actual speed along the track has to be measured accurately and compared with that at which the driving wheels are rotating. The current to the motors must then be controlled accurately to maintain the required degree of slipping to maximise the tractive effort. Such equipment

is fitted to the Class 60s as well as the various Co-Cos of General Motors design imported in recent years for freight duties.

In my September 1986 article I described how General Motors Type 5 No. 59004 brought a load of 2,284 tons up from Westbury to Southall. It was at Hayes, as we were easing the train across all the other running lines at 10mph, that this 'wheel creep control' suddenly cut in automatically. The only indication that this was happening was the whistling noise from the slipping wheels; the control system took over so quickly that the wheel slip warning light never lit.

This type of system copes automatically with almost any track conditions, and, as on my journey, is regularly called on to operate in normal weather conditions. Unfortunately there is no way in which the costs of similar equipment for every powered axle on the country's multiple unit fleet could be justified for use on a few occasions each year when conditions are particularly bad. Neither, of course, can we expect to be able to use our cars in every extreme of weather. ■

The terrible damage that can be caused by uncontrolled slipping: Tens of thousands of pounds worth of damage were caused to A2 Pacific No. 60532 *Blue Peter* in late 1994 when it was allowed to suffer a prolonged slip during a charter on the East Coast Main Line. The driving wheels were said to have attained an estimated speed of 120mph and the motion was bent and twisted beyond repair, forcing the loco to spend many months out of service.
MAURICE BURNS

The Furness section of the LMSR

Barrow-Carnforth train passing Dalton Junction – 4-6-4 tank locomotive No. 11102. O S NOCK

By O S NOCK, ACGI, BSc

MORE than 20 years have passed since any extended reference has been made in *The Railway Magazine* to the one-time Furness Railway.

The comparatively isolated position of the line has made it somewhat unfamiliar even to the railway student. A through traveller to Scotland by the West Coast route could get only passing glimpses of the Furness engines at Carnforth, and unless he were bound for some destination on the line itself, they were hardly likely to be seen by him anywhere else.

Throughout from Carnforth to Whitehaven, the main line follows the coast, and as would be expected pursues a very winding course. Although the Furness coast is nowhere very striking, some of the distant views are very fine, and include a number of the most famous peaks in the Lake District.

Leaving Carnforth by the sharply curved western platform, the line swings round almost at right-angles to the North-Western main line and joins the Carnforth-avoiding spur from the Midland. This connecting link is of great value in the working of mineral traffic to and from the Midland Division, and also of passenger specials from Leeds and other Yorkshire stations to Lakeside, the Furness station at the southern extremity of Windermere.

At first the railway runs through typical north-country pastoral scenery, passing Silverdale, until at Arnside comes the first of those wide sandy estuaries by which the Lakeland rivers enter the sea, that of the

At low water, Morecambe Bay seems one dreary interminable stretch of sand; at high tide, however, it is very lovely

Kent. Crossing the river on a low viaduct, the passenger has a fine distant view of the fells to the north of Kendal. The prospect seawards varies. At low water Morecambe Bay seems one dreary interminable stretch of sand; at high tide, however, it is very lovely, especially at night, when moonlight on the water can make the scene enchanting.

Past Grange-over-Sands and Kent's Bank, the railway is carried just above the shore, winding its way round the base of Lindale Fell. These two charming watering places straggle up the steep, wooded hillside behind the railway, and look out across the bay on a wide-flung panorama of mountain and sea, stretching far away to the east, where the flat summit of Ingleborough dominates the rolling ridges of the Pennines. Beyond Kent's Bank the line swings round to the right, and then Cark and Cartmel station is passed. Cartmel is a very ancient little place, nestling in the hills and possessing a venerable priory, while near the station is the curious old town of Flookburgh, renowned for its mussels.

We are now approaching the Leven estuary. Away to the north, in the far background, are the peaks of the Coniston range, while farther east are the Yewdale and Langdale mountains. Between these distant heights and the estuary lies Esthwaite Water, quietest of all the lakes. Across Morecambe Bay, Blackpool can be readily picked up by its tower, while the Furness coast can be seen stretching away from the pretty village of Bardsea, just across the water, right to Piel Island with its hoary old castle. The Leven

Viaduct was once the scene of a serious accident, when a train was literally blown off the line by a gale of hurricane force.

Immediately after crossing the viaduct, we pass Levens Junction, where the direct line to Lakeside, Windermere, diverges. The regular passenger service to Lakeside, however, is worked from Ulverston, leaving the main line at Plumpton Junction, about ¾-mile further on. Greenodd Junction is the third apex of this triangle. The spur from this latter point to Levens Junction is largely used by excursions to Lakeside from beyond Carnforth, and has been re-laid since the time during the war when the track was taken up and shipped to France for the use of the Railway Operating Division. From Greenodd Junction the branch reaches the foot of Windermere by the Leven gorge, a most delightful entry to the Lake District proper, which was Wordsworth's favourite route.

Plumpton Junction is an important box, as it also controls the junction leading to the Conishead iron mines and iron-works, which are on the shore near the viaduct, and can easily be located from the train by their blast-furnaces. The line is now rising steeply (for 2¼ miles at 1 in 76 to 107 out of a bank which is 3½ miles long), and passes on the right the conical hill on which is the Hoad monument; this lighthouse-looking erection is a prominent landmark for many miles round. Just below the hill lies Ulverston, the county town of Furness. The station is of some importance as the junction for Lakeside. Restarting, heavy collar-work for the engine is involved until reaching the summit at Lindal Moor, the scene of one of the most extraordinary accidents in British railway history.

The Furness Railway has always held a similar position in the north to that of the South Eastern in the south, in that its doings provided abundant and excellent 'copy' for humorists, but the climax must surely have been reached when one of its engines disappeared down a hole! This mishap has

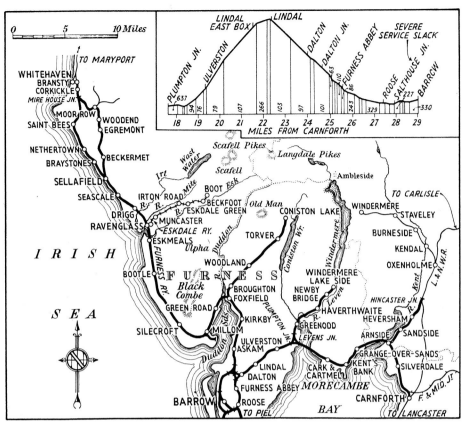

Map of the Furness section of the LMSR with a gradient profile of the line from Barrow to Ulverstone (inset).

been described several times in *The Railway Magazine*, but will bear re-telling. The district round Lindal Moor is honeycombed with iron ore workings, and a subsidence occurred right under the main line near Lindal station when a 0-6-0 goods engine was engaged in shunting at the spot. The driver and fireman managed to jump clear, but the engine went down to such a depth that it has never been recovered. Since then, timber longitudinals of great strength have been provided to support the track, and no further subsidence mishaps have occurred.

From Lindal station the line falls steeply through a short tunnel, which for a great part of its length is driven through rock hard

enough to require no lining, so that the Dalton end, a rough-hewn hole in the hillside, presents a most singular appearance. The descent from Lindal to Roose is 6½ miles long, the steepest pitches being 1¾miles at 1 in 100 from Lindal to Dalton, and ¾-mile slightly steeper from Dalton Junction. A winding stretch follows through Dalton and then, after another short tunnel, Dalton Junction is passed. Here the Barrow avoiding line goes off to the right to join the main line at Park South crossing, barely a mile away. A little further on comes the gem of the whole route, the magnificent ruins of Furness Abbey. While the train is waiting at the station an excellent view can be had from the right-hand side. A surrounding ring of wooded hills, and vivid green lawns among the ruins, make up an unforgettable picture.

Roose is now passed and we slow to 15mph past Salthouse Junction, where the branch from Piel joins, and the direct line to Barrow docks branches off. Piel castle can be seen well from here, and there are also glimpses of the varied shipping in the docks. Behind, a great array of electric cranes shows the whereabouts of the Vickers-Armstrong shipyard. The locomotive, carriage and wagon shops of the late Furness Railway and the running sheds are seen in the distance on the left, and then we reach Barrow-in-Furness.

Barrow is the headquarters of the Furness district, and the station is much the largest on the line, having four through platforms. ▶

Up iron ore train on the Furness section, hauled by an ex-Furness Railway 0-6-0 locomotive.

Ulverston station looking towards Carnforth. The view shows the down line with platforms on both sides. O S NOCK

The two main platforms are covered by a fine all-over roof enclosing a station of airy and spacious appearance; the other two platforms outside the main station are normally used only for excursions. A point of interest in the station yard is the small glass-sided exhibition building housing the historic Bury engine known as "Old Coppernob", from the appearance of its 'haystack' firebox – a relic of earliest Furness days.

After leaving Barrow and passing on the left the works of the Barrow Haematite Iron & Steel Company, the line runs due north for a while. A signalbox along here, Cocken, reminds us of the proximity of the little house High Cocken, which was the early home of George Romney, the great artist. At Sandscale crossing, the line turns eastwards, running near the picturesque and lonely sand dunes of Roanhead; then, curving very sharply to the left, we join the Barrow avoiding line at Park South, having travelled 8½ miles since leaving it at Dalton Junction, here only a mile away by the spur.

Past Askam and Kirkby, the line runs alongside, but not quite on the shore of the Duddon estuary. The mass of Black Combe dominates the view to the north-west, but the beauty is somewhat marred by the redness of the sand, due to iron ore workings, and also to the Millom ironworks across the water, which often add clouds of dense white smoke to the scene. Here the railway is making a great detour. The distance across the estuary from Barrow to Silecroft is 8½ miles as the crow flies, but by the railway it is no less than 19 miles.

Central station Barrow-in-Furness with a Furness Railway double-header.

Carnforth station looking towards Barrow view shows platform and crossover road used by trains for the Furness line. Beyond may be seen the bay platform used by Midland division trains for Leeds. O S NOCK

Beyond Kirkby, the Coniston mountains are seen at close quarters – a magnificent group – with the Ulpha fells a little to the left, up the Duddon valley. Foxfield is the junction for the Coniston line, which is a real 'scenic' railway. On the final stage from Torver, the branch is carried high up on the side of the Old Man range, and almost the whole length of the lake can be seen from the train. From Coniston station there is a glorious view of the Yewdale crags.

The main line now crosses the Duddon, just beyond Foxfield, and so enters Cumberland. From here the northern side of the estuary is followed, past Green Road and the industrial town of Millom, and then the railway curves round to the north again right under Black Combe, the most southerly mountain of the Lake District. Onwards to Whitehaven the line at last takes a fairly direct course. Past Silecroft and Bootle, a level strip of farming country separates high moor lands from the sea. At Eskmeals, among the lonely sand dunes on the sea side, is a range for testing the biggest naval guns. The Esk, which is crossed just beyond the station, sweeps right round among the sand hills, to join the Irt and the Mite before entering the sea. Up the valley rise tier upon tier of rough fells, crowned by the Scafell group, the highest mountain mass in England. Close at hand, on the right of the train, are the wooded slopes and grounds of Muncaster Castle, and then Ravenglass is reached.

This station is probably one of the best known of all on the Furness line, as the starting point of the Ravenglass & Eskdale narrow gauge railway, but Ravenglass itself is

a place of note. It was once a smuggling town, and in far earlier times was a Roman seaport. Near by is a Roman villa, in excellent preservation, and the straight line up Eskdale and over Hardknott Pass (where are found the remains of a Roman camp) and Wrynose Pass was once the route of a Roman road from Ravenglass to Ambleside. Immediately after leaving Ravenglass the confluence of the rivers Irt and Mite is crossed, and then from here onwards to Drigg, a magnificent array of mountains is gradually revealed to the east. Yewbarrow, Great Gable, Scafell, and the grim-looking Screes nearly surround the deep

The traffic which passes over the line is a curious mixture

trough wherein lies Wastwater; further south lies Eskdale, with the conical Harter Fell towering up behind.

At Seascale, a rising seaside resort, the line comes right out on the sea shore. The coast is now becoming much bolder, the sand dunes giving place to a line of low cliffs. Across the Irish Sea the Isle of Man is clearly visible in good weather, while Criffel in Dumfriesshire can be easily picked out.

At Sellafield, the next station, a branch goes inland to Egremont and the iron ore districts round Cleator Moor. From Sellafield to Whitehaven the main line is single, with passing loops at Nethertown, St Bees, and Corkickle. Here we travel on a ledge cut in the cliffs, and soon after passing the bungalow

colony of Braystones, we see the bold headland of St Bees ahead. This part of the coast is very wild, and in many places the base of the cliffs is protected against the sea by heavy masonry work. At St Bees the line turns inland, and a short run brings us to the Corkickle station at Whitehaven. Just before Whitehaven we are joined by the double line branch from Cleator Moor, which runs alongside almost until the station is reached. When the main line was first constructed, Corkickle was the terminus, from the south, of the Whitehaven & Furness Junction Railway. In 1854, a single line tunnel was opened joining Corkickle to the Bransty station of the Whitehaven Junction Railway, thus giving through communication from north to south through Whitehaven. The tunnel, which was of irregular section, has recently been re-lined to give full clearance for the largest rolling stock.

The traffic which passes over the line is a curious mixture; passenger traffic is heaviest during the tourist season, but there is always a steady flow of travel quite apart from the numerous excursion trains worked from large centres in Yorkshire and Lancashire. My earliest acquaintance with the line was in 1916, and at that time it formed a connecting link of great importance. Barrow-in-Furness, comparatively safe from raids by sea and air, had grown to be, not only a depot for building and refitting ships of the Royal Navy, but also an enormous munition-working centre. The goods traffic alone was prodigious, and such was the extent of the munition work that special trains were run morning and evening to and from Barrow to carry the vast numbers of workers who lived in ▶

the neighbouring towns of Dalton, Askam and Ulverston. There was no mistaking these trains, which were composed entirely of London & North Western six-wheeled stock and painted chocolate colour all over, without the characteristic upper white panels. Incidentally, a train for shipyard workers, not carrying ordinary passengers, still runs daily in the mornings from Greenodd and Ulverston direct to the shipyard, returning in the evening. Apart from the North Western coaches just mentioned, there was hardly any 'foreign' working during the war, the only exception that I can remember being the working of a Maryport and Carlisle 0-4-2 tender engine on the evening 'mail' from Whitehaven southwards. Her bright green livery made a vivid contrast with the dark red Furness engines.

Earlier engines of the Furness Railway were described in most interesting fashion by the late E L Ahrons in his articles on Locomotive and Train Working in the Latter Part of the Nineteenth Century in 1921, but during the present century great strides were made in the locomotive department under the superintendence of W F Pettigrew, while just after the war the new tank engines built to D L Rutherford's designs were among the largest in the country. Simplicity, both in outline and design, has always been an outstanding characteristic of Furness engines. As far as wheel arrangements are concerned, tender types in 1920 were 4-4-0 and 0-6-0 only, with three very old 2-4-0s; and tank engines were 4-4-2, 0-6-0, and 0-6-2, plus three ancient 2-4-2 tanks and one 0-4-0

Up express (with through coach for Euston) leaving Whitehaven, hauled by LMSR (ex-LNWR) 'Precursor' 4-4-0 locomotive No. 5201 *Egeria*. D S BARRIE

tank. It is notable that although some experiments were made with super-heating just prior to the war, one or two engines being fitted with apparatus of the Phoenix type, the idea never got any further and even the large 4-6-4 tanks of 1921 used saturated steam.

Neglecting the old engines built prior to 1895, there were three distinct classes of 4-4-0 engines at work before the Grouping. The first were built in 1896 by Sharp, Stewart & Company. They had 6ft 0in coupled wheels, 18in x 24in cylinders, 150lb boiler pressure, and a total heating surface of 1,208sq ft. In 1897, W F Pettigrew was appointed locomotive superintendent, and in 1902 he brought out an enlarged class, Nos. 126-129,

with 6ft 6in coupled wheels, 18in x 26in cylinders, 160lb pressure and 1,2705sq ft of heating surface. These handsome engines were doing a great deal of the faster and lighter passenger working just before Grouping. In his last design, Mr Pettigrew reverted to 6ft 0in wheels. The four engines of the 130 class were built by the North British Locomotive Co Ltd, in 1914, and had 18in x 26in cylinders, a boiler pressure of 170lb and a total heating surface of 1,246sq ft. The reduced size of coupled wheels gave these engines a considerable advantage over their predecessors in tackling the increasing train loads, whilst they have shown themselves capable of running at the highest speeds desirable on so tortuous a route.

Mr Pettigrew was a firm believer in standardisation, and in the case of both the 126 and 130 classes of 4-4-0 engines, he built 0-6-0 goods engines with identical boilers and cylinders; the 1901 0-6-0s had 4ft 6in, and the 1914 class 4ft 7½in wheels. The latter were ideal engines for dealing with the heavy wartime traffic. The 0-6-2 tank engines, of which the first were built in 1898, were powerful engines for the time, having 18in x 26in cylinders, 4ft 8in coupled wheels and 150lb pressure. In 1916 and subsequently, they were being used for widely varying duties, from working the munition workers' special and stopping passenger trains to banking goods trains in both directions to Lindal summit.

A handsome class of 4-4-2 tank engine was built by Kitson & Company in 1915 for working the Lakeside and Coniston branches and the Grange-over-Sands and Kendal service, in the latter case running over the West Coast main line between Hincaster Junction and Oxenholme, including a short length of the lower part of Grayrigg bank. The Coniston branch also has some hard climbing from Broughton-in-Furness onwards. Loads,

FR 4-4-0 locomotive No. 129, built 1902.

FR 0-6-2 tank locomotive No. 110 of the 1898 class.

however, were not very heavy and the engines, despite their moderate dimensions, did excellently. They had 17½in x 24in cylinders, 5ft 8in coupled wheels, 160lb pressure, and a total heating surface of 1,070sq ft.

The last Furness design was a powerful type of 4-6-4 tank engine brought out in 1921 by D L Rutherford. These locomotives were remarkable in two respects; that they were non-superheated has already been mentioned, but they were the first 4-6-4 tank locomotives to have inside cylinders, and still remain the only such engines in this country. They were built by Kitson & Co, and have 19½in x 26in cylinders, driving the leading coupled wheels, 5ft 8in driving wheels, a boiler pressure of 170lb per sq in and a total heating surface of 2,003sq ft. The total weight in working order is 92¾ tons, of which 55 tons are available for adhesion. Their introduction revolutionised Furness hill-climbing, especially on the semi-fast trains on which they were largely put to work, of which the morning service to London is an example.

Since Grouping great changes have taken place in the locomotive department. In the cause of standardisation it was inevitable that the Furness types, of which there were only a few examples of each, should soon be scrapped. In the years 1925-30, before standardisation was well under way, it was possible to make some very interesting comparisons between the Furness engines and such newcomers as had arrived. One of the earliest 'foreigners' was a large Glasgow & South Western 0-6-0 goods engine of Peter Drummond's design, which was at work in the autumn of 1923. Then came Midland Class 2 4-4-0s, North Western non-superheater 'Precursors' and 'Experiments', and at a later date 'George Vs' and 'Princes'. The Furness 4-6-4 tanks were still unsurpassed on the steep grades, but the 130 class 4-4-0s showed up poorly, even against the 'Precursors'. The latter did much excellent work, and one of them was usually employed on the fast early morning mail. The Midland 4-4-0s, however, were quite outclassed and were soon withdrawn.

They were the first 4-6-4 tank locomotives to have inside cylinders

After 1930, scrapping set in with a vengeance, so much so that on my last journey to Whitehaven, in April this year, I saw only one Furness engine, a 4-6-4 tank. Passenger traffic is now largely handled by LNW 'Princes' and 'Georges', and standard Class 2 4-4-0s, though one important turn, the 11.20am up from Whitehaven, is regularly taken by a standard 2-6-4 tank, working through to Preston. In many cases, as, for example, the 1pm out of Carlisle, the engine works through from Carlisle to Carnforth. A large number of L & Y goods engines are at work, and, of course, there are the standard Class 4 0-6-0s. The Lakeside and Coniston branches are being worked by L & Y non-superheater 2-4-2 tanks equipped for push-and-pull working. The Furness engine shed at Carnforth is no longer used, and at the northern extremity of the line the passenger engines are concentrated at Workington (LNW) shed.

Locomotive working does not present any great difficulty except between Barrow and Ulverston. The severe gradients between Ulverston and Furness Abbey have already been mentioned, but with such engines as the 'Princes' and 'Georges' loads of 250-300 tons are no great tax. With freight trains, however, a good deal of 'assistant mileage' is necessary over this section. Down trains stop at Plumpton for banking assistance to Lindal Moor, while in the reverse direction they are banked from Salthouse Junction. If coming from the north via the Barrow avoiding line, the banker is put on at Park South.

The fastest down passenger train is the 4.30am mail from Carnforth. This takes 47 minutes from Carnforth to Barrow and 89 minutes thence to Whitehaven, with stops only at Foxfield, Millom, Seascale and St Bees, which gives a total of 2hr 35min for the 74 miles. At one time it was booked from Carnforth to Ulverston, 19.4 miles, in 24 minutes, at 48.4mph, but the time has now been lengthened to 26 minutes. The 11.20am and the 2.23pm from Whitehaven, both with through coaches for Euston, and the latter with a buffet restaurant car – a recent innovation – from Barrow, are booked through to Carnforth in working times of 2hr 30min and 2hr 29min, respectively, and inclusive of nine inter-mediate stops in each case, the last-mentioned providing the fastest Furness service to-day. ■

FR 4-4-0 locomotive No. 131, built 1914.

Smoke effects

By F T BUDDEN

FAR and away the finest railway picture ever painted, in the opinion of many, is Turner's Rain, Steam, and Speed. It would be an impertinence even to praise so great a work, let alone to criticise it; but if I could help anyone to appreciate and enjoy the painting, I should feel it an honour. The railway-minded critic's first remark is: "Fancy putting the firebox in the front of the engine". But is it intended for the firebox? Turner travelled quite a lot in the Yorkshire Dales, and when he was in that neighbourhood is it not more than likely that he saw some of the old colliery engines, which used to carry a flaming brazier in front, as a kind of headlamp? And very picturesque it must have looked. Then again you hear the comment: "She's on the wrong road"; but what does that matter? Trains in America, and in many parts of Europe keep to the right. Turner never intended to present a correct mechanical drawing of an engine and train, but an impression of Rain, Steam, and Speed and how magnificently he did it! That train is certainly not standing still.

Thus, to follow the example of Turner, in making a picture of a train in motion, it is well to consider first what you mean to do. This is to describe to your friends, by means of a photograph, what you see and what are your feelings in watching an express passing. In describing a scene in words you have to observe certain rules of composition, and the same applies in making a picture. The background should be picturesque if possible, but not obtrusive; there must be a certain balance of objects on each side of the picture, transverse lines being balanced by upright lines; and there should be nothing to detract from the train, which must be the chief point of interest. Personally I prefer to have the camera on a level with the carriage windows, but many good views can be obtained from rail level or bridges. In my judgment the photographer should not try for minute detail; in fact, detail should be suppressed as far as possible, so that a general effect may be striven after.

Down 'Flying Scotsman' emerging from Greenwood tunnel behind LNER streamlined 4-6-2 locomotive No. 2511 *Silver King*.

▶ PHOTO: C R L COLES

Down goods train climbing Shap, LMSR Stanier 2-6-0 locomotive No. 2951 banked in rear by 0-6-0 tank No. 7338. PHOTO: J G MUIR

Newton Abbot-Laira goods train on Rattery bank, GWR 4-6-0 locomotive No. 4966 *Shakenhurst Hall.* PHOTO: H K HARMAN

The pre-war 'Golden Arrow' continental express near Bromley, SR 'Lord Nelson' 4-6-0 locomotive No. 863 *Lord Rodney* with Lemaître chimney.
H C CASSERLEY

Glasgow express near Carlisle about 1898, Caledonian Railway McIntosh 4-4-0 locomotive No. 774. PHOTO: F T BUDDEN

From *The Railway Magazine*, March 1941

'The Flying Dutchman' near Acton in 1892. The smoke effect is the same as that on Caledonian No. 774 opposite.

The most important thing is the smoke effect, as it is chiefly through this that the idea of power and speed can be conveyed. One must take the weather into account, for on warm dry days there is no steam at all to be seen. Another very important thing is to secure, if possible, the co-operation of the driver and fireman; a shovelful of coal at the right moment and the closing of the firebox door will make all the difference in the world to your picture. If you can get a good cloud of steam tinted with smoke your friend will say: "My word! She's moving"! and that is just what you want. Don't have the smoke too dense or the locomotive authorities may not be pleased. If you can choose your spot so as to have a high bank or a clump of trees to form a background to the smoke, so much the better. A group of men working on the line improves a picture, but be careful not to get them nearer to the camera than, say, the first coach of the train, or the engine will be dwarfed.

Having obtained a satisfactory negative with excellent smoke, you may be greatly disappointed with the way it prints, the smoke being too dense to appear in the print. In such cases I put the negative in the enlarging camera, and take a large piece of white cardboard in the centre of which a pear-shaped hole has been cut, about the size of the smoke

wreath. Having exposed the printing paper for the time I think necessary, I hold the card so that the light through the hole exposes the smoke only, keeping the said card slowly moving so as to prevent an 'edge' being made. I find that it may take from three to five times as long to print the smoke satisfactorily as to print the rest of the negative. If in developing the smoke does not come up as soon as is desired, it may be accelerated with a tuft of cotton wool dipped in developer and gently rubbed in. Sometimes it is worth transferring the smoke from one negative to another that has none. Choose a good negative, but one which has a large space of blank sky where the smoke should be, and this space should not be cut by any object such as a signal, or a branch of a tree. Next choose a negative with a good smoke effect, from which you wish to transfer, and cover it with a piece of clear glass of the same size, binding the edges as one does in a lantern slide. On this cover glass paint out all the rest of the negative with black paint, leaving only the smoke wreath clear. Thus the paint will be solely on the cover glass, leaving the negative quite untouched. Having made sure that your enlarging apparatus is absolutely rigid, take a piece of white paper the exact size that you mean to use for the enlargement, and fix it to the board of the enlarger; then insert

the smokeless negative in the enlarger, focus it on the piece of white paper, and with a pen and ink trace out the top of the chimney.

Now cover the lens with the cap, and place the piece of sensitised paper exactly over the white paper, securing it in place. Expose this for the time you think necessary, put back the lens cap, and transfer the sensitised paper to a box or dark envelope, making certain that you will be able to recognise which is the upper edge. Remove the negative and replace it with the smoke negative, so arranging it that the base of the smoke-wreath comes exactly over your drawing of the top of the chimney. Put on the cap, take the piece of sensitised paper from the box, and having verified which is the right way up, place over the white paper. Then expose for about three to five times as long as you gave the other negative, according to the relative densities of the two negatives, and develop as usual.

If in the result the smoke does not exactly fit the chimney, the superfluous edges can be painted out with a solution of 'hypo' and ferrocyanide of potassium, which, incidentally, is a very poisonous solution and requires careful handling. In the photographs above, the smoke was transferred from ex-Caledonian 4-4-0 No. 774 to my GWR broad-gauge picture in this way. ∎

Diesels in Devon and Cornwall

Top: The curve near Teignmouth station – taking the GW main line from alongside the Teign estuary to run along the sea wall to Starcross – is the location for Class 50 No. 50027 *Lion* working the 09.24 Paignton to Birmingham New Street on September 7, 1985.

Right: For many years the china clay hood wagons were a characteristic of Cornwall, and here Class 37 No. 37273 runs into the yard at Par with empty wagons on July 26, 1984.

Bottom: With its white embellishments, Class 45 No. 45022 powers away from Teignmouth towards Shaldon Bridge with the 09.11 (SO) Manchester Piccadilly to Newquay service on July 28, 1984.

Top: Class 45 No. 45003 crosses Coombe St Stephen Viaduct on September 6, 1985, with a Penzance to Bristol Temple Meads working.

Left: On July 26, 1984, the 10.24 Penzance to Liverpool was double-headed, giving freshly overhauled 'Peak' No. 45070 a test run in the process with Class 50 No. 50017. The pair are seen entering Liskeard station.

Below: Newton Abbot once boasted a fine array of GWR semaphore signals, but is now much rationalised. Class 47 No. 47074 eases away with the 09.14 Brighton-Penzance train on July 27, 1984.

ALL PICTURES:
TRACKS NORTH

Three engines passing slowly through the floods between Leigh and Benfleet, on the Fenchurch Street-Southend line, on February 3, 1953.

British railways and the January floods

HIGH tides and severe gales are by no means uncommon on the East Coast of England, and in the Thames Estuary, but on the night of January 31, 1953 the two acted in concert to such an extent that the sea rose several feet higher than was predicted, with the gale whipping up wave action. Coastal defences were breached at many places from the Humber right round to the outskirts of London, and the inundation of low-lying lands caused damage on a scale unequalled within living memory. The Eastern and Southern Regions of British Railways suffered severely, and train services on several lines had to be suspended.

On the Lincolnshire side of the Humber, the Pier station at New Holland was put out of action when the ferry boat plying to and from Hull broke loose from its moorings. The ship's funnel wrecked a signal gantry, and the pier roadway and the pontoon buffers were damaged. Trains were terminated at New

Holland Town until 1.30pm on February 1, when the service to the pier was restored with hand signalling. In the Immingham district, the railway to Coxhill was flooded at Killingholme, and damaged to such an extent that it could not be used until February 6. Immingham Dock station was put out of action by water sweeping between the platforms, but was reopened two days later. The water supply of the locomotive shed was contaminated with salt. The electric railway from Grimsby to Immingham, and the adajcent goods lines, sustained minor damage, which was quickly repaired. Flooding also occurred at Cleethorpes, and services were not fully restored until February 8.

Further south, on the Lincolnshire coast, at Mablethorpe, and Sutton-on-Sea, the inundation was more serious. By the evening of February 2, a shuttle service was in operation between Louth and Mablethorpe, but four miles of track south of the latter station were still under water. Trains carrying

slag for the repair of the coast defences were able to approach Sutton-on-Sea from the south two days later, but it was not until March 2 that normal services could be resumed throughout the line from Louth to Willoughby via Mablethorpe.

In West Norfolk, the main line from London to Hunstanton was breached in several places north of King's Lynn, and by the flooding of the River Ouse at Magdalen Road, a few miles to the south. The marshalling yard and station at South Lynn also were flooded. At Wells-on-Sea, the water rushed along the line from the harbour, and flooded the station and yard to a depth of 4ft, and the line to Heacham was damaged near Holkham. Wells station was reopened on February 4, and the main line to Hunstanton was restored a week later, but the Wells-Heacham line, now used only for goods trains, remained closed for through traffic.

At Hunstanton, the onset of the flood almost coincided with the departure of the

7.27pm train, which struck a wall of water about three-quarters of a mile south of the station. A bungalow floating on the crest of the wave struck the engine squarely on the smokebox, and damaged the vacuum brake pipe, so that the engine became immovable. Water rose rapidly to the level of the seats in the compartments, the lights failed, the engine fire was extinguished, and, from time to time, heavy debris crashed against the coaches. For six hours the enginemen and the guard kept up the morale of the passengers, and at length succeeded in effecting temporary repairs to the brakes, and, by using the floor boards of the tender as fuel, in raising sufficient steam to propel slowly back to Hunstanton.

Shortly before 10pm the flood breached the north bank of Oulton Broad, and flooded the station and other railway premises of Lowestoft to a depth of 3ft. A few minutes later, at Yarmouth, the south wall of Breydon Water burst, and the station and motive power depot at Yarmouth South Town were inundated. An hour later, the north wall of Breydon Water gave way, and a similar fate befell Yarmouth (Vauxhall). Further inland, water in the tidal rivers breached the railway from Yarmouth (Vauxhall) to Reedham at Berney Arms, the main line from South Town to London near Belton, and Aldeby, and the Lowestoft-Norwich line at several places at Haddiscoe. Some of the damage in the Yarmouth area was relatively slight, and was repaired within a few days, but more than a fortnight elapsed before both tracks were restored at Haddiscoe.

By midnight on January 31, the goods branch to Snape, at the head of the tidal River Alde, near Aldeburgh, had been flooded; the River Deben had breached the East Suffolk main line between Melton and Woodbridge; and the Pier and Beach stations at Felixstowe were inundated. Fortunately, most of the damage was relatively slight.

On the south bank of the Stour Estuary, the branch from Manningtree to Harwich was damaged at several places between Wrabness and the terminus. Harwich, Dovercourt, and Parkeston stations were cut off, or under water, and the marshalling yard and motive power depot at Parkeston were inundated. Despite some damage to the quays, the passenger services to and from the Continent were maintained at Parkeston without interruption. The railway between Wrabness and Parkestone was restored on February 5, but it was not until February 23 that normal working to Harwich could be resumed. The 120-ton double-track bridge ramp of the Harwich-Zebrugge train ferry was seriously damaged when the ferry Essex was lifted on the flood tide to an abnormal height, but was fully restored on March 5.

The high tide at the mouth of the River

The tracks suspended over a 100ft breach in the Norwich-Lowestoft line between Reedham and Haddiscoe.

Colne caused breaches in the railway from Colchester to Clacton between Hythe and Wivenhoe, and the Brightlingsea branch was washed out over a length of about three miles. Services to Clacton were resumed within a few days, but the Brightlingsea line has not yet been reopened.

In the Thames Estuary, the disastrous inundation at Canvey Island was accompanied by serious flooding of the main line from London (Fenchurch Street) to Southend, where three miles of track

A bungalow floating on the crest of the wave struck the engine squarely on the smokebox

between Benfleet and Leigh were submerged to a depth of 10ft. Single-line working on the up line was resumed on February 6 and the down track was restored three days later. Meantime, services were maintained between Fenchurch Street and Benfleet, and these were increased after February 3, when engines and rolling stock isolated at Shoeburyness were moved through the flooded section.

As much as possible of the heavy residential traffic between London and the Southend area was diverted to the alternative route from Southend (Victoria) via

Shenfield. There were sufficient engines at Stratford to cope with these additional services, but only three trains of high-capacity surburban coaching stock were available. At least three trains an hour were required during the peak periods, and it was decided to run steam services to Shenfield, and special non-stop electric trains thence to London. To relieve Liverpool Street, and to bring regular passengers to their usual terminus, these electric trains ran to and from Fenchurch Street. As the line between Bow Junction and Fenchurch Street was not in normal use for electrified services, special trains were run to clear the soot from the overhead conductors.

The emergency timetable came into force on Monday, February 2, and provided for a journey of 77 minutes from Southend (Victoria) to Fenchurch Street. It remained in operation for a week, by which time both tracks between Benfleet and Leigh had been reopened, with a speed restriction of 20mph. The electric trains were then returned to their normal working between Liverpool Street and Shenfield, and four steam relief trains were run from Southend (Victoria) to Fenchurch Street via Shenfield. The full services between London, Benfleet, and Southend were restored on February 19.

Tilbury Riverside station was inundated, and a length of track near Low Street was damaged. The branch serving the oil refineries at Thames Haven shared the same fate, and two miles of railway at Purfleet were rendered unusable when the adjacent industrial area was flooded. The track at Low Street was ▶

restored on February 9, but 10 more days elapsed before traffic was able to pass through Purfleet. Meantime, a shuttle service was run between Purfleet and Barking, and between Tilbury and Upminster over the single-track loop line from Grays, through Ockendon. The loop line also was used by ocean liner specials to and from Tilbury, when they were resumed after a two-day interval, and for heavy freight traffic, as soon as Thames Haven was again in working order.

Higher up the Thames, in the London area, the running lines and sidings at Canning Town and Stratford Market were flooded, and the Blackwall branch was blocked. Fortunately, no serious damage was caused, and services were speedily restored.

On the Southern Region, the main line from London to Ramsgate via Faversham, was breached at Graveney, near Whitstable, and between Herne Bay and Birchington. The damage at Graveney was made good within a few weeks, and the line was reopened for materials trains on February 23, and for passenger traffic between Faversham and Herne Bay on March 2. The branches from Sittingbourne to Sheerness, and from Gravesend to Allhallows, and Grain, both of which had suffered severe damage, also were reopened on March 2. In the London area, the North Kent line to Dartford was affected, but to a lesser extent.

Between Herne Bay and Birchington, the damage was more serious. The sea-wall was breached in several places, and some 5,000 acres of low-lying land were flooded by seawater to a considerable depth. The railway, which runs nearly parallel to the coast, on a low embankment about half a mile inland, was damaged over a length of 1¾ miles, and long sections of track were either washed off the embankment or seriously distorted. Subsequent high tides continued to reach the railway, and to run over it in places, and it became evident that restoration of the line could not be undertaken until some measure of protection was provided.

The Kent River Board, faced with the problem of saving a considerable area of agricultural land, and of protecting the railway and the main road to the Isle of Thanet, decided to build a new wall between the railway and the coast. It was evident that the construction of this wall could be expedited if supplies of filling material (in this case chalk) could be brought in by rail, as well as by road, and a site a few yards north of the railway was selected. It was decided that when the new wall had reached a certain height, it would be possible to proceed with the restoration of the railway.

The down line was restored temporarily, and crossovers and other special facilities for the trains of chalk filling installed, by February 23. To enable the work to proceed by night as well as by day, groups of powerful electric lights were provided at intervals of about 75 yards. These lamps were mounted on steel scaffolding towers erected on the

site of the up line, and were supplied with current from portable generators placed beside the track.

Concurrently with the restoration of the service line, a search was made for sites from which chalk filling could be obtained and loaded into railway wagons. These were found at Manston, on the outskirts of Ramsgate, and at Knockholt, and the Kent River Board's contractors immediately moved in heavy excavating plant. At Ramsgate, a new siding, about half a mile long, which necessitated tipping over 4,000 cu yd of material to form an embankment, was laid in three days.

Deliveries to the site at Birchington began on February 24, and in the first six days more than 100 trains carrying some 15,000 tons of chalk were run without interference to normal passenger and goods traffic. The number of trains subsequently was increased, and chalk is now reaching the site by rail at the rate of about 7,000 tons a day.

Subsidence of the Kent Coast main line of the Southern Region near Graveney, between Faversham and Whitstable. PHOTO: F DEBBAGE

Mechanical equipment is being used to unload the trains, and the material is moved into position by bulldozers. Additional supplies of chalk are being obtained from a site near Ramsgate, and delivered by road.

The new wall begins nearly two miles west of Birchington station, and extends for about 1¾ miles in the direction of Herne Bay. It will be carried up to a height of some 14ft above the level of the surrounding marshes, which stand at about 6ft above sea-level. Drainage channels are to be carried through the wall in double concrete box-culverts, supported on two rows of steel piles, about 20ft apart. The bridges carrying the railway over the drainage channels appear to have escaped serious damage.

Permanent restoration of the track will be undertaken as soon as the new wall has reached a height adequate for the protection of the railway. Deliveries of chalk by rail are then to cease, and the material required for

the completion of the work will be carried by road. It is the ultimate intention of the Kent River Board to construct a new seawall from Birchington to Reculver, a distance of about three miles. The new chalk wall will then

Subsequent high tides continued to reach the railway, and to run over it in places

become the second line of defence for the railway and the area lying to the south of it.

For the first three weeks after the inundation, trains between London and Ramsgate were diverted at Faversham via Canterbury (East), the Kearsney loop, and Deal. On February 23, however, this circuitous journey was short-ended

considerably by the reopening, as a fully signalled double line, of the spur connecting the Faversham-Dover line with the Ashford-Ramsgate line at Canterbury. This spur was built as a double line during World War One, at the request of the War Department, and was opened on May 5 1918. It was taken out of use in November 1920, and the track was removed in 1935. A single line was restored in March, 1941, and used for the movement of heavy rail-mounted guns, but the connections with the main lines were removed in the autumn of 1951.

Easter holiday traffic for the Thanet resorts was worked via the Canterbury spur, and through trains between London and Whitstable, and Herne Bay were provided during that period. Similar services are to be run at Whitsun, and it has been announced officially that normal working between Faversham and Ramsgate will be resumed on June 1. ■

Some railway myths

By CHARLES ROUS-MARTEN

AT first sight it may seem not a little strange that such essentially prosaic and scientific things as railways should be able to produce any 'myths' at all. But it must be remembered that the vast possibilities of railway locomotion have a tendency to appeal to the imagination of marvel-lovers, and imagination of that sort is apt to clamour for the out-marvelling of marvels. Hence have arisen the wondrous tales of manifest impossibilities which have been current ever since railways were given to a grateful world.

Nor is it perhaps surprising to find this craving for the marvellous with regard to railway speed. For speed is the one characteristic in which railways so far stand alone and unapproachable. By no other means as yet feasible on this earth can a human being experience so swift a rate of motion as on the railway. In mere weight-carrying, a railway is surpassed by some other modes of conveyance – by water carriage particularly – given only the necessary time. Even a horse or a man could convey a load as heavy as that of a train if allowed the requisite time in which to do it. But in no other way than by rail can anybody, or anything, as yet be conveyed at the rate of 70 or 80mph. And so it is the rapidity of railway-transit that specially and justly appeals to the admiration, and to the imagination also, of the world in general.

And thus it is that railway speed has been the subject of so vast a number of mythical romances. Their prevalence is at times apt to be mortifying to careful and accurate observers of locomotive performances. If one happens to mention to a railway mythologist one of the notable locomotive feats of the past two years, such as the averaging of 67mph from start to stop, the prompt reply is: "My dear fellow, that's nothing. Why, in the old broad gauge days, Brunel went down from London to Bristol, 118½ miles, in an hour!" It is useless to argue or to lose temper. The temptation may be great, but to yield is idle. The railway mythologist is not to be undeceived.

The railway myth has never blossomed so profusely as upon the old broad gauge system and its 8ft, single-wheel engines, one of the most famous of which, *Great Britain,* I now illustrate. It was entirely natural that the magnificent scale of the 7ft gauge, and the high speeds of the single-wheelers, should impress the public imagination. And it is quite true that they did many things which, in those days, must have seemed marvellous, and, which, even in these times, we are warranted in regarding with warm admiration, But they did not do – and no engine ever did – the miraculous things attributed to them.

That myth, that Brunel once ran down to Bristol in an hour, is often to be heard. And I suspect it had the same origin as the equally fabulous story that the horse Eclipse ran a mile in a minute. The horse, I believe, really did run a mile in a minute

> ## In the old broad gauge days, Brunel went down from London to Bristol, 118½ miles, in an hour!

– and so many seconds; in fact, a little under two minutes. And I have reason to think that Brunel and Gooch did once go to Bristol in 1hr 55min – that is to say, five minutes under the two hours. But those 55 minutes make all the difference! The one performance was quite possible on that very easy road. The other was, and still is, impossible with any engine yet invented.

Even so lately as May 1892, when the broad gauge was done away with, a statement was gravely made by a leading daily paper in London, that the 8ft, single-wheelers frequently ran the 12 miles from Bath to Bristol in eight minutes, or at the average rate of 90mph! The actual distance is less than 11½ miles, but that is a mere detail. If the engine could have done the 11½ miles from start to stop in eight minutes, perhaps she could have squeezed in the extra half mile. But as that length happens to be a rather awkward bit of line for fast running, with many curves and tunnels, and as, moreover, the first three miles usually occupied fully five minutes, and the last one

and a half (slowing into Bristol) at least three, the remaining eight miles would have had to be done in no time at all, or, at any rate, with the swiftness of a lightning flash. Yet that silly story was widely read with implicit credence! As a matter of truth, the engines always found it a tight pull to make the run in much less than double that time.

There is another tale about an ancient feat on the Great Western, which has a good deal more of genuine basis than have most of the others, but which, nevertheless, has embodied some manifest exaggeration, and, I suspect, more which can only be guessed at. I refer to the oft-quoted feat of the engine *Great Britain*, which is alleged to have run, on May 11, 1848, the 9.15am express from Paddington to Didcot, start to stop, in '47

From *The Railway Magazine*, August 1897

Great Western broad gauge express engine (Gooch) as originally built. Driving wheels 8ft, cylinders 18in x 24in.

minutes, the distance being 53¼ miles'. Now, in the first place, the actual distance from start to stop was not 53¼ miles, but barely 53, even assuming the time to have been taken from the usual place of starting to the usual place of stopping. In the next place, the run was stated at the time as 47½ not 47. The fraction was dropped by degrees for the sake of improved effect. Now, 53 miles in 47½ minutes represents an average speed of 66.9mph.

I do not say that was an impossible performance for one of those engines on that nearly level length with only four small coaches behind her – a load of some 50 tons. But I do say that whenever an authentic repetition of the alleged feat was attempted it proved impracticable. It was never again

done by those engines; and it has yet to be proved that even Mr Dean's much more powerful modern engines could get to Didcot in the time.

How then, it will be asked, did the report originate? I understand that the time was taken from the guard's journal. I would not say one word to disparage the accuracy with which guards keep their books. Generally they keep them with scrupulous care and accuracy. To this I can testify after close comparison of returns. But precise timing is not their particular métier; and, now and then, especially when a 'record' has to be established or 'broken', one does find a guard too enthusiastic or too much carried away by natural excitement to be entirely trustworthy.

To give an instance in point. On one

occasion, when a 'record' was undoubtedly achieved, the time from start to stop was so fast as to create great surprise, considering the nature of the road. Upon application, the guard's intermediate timings were furnished to me with the ready courtesy I have almost always experienced at the hands of the British railway authorities. On examining these figures, I discovered that the distance from the last station passed to the final dead stop – exactly three miles – was recorded as having been done in two minutes, or at the average rate of 90mph, about one-third of the length being on an ascending grade of 1 in 78. Clearly that reported average of 90mph to the stop was never attained, and in subsequent experiments I was only once able to get the same run done in three minutes, or ▶

a whole minute longer than the impossible time recorded by the guard. No doubt he took his time just as the terminus came in sight. Is it not possible that the Great Western guard of 50 years ago may have done likewise?

Again, I have been informed that the departure time was occasionally recorded as from Westbourne Park, then merely known as the London ticket-platform, a mile from the terminus. All these wonderful things happened before my day, so I do not pretend to have any personal knowledge of them; but in view of the possibilities I have suggested as the result of more recent experiences, it would be rash to accept without more detailed verification all the traditions of bygone wonders.

Then as to the maximum speeds attained by those engines, few of their enthusiastic champions are content with less than 90mph. Let me offer a case in point. A scientific friend of mine happened to be present when *Great Britain* made one of her earliest express trips in the year 1847, or 1848, and was requested to 'take the times', as he had a particularly good chronometer. He did so, and found that for some distance down a falling gradient each mile was run in 48 seconds, or at the rate of 75mph. He mentioned this to me some time afterward, and I carefully recorded the facts. But as years rolled on and his memory faded, he used to say that the speed was 'a mile in 40-odd seconds'; and in his later days the "odd" was dropped, and the speed became "a mile in 40 seconds", or 90mph. Had I not retained the original notes, this would have seemed to be a well-authenticated instance of that speed having been reached on the Great Western, whereas the true rate was 75.

It may not unreasonably be asked here: "What was the maximum speed actually attained by those engines?" It is much to be

regretted that fuller and more obviously authentic records were not taken and preserved than any which now seem available. But we have at least something to go upon.

Twelve years ago I had some very interesting conversations with the late Charles Sacre, the eminent engineer-in-chief of the Manchester, Sheffield, and Lincolnshire line. When Brunel and Gooch were trying the speed capacity of the then new 8ft singles, nearly 50 years ago, Mr Sacre also was present and took notes. The engines tried were *Iron Duke*, *Courier*, and *Great Britain*, and they were run at their highest possible velocity down the Wootton Bassett bank of 1 in 100. The result was that the maximum possible proved to be a small fraction over 78mph. This, I believe, is the highest speed ever authentically recorded

The engines used on the 4ft 8½in gauge can run as fast as any yet tried on the 7ft, and perhaps faster

with those famous old engines. Some years back I had two or three opportunities of seeing them doing their best, with a much-augmented steam-pressure, and then, too, 78.2mph was the maximum that could be obtained.

Undoubtedly the fastest work ever done on the 7ft gauge was that of Mr Pearson's 9ft single-wheelers on the Bristol and Exeter line. These, when new, attained 81.8mph down the Wellington bank; and many years afterward I myself recorded the same rate with one of them at the same spot.

Curiously enough, these notable engines which, with their huge single-driving wheels 9ft in diameter, might have been expected to inspire a cloud of myths, do not seem to have been the subject of more than one or two. Perhaps the most circumstantial of these is the allegation that one of the 9ft engines took the 'Emperor Napoleon III' in a special train from Bristol to Exeter, 75½ miles, in an hour. Of course, no such thing was ever done. Nor could it be done even today with the more powerful locomotives in use. I have not been able to ascertain definitely what was the true time occupied. It was, no doubt, as in the London-Bristol case, an hour, and so many (probably 15 or 20) minutes.

Three illustrations are given of these remarkable engines, the fastest that ever ran on a broad gauge, showing one in its original form, then as first rebuilt for the Great Western line when that absorbed the Bristol and Exeter, and finally as again rebuilt, this time as a tender engine, the driving-wheels reduced to 8ft in diameter, and the trailing bogie done away with, so that the engine might be virtually identical with the 'Great Britain' class and 'work round' with the locomotives of that type in the same 'link'. As thus converted they ran until the abolition of the broad gauge in 1892. They always, in my experience, did excellent work, relatively to their power, and ran just as fast as with the larger driving-wheels. But neither as 9ft nor as 8ft engines did they ever authentically equal the speeds since attained by several classes of engines on the narrow gauge.

And so disappears the 'mythest myth' of all – the fallacious idea that higher speeds were feasible on the broad gauge than on the narrow under conditions such as have hitherto existed. The engines used on the 4ft 8½in gauge can run as fast as any yet tried on the 7ft, and perhaps faster. At all events they do run faster than any broad gauge engine can be proved ever to have done.

But another equally 'mythical myth' is the notion held by many people that the broad gauge has been demonstrated to have been a mistake per se, and to have no greater capacities than the narrow. The late Sir Daniel Gooch clearly showed that the 7ft gauge, while more costly at the outset, possessed many advantages in respect of superior economy in working and maintenance. Its abolition was necessary simply to get rid of that intolerable obstruction of traffic-break of gauge. The co-existence of two different gauges was unendurable. The narrow gauge mileage was in the majority; so the broad gauge had to go. But there are few railway engineers indeed, if any, who pretend nowadays that the 4ft 8½ gauge, almost accidentally adopted by Stephenson in the infancy of railways, is the most suitable to present and prospective requirements, or is even adequate for existing

Bristol and Exeter broad gauge express engine (designed by Pearson) as originally built. Driving wheels 9ft, cylinders 16½in x 24in.

Bristol and Exeter express engine
as first rebuilt and renumbered.

locomotive purposes. Far from it. On all the principal lines the great and crying need is for increased locomotive power, so as to avoid the costly duplication of trains and frequent use of pilot engines. But where is the additional power to come from? Its source must in all cases be the boiler, and how are larger boilers to be got between two rails 4ft 8½in apart without resorting to devices which are not only inconvenient, but also costly?

Numerous plans have been tried, and are still in course of trial, but many have proved failures. The crowding together of tubes to obtain increased heating surface within practicable space limits produced mere froth instead of more steam. The extensive lengthening of the boiler barrel proved that tube heating-surface is of small value beyond a limited distance from the firebox. To meet this difficulty F W Webb is trying an intermediate combustion-chamber, which appears to be giving good results. The high-pitched, large-diametered boiler adopted by J F McIntosh in his 'Dunalastairs' (Scottish estates) undoubtedly produces excellent work, but greater power is already demanded by the heavy and swift Caledonian trains. Moreover, boilers of such a size limit the size of the driving-wheels to 6ft 6in, over which

the 'Dunalastair' boilers bulge out sideways. Then there are the Flaman double-boilers, one above the other, as used on the Est Railway of France, and the various types of compound locomotives. All these are ingenious, and some do admirable work, but how enormously would the task of the modern locomotive designer be simplified if he had a width of 7ft within which to get his boiler and cylinders! It is hardly conceivable that we should ever revert to the 7ft gauge, but it is a fallacy of the deepest dye to imagine that our present gauge is adequate, or that immense advantages would not attach to a wider gauge. Possibly one of 6ft would be sufficient, and it may be that had Brunel been less ambitious in his chosen dimensions the wider gauge might have carried the day. It is too late now to lament lost opportunities, but, it would be disingenuous to pretend that great opportunities have not been lost – and to all appearance irrevocably.

Another type of locomotive which has given rise to many mythical tales is that, now, extinct, which used to do most of the express work on the southern division of the London and North-Western Railway, the so-called 'Bloomer' class. When the Great Western threatened keen competition to Birmingham,

in spite of its 16 miles longer road, and a two-hours' broad gauge service was talked of, the 'Bloomers were built with the alleged intention of running between Euston and Birmingham; if necessary, in two hours exactly, the distance being 113 miles.

The two hours' service, however, proved another myth. No such timing was ever adopted by either route. That it would have been feasible in each case with light loads there is little doubt. 'Indeed, the North-Western could certainly have accomplished it with ease, even in those days. Yet to this date, so far as I am aware, Birmingham has never 'been reached in two hours from London, although the same distance from Euston has several times been run by the ordinary Scotch expresses in some minutes less. Perhaps, when the Great Western gets its shortened route to the Midland metropolis, we may see a 'race' thither, with the result of bringing down the time to 1hr 45min – an easy possibility.

Some years ago, when the fiat had gone forth for the destruction of the 'Bloomer' engines, and was made known to the public through their numbers being changed to some among the 1800s, various romantic tales found publication having for their texts ▶

Bristol and Exeter express loco as finally rebuilt for Great Western. Wheels reduced to 8ft.

the marvellous feats achieved in bygone days by the doomed locomotives. 'Logs' were even given in elaborate detail, and timed to seconds, of highly apocryphal runs. One 'Bloomer' was accredited with an average of 72mph between Weedon and Welton, part of the way being uphill. On examination, this proved to have been arrived at by overstating the distance by just a mile, on the authority of an erroneous timetable. Another was alleged to have averaged 84mph from Watford to Harrow, full details being given. As, however, the writer also gave the dimensions of the engine, all grossly inaccurate, and the composition and weight of the train about four times as much as a 'Bloomer' could have pulled, grave scepticism was unavoidably suggested as to his trustworthiness. This distrustful feeling was enhanced by a second record on his part, the latter being of 100mph having been run down the Tring bank.

There is no authentic information of a 'Bloomer' having attained 80mph. I have known them often do 70 to 73 downhill, and once more than 75. But all allegations of greater velocity than that in their past have invariably dissolved into thin mist when subjected to critical analysis. That they were very fine engines in their day is unquestionable, and to the last they did excellent work with loads proportional to their power. But, like the old Great Westerns, they never accomplished impossibilities. Indeed, I have not found that a common achievement, even by the most modern of their descendants.

Nearly coeval with the 'Bloomers' were the once famous 'Jenny Lind' engines, built by E Wilson, of Leeds, and noticeable for their fluted iron dome-covers and similar

safety-valve columns. They had 6ft single driving-wheels, and cylinders varying from 15in to 16in in diameter, with piston stroke varying from 20in to 22in, the driving-wheels having inside bearings; the leading and trailing wheels outside bearings. These, too, did relatively admirable work in their day, and their main features of construction are reproduced, though on a far larger scale, in the newest Great Northern inside-cylinder single-wheelers.

For some years engines of this class ran the Brighton expresses, including the 5pm down, when it was timed, as it now is, to do the 50½ miles in 65 minutes, though of course the load then was far lighter. The corresponding express from Brighton was allowed in those days five minutes longer than at present, taking 75 minutes to London Bridge.

This train was at one period a favourite theme for romancers. The down one was usually reputed to be allowed only an hour to Brighton, and was asserted with much positiveness to have made the journey in 52 and even 49 minutes! This performance still awaits accomplishment.

But the up train produced a double-barrelled myth of curiously perverse ingenuity. It was stated as being timed to do the '60 miles to London in exactly one hour'. The actual distance, as I have already said, is 50½ miles, and the time was then 1hr 15min. This, however, is the way railway mythology is built up. 'More than 50 miles' – half a mile more! – becomes '60 miles'. One hour and a quarter drops the fraction. This is only one case of many.

It was not to be expected that when Patrick Stirling's 8ft single-wheelers first came on the scene their capacity as

myth-subjects should be overlooked by manufacturers of those articles. Nor were they. One romance much published and repeated, attributed to the first of these splendid engines a run of 12 miles in eight minutes – or at the rate of 90mph down the incline of 1 in 178, and 1 in 200, extending from the 100th mile-post on the Great Northern Railway toward Peterborough. They have been tried over and over again, and have never even touched that speed, much less maintained it for eight miles. I have known them average 80mph for 10 miles down that bank, and touch a maximum of 83.7 more than once; but then they were doing their

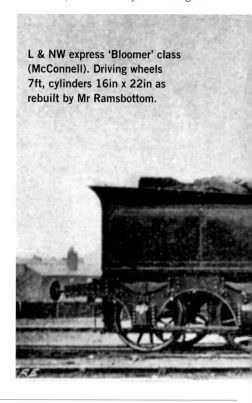

L & NW express 'Bloomer' class (McConnell). Driving wheels 7ft, cylinders 16in x 22in as rebuilt by Mr Ramsbottom.

best, and the experimental admission of a little more steam had a prompt retarding effect through back pressure. What has been done by them several times is to run more than 11 miles in less than nine minutes; for instance, 11¼ miles in 8¾ minutes, or at the rate of 77.1mph, and this is, of course, the origin of the 'yarn'. More than 11 miles easily becomes 12. From the 8¾ minutes the fraction is readily ignored, and so we get 12 miles in eight minutes. But that run has never yet been authenticated on any line in the world.

About 10 years ago a 7ft single-wheel express engine was built for the Caledonian Railway to the design, I believe, of Dugald Drummond the locomotive superintendent of that line. It is, at any rate, merely an enlargement of the type of which he previously built two for the North British Railway (Nos. 474 and 475), with a leading-bogie added. As No. 123, it ran the "racing" train from Carlisle to Edinburgh every weekday in August 1888, and on the strength of its performances during that month it has acquired a reputation for exceptional speed and power which is very largely mythical. I do not wish to be misunderstood in this connection. I do not say that No. 123 did not do what she was stated to have done. On the contrary, I state distinctly that she did do all the best performances attributed to her, for I possess minute records of them taken for me by friends of whose capability and trustworthiness there cannot be the smallest doubt whatever. The performance and excellence of the work are unquestionable: it is its alleged exceptional merit that is

mythical. The work was no doubt better than had been actually done previously on that line. But it has since been greatly surpassed in every respect by the 6ft coupled engines, designed and built about the same time, and earlier, by Mr Drummond, and still more by Mr McIntosh's 'Dunalastairs'.

What made the fame of No. 123 was her run from Carlisle to Edinburgh, 100¾ miles in 102min 33sec. That was it most creditable performance. But the load was only 76 tons, and the engine took 75 minutes to pass Carstairs (73½ miles). Some

The Bloomers were built with the alleged intention of running between Euston and Birmingham in two hours

years later an older 6ft 6in coupled Drummond engine, No. 78, covered the same distance from Carlisle with a load 25% heavier in barely 70 minutes, or five minutes less. Yet it has been a most frequent remark that had No. 123 run the Aberdeen "Racing Trains" in 1895, the West Coast would have won even more decisively than it did. Manifestly the facts do not warrant such an assumption, in view of the actual performances of the different classes of engines. But it has been said that although the coupled engines might have beat No. 123 up the Beattock and Dunblane banks, the single-wheeler would have won in the

long run with a light train by dint of her higher speed on the level and downhill.

This also has, however, been put to the test. Pressed to her utmost capacity, No. 123 on two occasions did the mile in 44 seconds – 81.8mph. But No. 79, one of the coupled engines, attained the same speed easily with a heavier load, running in the ordinary course; and during the race of 1895 a speed of 85.7mph was more than once reached by the coupled engines, both of Mr Drummond's and Mr Lambie's build, as it has frequently been by Mr McIntosh's 'Dunalastairs', which latter, moreover, have equalled the record time of No. 123, with loads nearly thrice as heavy. Possibly, with greater boiler-power, No. 123 might do better things; and an attempt was made last year to put this to the test, but, unfortunately, it was found impracticable to fit her with one of the larger boilers, and so she continues to run light, moderately-timed trains.

As a matter of fact, her 'record' feat was beaten in point of merit, even during the 'race' of 1888, by one of the smaller and much less (nominally) powerful 6ft 6in coupled engines on the London and North-Western Railway, which took the same load from Preston to Carlisle, 90¼ miles, in 90 minutes, the road being very nearly, if not quite, as heavy; while another engine of the latter class beat even that remarkable time by 9¾ minutes in 1895, reckoning, however, from passing Preston at reduced speed, and not from an absolute start. Still, the complete run from Crewe to Carlisle, 141¼ miles, was done in 126 minutes, or at the average rate of 67.2mph. I fear, therefore, that No. 123 ▶

must descend from the pedestal she has occupied as a mythological railway deity, and must be regarded simply as a very good ordinary engine which was forced into factitious fame by peculiar circumstances. It is noteworthy that no more of her type have been built.

It is impossible to deal with the subject of railway speed myths without a passing notice of the gorgeous and gigantic contributions so generously furnished by the United States to the long list. To review them all in detail would require a whole volume's space. I must content myself with touching upon a few of the most remarkable.

Some years ago, before a speed of 84 miles had ever been authentically recorded in Great Britain, a very eminent engineer claimed that a new locomotive of his design had run, with a fair load, a distance of 2.8 miles, on a road practically level, in exactly two minutes, that consequently being at the rate of 84mph. Doubts being expressed as to the feasibleness of this alleged achievement, the engineer promptly and indignantly forwarded his detailed figures in proof of his assertion. But these figures showed that the run of 2.8 miles occupied 2½ minutes – not two – and so the speed was only 67.2mph – not 84. This is how one American myth collapsed.

But when the much-betrumpeted No. 999 came out, mere rates of 80 and 90mph seemed infinitely too poor and mean to be worth noting. For her it was claimed that she had accomplished speeds of 102 and 112mph respectively. It happened that two friends of mine, both being engineering writers and train-timers of much experience, travelled by the same train which was alleged to have achieved this marvellous feat. Their timing, taken quite independently of one another, brought out the rate of travel as a mile in 44 seconds, or 81.8mph. But after the English record had been made in the 'race' of 1895, the Americans, as in patriotic duty bound, at once set to work to beat it, and used No. 999 for that purpose. A 'tie' was the virtual result. But in the official report it is expressly stated that the maximum speed attained by No. 999 during that supreme effort at record-breaking was 'about 81mph'. I may well leave these indisputable facts to speak for themselves.

It will doubtless be expected that I shall say something about that oft-quoted Lake Shore run, when an average rate of 72.9mph from start to stop is said to have been maintained, and a maximum, of 92.5 reached. But in the first place I do not feel warranted in classing that performance among the 'myths' of railway speed, because I have not yet had the opportunity of subjecting the recorded figures to such a process of analysis or dissection as would justify me in accepting or rejecting the alleged results. For it should be

carefully noted that all through this article I most studiously avoid all expressions of more personal opinion, and deal solely with established facts. Still, I do feel it incumbent on me to point out that, assuming the published figures to be accurate as regards the Lake Shore run, all existing ideas as to the types of locomotives suited to high speeds must be included in the list of railway myths. For the locomotive which is stated to have broken all speed records was merely an old six-wheel coupled goods engine with 5ft 6in wheels, and cylinders 17in x 24in. This old goods engine is credited with beating hollow, not nearly all the British engines specially designed for high speeds, but also every American engine so designed. Thus, if that feat can be authenticated, then the proper course would be to put six-coupled goods engines on our fastest trains, and to break up all our express locomotives.

I do not expect to witness such a practical acceptance of the Lake Shore results as this. Yet it would be the strictly logical outcome.

There are other myths whose dissipation

This train was at one period a favourite theme for romancers

would require a more elaborate and technical method than is adapted to the pages of a magazine – such, for instance, as the old and long-accepted theory of train-resistances, wind-force, etc. The '15-coach-test' myth has long faded into thin air. Twenty years ago it was held that an engine must have 100lb of tractive force for every 1lb of effective steam pressure in the cylinders to be able to perform this test – i.e., to haul fifteen 10-ton coaches, 150 tons in all, on the dead level, at the rate of 60mph. It has been found, times without number during the past few years, that locomotives possessing less than that amount of nominal tractive force could haul not only 150 tons, but more than 200 tons on the level at 60mph.

It is perhaps hardly accurate to include wrong phraseology among myths, but I cannot refrain from noticing in passing the curious inappropriateness of the term 'journey speed' applied in the customary way to the rate including stoppages. For the journey 'speed' is thus made to include the time when the train is at absolute rest – at a dead stand. Total absence of motion is an eccentric kind of 'speed'. What was no doubt intended is 'journey-rate'.

In a previous article I referred to the phase of railway speed which some writers call 'flying average' as fanciful and untrustworthy. I think I am justified in adding it to my list of railway myths; for to adopt a

wholly arbitrary allowance for loss of time in starting and stopping, and to base an average upon that allowance, is clearly misleading. This, let me say, is again not a matter of personal opinion, but of careful scientific experiment. The 'flying average' idea was first put forth some 22 years ago, although not under that name. I fully accepted it, and until I had the opportunity of thoroughly testing it I implicitly believed in it. The original theory was that to get the 'true' average speed of an express you must allow two minutes for starting and two minutes for stopping. With the general adoption of continuous brakes, the stopping allowance became reduced to one minute. In many cases such allowances do give a fair idea of the average running, but as they take no account of uphill or downhill work, of gradients, curves, junctions, weather, state of road, length of run, signal checks, or relaying slacks, they really give no information at all of the slightest value as to the locomotive work done; while from no other view point, would any interest attach to 'flying averages'.

Again, the nature of the start is a factor of the most variable kind. How can the same allowance reasonably be made for such starts as those from King's Cross, Euston, or Liverpool Street, with their rising grades of 1 in 103 (through a slippery tunnel) and 1 in 70, and those from Paddington and Waterloo, almost at a dead level till speed is attained? Or, how can the quick stop at some country station be compared with the necessarily slow approach to London or to the large provincial town? Also, what average would give any accurate view which took no account of such hindrances as the slacks at Peterborough, Selby, Crewe, Preston, Gateshead, or Bristol? Manifestly, a heavy express may need an allowance of six or eight, or even 10 minutes, before its average can be fairly compared with that of a light one, which may need less than two minutes' allowance.

A *reductio ad absurdum* promptly followed the original promulgation of this uniform allowance theory. The four-minute allowance was claimed for a run of seven miles in nine minutes. This made the average speed 84mph. Then it had to be explained that a smaller allowance might have to be made in certain cases. This, of course, virtually 'gave away' the whole theory, and when one enthusiast quite logically claimed that a run of three miles in five minutes meant 180mph, the theory disappeared for some years.

Plainly, no uniform or even approximately uniform allowance for starting and stopping loss can be adopted which will give anything like an accurate idea of locomotive performance, and I must hold, therefore, that I am warranted in including the 'flying average' theory among my list of 'Railway Myths'. ∎

From *The Railway Magazine*, August 1897

THE WHY AND THE WHEREFORE

The Worcester Railway

THE Worcester Railway is really a short mineral branch line linking the Lowesmoor vinegar works of Hill, Evans & Co Ltd, with the GWR at Shrub Hill, Worcester. The firm was established in 1830 by William Hill and Edward Evans, and 40 years later applied to Parliament for powers to build this railway. The result was the passage on August 1, 1870, of the Worcester Railways Act, which authorised 2 furlongs 9 chains of line, subject to a speed limit of 4mph, but conferred no powers for the compulsory purchase of land. The undertaking was described in the Act as the Worcester Railways, and the proprietors were named as the partners for the time being in Hill, Evans & Co. The firm has often been called the Worcester Railway Company, but the Act did not incorporate a statutory company. A maintenance agreement regarding the railway was made with the GWR on May 28, 1872, and this still continues to operate. The owning firm was converted into a limited company on May 31, 1900, and this

company presumably replaces the old partnership as proprietor of the railway. An unusual feature of this railway is its semaphore signalling system at the point where it crosses Shrub Hill Road, Worcester, on the level. For the protection of road traffic two ordinary semaphore railway signals are placed in the footpath and are kept normally in the off position. When a train is due to

pass over the roadway they are set at danger by hand by a member of the staff working the train across. The lever operating each signal is controlled by a key so that the mechanism cannot be tampered with. The signals are also interlocked with a near-by ground frame which cannot be used to permit of rail traffic until the road signals are placed at danger.

[Reply to A F Wilkerson, April 1939 issue]

Rail Coaches on the LNER

THE LNER has now completed its orders for a fleet of 50 rail coaches to be supplied by the Sentinel Waggon Works and Cammell Laird & Co Ltd, and by Clayton Wagons Limited. These are the largest individual contracts ever placed by a railway company for self-propelled rail coaches, and as the new vehicles are received they are being named and placed into service. The intention is to operate them on selected sections of the LNER in order to provide more intensive services, and to follow the fluctuations of public requirements, including market days, shows, local events, sports meetings, etc.

The steam rail coaches have seats for 60 passengers and straps for additional travellers should the necessity arise. Each coach is equipped with steam heat, electric light, and automatic brakes, and is signalled throughout as safely as an ordinary train. A high boiler pressure of 275lb per sq in enables a speed of between 40-50mph to be attained, and special attention has been given to the powers of acceleration of these rail cars, which can be run in either direction without reversing.

The steam coaches are to be decorated in two distinctive colours - vermilion and cream, and green and cream - and in order that they may be better known to the public, each coach will be named after a famous road stagecoach of olden days.

In the interior of each coach an interesting framed notice is fitted, giving particulars of the running of the old stagecoach after which the rail coach is named, and offering 5s reward for supplying to any LNER stationmaster hitherto unpublished information relating to the old horse coach.

The following names have already been allotted:

Tally Ho, The Highflyer, The Rockingham, The Phoenix, The Perseverance, The North Star, The Neptune, The Liberty, The Hero, The True Briton, The Trafalgar, The Transit, The Teazle, The Rob Roy, The Rapid, The Red Rover, The Royal Sailor, The Yorkshire Hussar, The Wonder, The Wellington, The Express, The Union, The True Blue, The Rodney, The Railway, The Eclipse, The Ebor, The Comet, The Bang Up and The Chevy Chase.

Electrification of a main line

Station and track alterations on the London & North Western

The electrification programme of the London Midland Region of British Railways is being followed by railway engineers throughout the world, much of the interest being centred on the problems involved and the methods adopted for their solution. The southward approach to Euston is again emphasised by the extension of electric working from Stafford to Nuneaton.

Electrification of the former London & North Western main line between London, Manchester and Liverpool, and Birmingham, not only is necessitating the reconstruction of some stations and alterations to the track layout, but advantage is being taken during the heavy civil engineering work involved to improve and modernise wherever possible existing stations and track layout. The stations which have been rebuilt, or are now in course of rebuilding, are Euston, Birmingham New Street, Manchester Piccadilly, Manchester Oxford Road, Macclesfield, Stafford, Coventry, Tamworth, and Northampton.

At other stations alteration, rather than rebuilding, is being undertaken, as at Liverpool Lime Street, Crewe, Wolverhampton, Rugby, Lichfield, Nuneaton, Bletchley, and many other places.

The rebuilding of Manchester Piccadilly – formerly London Road – station was commenced in 1958 and continued until

1961, when work was temporarily suspended. Final approval to the plans has now been given by the British Railways Board, and subject to acceptance by the Manchester City Council, work is scheduled to recommence in October 1964, for completion in October 1965, in time for the introduction of through main line electric services to London.

The original station, more than 100 years old, was the terminus of two pre-Grouping lines, the former London & North Western Railway and the Great Central Railway. The station and its approaches are on a viaduct and the space beneath forms a goods yard. Mayfield Station, built by the LNWR as a subsidiary suburban terminal, never fulfilled its original purpose, and under the modernisation scheme has become a parcels depot.

Under the 1923 Grouping, the GCR became part of the London & North Eastern Railway and in 1930 the Manchester South Junction & Altrincham line was electrified on

Electric loco No. E3038 (later 84003) roars north through Wilmslow with an engineers train from Crewe towards Manchester in 1961. RAIL PHOTOPRINTS/ALAN H. BRYANT, ARPS

The stylish blue livery and white roof suited BR's new AC electric locos. No. E3074 sits at the buffer stops at Manchester Piccadilly on October 16, 1963. COLOUR RAIL/G C GORDON-STUART

the 1,500v DC, overhead system which, in 1938, was adopted for the LNER Manchester-Sheffield-Wath electrification. The war and the decision to build a new Woodhead Tunnel delayed the completion of the electrification until 1954. By then, the whole of London Road station and the Manchester-Sheffield-Wath line as far as Dunford Bridge was the responsibility of the London Midland Region and the 25kv AC system was being developed by the railways.

London Road station had long been inadequate; the platforms were too short, the track approaches were bad, necessitating frequent crossing movements, and the concourse was narrow. When electrification to Crewe and Euston was agreed, this provided the opportunity to improve the station layout. On the west side, the electrified 1,500v DC MSJ & A lines created more difficulties with the 25kv system than did the Manchester-Sheffield-Wath lines on the east side, the latter being already fairly independent of the lines to Crewe and practically the only alteration here was the addition of a platform road. The solution adopted on the west side was to make Oxford Road station the changeover point between 25kv and 1,500v DC so that some of the new electric suburban trains from the south could terminate at Oxford Road, which is nearer the business centre of the city. These works were completed in 1960.

The removal of the turntable and the rebuilding of the MSJ & A station on Fairfield Street Bridge, as an island platform with two tracks, gave additional space on the west side, and the number of main line platforms, excluding the MSJ & A, has been increased from 10 to 12 and the length from 7,800ft to 11,800ft. These works were completed during 1958 and 1959. All this was done within the boundaries of the existing roof which, although

in good condition, has been completely re-covered, and awnings provided over the extended platforms.

Two bays of the main roof at the buffer stop end of the station have been removed to suit the widened concourse and a gable screen provided. The concourse and trucking-way behind the ticket barrier extends over the whole width of the station and is roofed. This roof extends from the buffer stops to the line of the cafeteria and booking hall. This work was completed in 1961, as was the 10-storey office building.

The demolition of the remaining portion of the former buildings will commence in October, with the construction of the passenger facility building and booking hall to follow. The passenger facilities building will have two storeys and will include a cafeteria, ladies' waiting room, bar, enquiry offices and shops within one enclosed area which will be linked to the office block by a two-storey booking hall and general waiting area. Part of the cafeteria will also be two storeyed. The roof of the passenger building will include a series of north lights. The bridge over Fairfield Street, carrying the new MSJ & A island platform, is of interesting construction. It is of part post-stressed and pre-stressed concrete with the tracks supported on cantilevers on each side. ▶

London Road station had long been inadequate; the platforms were too short, the track approaches were bad

The new island platform on Fairfield Street bridge, Manchester, nearing completion. The concrete main beams of the bridge double up as the platform, the tracks on each side being supported on cantilevers.

Platforms have been lengthened at most stations between Crewe and Manchester and Liverpool. A pre-fabricated station building was developed by the London Midland Region for station rebuilding and modernisation, and a series of standardised components were produced in factories and assembled by numbers at the sites. By using the system of numbered standard components it was possible for a station structure to be erected in three weeks or, with drainage and all services, in two months. Several stations between Crewe

and Manchester and Liverpool were rebuilt on this pattern. A feature common to all these stations is a large clerestory roof, as well as large glazed areas and extensive use of aluminium and vitreous-enamel steel for the external walls. Push button-operated electric heating in the waiting rooms is provided.

At Crewe the Nantwich Road Bridge has been rebuilt and the station entrance has been improved by a new booking hall and footbridge. South of Crewe, excluding Birmingham New Street and Euston, the stations which have

A double-header of Nos. E3039 and E3036 waits to leave Manchester Piccadilly in September 1960 with the 12.15 to Plymouth.
COLOUR RAIL/ J D GOMERSAL

been or are to be completely rebuilt are Stafford, Coventry, Tamworth, and Northampton Castle.

The track layout in the vicinity of Stafford has been changed considerably, the main lines from Rugby having been redesignated to correspond with the lines from Birmingham and the lines going north to Shrewsbury and Crewe. The one-time order of down slow, down fast, up fast, up goods, has become down slow, up slow, down fast, up fast. This change commences where the two tracks between Colwich and the north end of Shugborough Tunnel become four; it eliminates the cross-over movements at Stafford which were productive of delays. The connections to the up goods yard have been remodelled so that shunting operations, which often fouled the main lines, can now be carried out at the south end without so doing.

At Stafford station the bay-line platforms and the former island platforms have been

The completed Fairfield Street bridge, viewed from Travis Street, showing the cantilever crock supports springing from the island platform in the centre.

extended so as to make two island platforms, long enough to deal with all main line express trains and to provide platform facilities on the up and down slow lines. These arrangements permit trains from the south and from Birmingham to be dealt with simultaneously without crossing the main line. A luggage and footbridge provides access to all platforms. Bridge No. 84, at the south end, carrying a main road, has been rebuilt to a modern design in pre-stressed concrete.

At Colwich Junction, where the main line is joined by the line from Stoke, major track alterations were made primarily to assist in realignment for high-speed running, and the route continues south as four-track, with the down fast on the outside of the down slow line, so that the arrangement is down fast, down slow, up fast and up slow. This arrangement of tracks continues south as far as Armitage and through Rugeley, where

there is a branch to Walsall which is not at present being electrified.

The double-track connection from the high-level line to Lichfield City station and down to Lichfield Trent Valley station has been made into a single bi-directional

At Coventry the whole station has been rebuilt and track layout revised

goods line connecting with the up slow line near Bridge No. 100. This eliminated a cross-over road underneath the bridge and reduced the amount by which this bridge had to be raised to give electrical clearances. At the north end, the connections to the groups of sidings on each side of the main lines have been simplified and improved and some sidings have been

removed to provide for overhead structure masts.

Tamworth is a railway key point for transfer of mails and parcels between the West Coast route and the high-level Derby-Bristol line. The former station was 115 years old. No track alterations have been made, but the platforms have been lengthened, the high-level to take 14-coach trains and the low-level to accommodate 15-coach trains. The whole of the station buildings has been rebuilt, with stairways giving access from high- to low-level and work was completed in 1961.

The up and down platforms at Nuneaton station have been lengthened to 1,100ft, bridge No. 45 has been raised and widened, and the track connections at each end of the station have been simplified and improved. Modernisation of the booking hall and office has been carried out.

At Coventry the whole station has been rebuilt and track layout revised, the latter ▶

being of some interest. The former station comprised two platforms with the up and down fast lines in the centre and between the up and down platform tracks. There are now four platforms, all longer than the original ones, and capable of dealing with 16- or 17-coach trains. The connections with the Leamington branch at the south end have been modified so that trains from Leamington can operate clear of the main lines to Birmingham, further assisted by signalling the down slow line for bi-directional working. An up and down goods line running parallel with the Nuneaton branch has also been provided.

A power signalbox at the Rugby end replaced five mechanical boxes. The two overbridges – Stoney Road and Warwick Road – at the London and Birmingham ends of the station respectively, were completely rebuilt to suit the revised track layout and for overhead electrification clearance and were widened to meet local requirements. A footbridge and luggage bridge were provided at the centre of the station giving access to all four platforms, built as an extension of the high concourse structure. The station was opened on March 1, 1962.

Rugby station is essentially a large island platform with bay platforms at each end and located between the down platform No. 1 and the up platform No. 2. The down fast and up fast lines are located on the outside of the station, and outside these two tracks are the down goods and the up goods lines. There are four bay platforms at the north end, Nos. 3, 4, 5, and 6, and two bay platforms at the south ends, Nos. 7 and 8.

BR No. E3012 arrives at Stockport Edgeley with the Manchester Piccadilly to Bournemouth 'Pines Express' on September 18, 1961. A H BRYANT

The platform layout remains unaltered, except for extensions to Nos. 8, 4 and 5 platforms, and the present platform gas-lighting changed to electric. The track layout at the north end has been simplified and improved by the elimination of the connections to the former Leicester branch which previously crossed all up lines. The tracks from Nos. 3 and 4 bay platforms have been turned away to the west and connect with the up and down slow lines. At the south

end of the station there is no major change, but connections, particularly to Nos. 7 and 8 bays, have been improved. In the groups of sidings to the north the tracks will be rearranged and certain sidings eliminated. Further north, the flyover, a feature of the Rugby area, carries the up Birmingham line over the down main lines and helps very considerably towards free traffic movements. It is 450 yards long and was completed in 1962. There will be a power signalbox and a

A freight train, headed by a Class 5 4-6-0 locomotive, crossing the Rugby flyover, in September, 1962. The object of the flyover was to take the up Birmingham line over the Trent Valley lines and thus free the latter from interruption by unnecessary traffic movements.

A view of the rebuilt Coventry station, opened on March 1, 1962, showing Nos. 1 and 2 platforms with a DMU and EMU awaiting passengers. The clean and modern design of the station buildings and platform awnings is in evidence.

district electric locomotive depot where electric and diesel locomotives will be maintained.

The permanent way at Bletchley has been realigned for high-speed running and cross connections, improved, while the fast-line platforms are being lengthened to deal with 12-coach trains. A district electric maintenance depot and new carriage-cleaning sidings are being provided. Alterations to be made to the passenger

A power signalbox at Rugby replaced five mechanical boxes

station include the remodelling of the booking hall and rearrangement of the passenger amenities, and a new passenger and luggage bridge. A new power signalbox has been constructed on the down side at the south end of the station and is now being equipped for commissioning in June 1965.

The importance of Hemel Hempstead station is enhanced by the new town. Platforms have been lengthened to facilitate 10-coach trains and the station buildings are being modernised.

Willesden Junction main line station has been closed and is being demolished. Cross connections between the main lines and the various sidings groups are being simplified and improved to permit of fast running. The Sudbury arrival sidings will all be electrified

and individual tracks are being stewed to provide space for OLE structure masts. The carriage sidings and high-level storage sidings (new E) are to be wired for most of their length, but not the Sudbury low-level sorting sidings or the high-level sorting E sidings. Brent sidings will be wired for about half their length and three sidings are to be removed. On the down side, the north carriage shed and the associated sidings have been removed and the Motive Power Depot will be closed. The new power signalbox is under construction on the up side, opposite the Motive Power Depot. The A/B sidings have been remodelled and will be electrified wholly or in part. On the up side, south of Bridge No. 5 which carries the North London lines, a new district electric depot is being built.

The Motive Power Depot at Camden will be closed, buildings removed, and new sidings will be provided with simplified connections to the main line. These new sidings will be used for the storage of electric multiple unit stock during off-peak periods. ∎

Stafford station as rebuilt: In the foreground is the down relief line and, beyond, the down and up fast, and up loop lines respectively.

The "Jaffa Cake" express livery was used by British Rail on some Class 309 Clacton EMUs and also a number of 4-Cep EMUs, as seen here on No. 1582 passing Wandsworth Road with a Victoria to Dover Western Docks service in April 1993. Note the luggage van on the rear.

Multiple Unit Slam-Door memories

Designated AM4, these units were built for suburban services around Liverpool and Manchester, and unit No. 029 is seen entering East

Top: Three car 'Hampshire' DEMU No. 1107 slips away from the west end of Bournemouth station on May 25, 1968, with the 18.25 service to Swanage.

Left: Stalwarts of the Portsmouth line for many years were the 4-Cor EMUs. On April 9, 1965, unit No. 3122 leads a 4-Buf unit into Woking station with a semi-fast service to Portsmouth Harbour.

ALL PICTURES: TRACKS NORTH

AM2 EMU No. 274, later TOPS Class 302, stands at Grays station, Essex, on August 19, 1962 with an Ockendon branch train.

4-Sub EMU No. 4620 waits at Waterloo for departure with a service to Chessington South in March 1979.

The escape of Koravitch

By VICTOR L WHITECHURCH

IN Issue Number One of *The Railway Magazine* was detailed the attempted capture of the Russian Ambassador, Sklavotski, by the agent of a secret society named Koravitch, assisted by two comrades, one of whom told the story of Sklavotski's clever subterfuge by which the daring plan of Koravitch, successfully carried out as it was in every other detail, came to nought. The story about to be related comes from the same source of information, and describes how Koravitch in his turn baffled the plans of Sklavotski. It will be told, as was the last, in the narrator's own words.

✳ ✳ ✳ ✳ ✳

The adventure which I am about to relate is another of the annals of the Secret Society which at one time claimed me as a member – an adventure, too, in which Koravitch again was the principal actor, only this time the tables were turned, and he stood on his defence rather than on his attack. The relation of the episode in question, which may safely be done now, will also clear up a mystery which at the time baffled police agents and railway officials alike, but which, like many other so-called 'mysteries', was in reality simplicity itself.

In my last story I told how Koravitch had been hoodwinked by the astute ambassador Sklavotski, who had hit upon the plan of disguising himself as an old clergyman and allowing his trusty servant to 'make up' as himself, the consequence being that he eluded our hands, and the secret treaty by which the threatening war clouds of Eastern Europe were dispersed was safely concluded. But, as far as Koravitch was concerned, the matter did not end here. He had been a marked man in Russia, and had fled to England some years previously in order to avoid the chance of a journey to Siberia, on which 'no return' tickets were issued. And there was one man especially – a terrible man, too – by whom he was not forgotten. That was Sklavotski himself. It will be remembered that the latter had been a police agent of the Russian government before he was promoted to the higher post of Ambassador Extraordinary, and in his former capacity the name of Koravitch in connection with sundry little quiet undertakings 'against the Czar' had been familiar to him.

Koravitch, like others of his kind, lived in an atmosphere charged with danger and suspicion. He was still a Russian subject, and he knew that Russia had watched him with that solicitude which she so often displays for her wandering children. He had more than once recognised a secret police agent in the man who sat opposite to him in an omnibus, or the stranger who sometimes, aimlessly enough it seemed, dogged his footsteps through the streets of London. But so far all had gone well with him; he had kept his movements perfectly secret; our meetings, at which he took the chair, had been arranged with the utmost caution, and for months past he had felt almost secure.

It was a few weeks after our unsuccessful attempt to kidnap Sklavotski that I was walking across Waterloo Place when I felt a light touch on my shoulder, and looked round to find Koravitch.

"Hush," he said, as I began speaking to him; "I want a few minutes' conversation with you. Let us go into St James's Park."

We went past the Duke of York's Column, down the steps; reached the park, and found a secluded seat near the water.

"What is it?" I asked.

" Well, you wouldn't think it of me, I expect, but I'm getting nervous," and he laughed an uneasy little laugh.

"What about?"

" Well, you'd feel a little nervous if you had the thought of Siberia constantly running in your mind."

"What has happened?"

"Nothing – as yet; but look here."

He drew from his pocket-book a letter with a Russian stamp upon it and handed it to me.

It contained a scrap of paper with these words:

"Sklavotski never forgets!"

"Who sent this?" I asked.

"I don't know. Probably Sklavotski himself."

"What makes you think that?"

"Because it's just the sort of thing he'd be likely to do. Listen! I had word last night that the house of one of the 'brothers' in St Petersburg was searched by the police some days ago, and before those inside could destroy certain papers they had to escape. These papers incriminate me, because they prove that I am the chief agent in England. Probably, too, Sklavotski knows very well of his escape six weeks ago, and I fancy he's putting the police on my track. As to the warning note, it's the sort of thing he used to delight in doing, making those whom he was after suffer beforehand. It's done to make me feel I'm a marked man – more, a hunted man. See there!" and his voice sank as he pointed to a man lounging on a seat near us.

"That's the fourth time I've noticed that fellow today. I'm being watched!"

"What do you propose doing?"

"Well, if Sklavotski means business, I'd better be off."

"Where?"

"America eventually; only that's more easily said than done. If I'm being shadowed now it probably means they're waiting for more evidence against me so that they can manage to arrest me by extradition. So the thing is to get away before any further

" I felt a light touch on my shoulder."

He had fled to England some years previously to avoid a journey to Siberia on which no return tickets were issued

developments. Now, I want your help to a certain extent – in this way; I can see about getting out of England: I've got a friend who'll work that quietly enough. But I may want a hiding-place for a day or two after I've thrown the spies off the scent. Can you manage this?"

"How?"

"Well, you've got diggings in Oakley Square, haven't you? Is there anyone else lodging in the house?"

"No, not just at present. There's a set of rooms to let."

"Good! You take them for me, and say they're for your brother who is coming on a short visit to England. Stay in the house, keep a sharp lookout, and expect me when you see me. Take care, too, that you're not 'shadowed' yourself, as that would spoil the game. And now I'll be off and lead our friend yonder a bit of a dance. Good-bye!"

"Good-bye and good luck!" I answered.

✳ ✳ ✳ ✳ ✳

Four days passed and I heard nothing of him. I kept indoors the whole time, telling my landlady, who was fortunately a rather deaf widow, that my brother might arrive from abroad at any time. At four o'clock on the morning of the fifth day I heard a knocking at the street door, and descended very cautiously to open it. Koravitch, looking worn and tired, entered quickly and came up to my sitting-room. His first movement was to go to the window and carefully watch the square, which was beginning to grow distinct in the dawning daylight.

"Good!" he ejaculated as he presently came away from the window and threw himself into a chair; "I think I've eluded them at last. And now let me tell you the news. When I got back to my rooms the evening after seeing you I found that they had been entered and rifled. Some papers were missing. Certainly they were written in cipher, but I doubt if the cipher was sufficient precaution to conceal the contents. Worse than that, too, I have received intelligence that the warrant for my arrest under the extradition treaty is out, and that any moment I am liable to be taken. I've been hunted about like a hare, but I've managed to give them the slip for a time, and if only I can get out of the country unobserved it will be all right, for they're on a false scent and think I'm making for Paris. As it happens, though, I'm going on board a vessel at Manchester."

"Manchester?"

"Yes; she's going down the ship canal and then over to Ireland. I want to lie low for a few weeks in a place I know well. It's too risky trying America yet. The captain of this boat knows me, so it's all right."

"When does she sail?"

"This evening, so you see, I must get off

If I get out of this, I shall retire from the business altogether. Life isn't worth it at the price

" Now let me tell you the news "

today. I should have done so last night, but it was impossible."

"How shall you go?"

"Got a Bradshaw?"

I handed him one, and he studied it for a few minutes, carefully comparing different routes.

At length he said: "Well, it's an awful risk, but it's my only chance. I shall take the 2pm from St Pancras. It's safer than going by the London and North-Western, I think, as they're not so likely to be watching, and that train will land me in Manchester just in the nick of time. But I'm ravenously hungry, my friend, so let us put off discussing these details until you've given me some breakfast."

I got him some cold beef, and brewed him a cup of strong tea. He fell to heartily, and after his meal lit a cigar and leaned back in his chair.

"I'll tell you what, my friend, if I get out of this safely I shall retire from the business altogether. Life isn't worth it at the price, although the 'cause' is a grand one, I admit. I'm dead beat with the exertions of the last few days. Think of it: you see the crowd of thousands rolling along the Strand, Cheapside, or over London Bridge; you yourself float with them, a little pygmy on life's stream, and feel lost and isolated. But when you are hunted, and your dear freedom is at stake, then do you feel the impossibility of losing yourself among the millions and the awful difficulty of isolation. See here: for three days and nights have I been trying to get to you or out of London unobserved, and till this morning it was impossible. My very thoughts seem to have been dogged by spies. It's enough to make a man turn aristocrat and live peaceably. But there, I want to sleep, so let me go to my room. Give me some food before I start; I have plenty of money on me. We're close by St Pancras, and we won't

leave too early. It's much better to be there just before the train starts, in case anything might happen."

I showed him to his room, and in a few minutes he was sound asleep. The morning dragged itself away slowly. I did not dare to venture out of doors, but now and then I glanced out of the window to see if any suspicious personages were about, but saw no one likely to be a detective. At twelve o'clock Koravitch came and asked me for a razor, and after some little trouble he removed his beard and moustache. A little before one we had a meal. He had recovered his spirits, and was quite cheerful.

"You'd better come with me to the station," he said.

"If I can get a compartment to myself so much the better. I always carry a carriage key, and I shall lock myself in. The train arrives at Manchester Central at 6.20, so it's a long journey. Thanks, I will fill my cigar-case. Now, it's twenty to, and we ought to be off. Yes, fill your glass. Success to my escape!"

"Success to your escape, Koravitch!"

He put on his coat, took up his small handbag, and we set forth together. As we went out of the door we noticed a man lounging against the railings opposite. Koravitch turned off quickly.

"Come!" he said; "I don't like the look of that fellow. Glance back at him as we turn the corner, will you?"

I did so.

"He's coming our way," I said.

"Then let's hurry and get out of his sight; he mustn't see us go to St Pancras."

It seemed when we arrived at the station that we had succeeded in eluding the spy, if spy he was.

"You'll have to be quick, sir," said the booking clerk as he handed over the ticket; "only three minutes before she starts."

We ran to the departure platform. ▶

Koravitch hastily scanned the train. A fine 'bogie' carriage in the centre had two vacant compartments – one right at the front end and the other about the middle. To the first of these compartments he hurried.

"Take your seats, please!"

The door slammed, and Koravitch slipped his hand out of the window and locked it. Then I saw him move to the other side and lock that door also.

"Any more, going on?"

There was a little stir near the door opening into the booking hall.

"Right away!"

The whistle sounded, there was the first sonorous puff, and then, just as the train began to move, two men, one of whom I recognised as the one who had been following us, came rushing on to the platform and ran along the train.

"Here he is!" shouted one, as they saw Koravitch, and tried to open the door. But it was locked.

"Stand away there!"

"Stand away yourself!" said the man, pushing the porter on one side and springing, with his companion, at the compartment nearest to them as the train steamed on, opening the door, and jumping in. The other followed, shut the door, and, as the train cleared the platform, I could see that they were stretching their heads out of the window, one on either side of the compartment, in the middle of the coach, watching lest Koravitch should attempt to jump from the train and escape. I did not wait to see any more, as I thought it wise to disappear myself, and I did so with the sad thought that one whom I had known well, and with whom I had shared several perils, was booked for Siberia instead of Manchester. There seemed no chance of his escape with two detectives so close to him, and I had no doubt in my own mind that at Kettering, the first stopping-place of the

train, Koravitch would be arrested, unless, indeed, he were mad enough to risk his life by jumping before that event.

At an early hour the following morning I went out and bought a paper, hoping that it would contain some news concerning poor Koravitch. Eagerly I scanned it until my eye was caught by the following heading:

"EXCITING CHASE AFTER A NIHILIST"
"MYSTERIOUS DISAPPEARANCE."

And then I read the paragraph beneath:

"For several days the authorities of Scotland Yard, in conjunction with a couple of Russian detectives, have been on the eve of arresting a member of one of the Nihilist societies, a man who has been residing in England for some years past, and dictating to a large extent the movements of the society in this country. For political reasons the police have not thought it wise to mention the particulars which led to a warrant for his apprehension being issued under the extradition treaty at a late hour the day before yesterday.

"Almost at the time that it was to be put into force, however, Koravitch, the individual in question, managed to elude the vigilance of those who were 'shadowing' him, and for a few hours his whereabouts was unknown, though it was imagined that he was endeavouring to make good his escape from the country.

"Yesterday, however, it was ascertained that he was concealed somewhere in the neighbourhood of Euston; but almost at the time that his capture seemed imminent he again eluded for a few minutes the watchfulness of the police and proceeded to St Pancras Station, where he took a ticket for Manchester by the 2pm express.

"Just as the train was about to move out of the station Detective Armstrong and a Russian colleague rushed upon the platform and saw their man in a compartment alone. They at once endeavoured to get in with him,

but it appears he had locked the door, so, failing in their attempt, they jumped into an empty compartment in the same carriage behind him. For some little distance both men kept their heads out of the windows, one on either side, in order to watch lest he should jump from the train. No such attempt, however, took place, and as he himself glanced out of his window just before Child's Hill station they felt satisfied that he was in the train and that they would capture him easily at Kettering, the first stopping-place. Therefore they withdrew their heads and sat one on either side of the carriage.

"The engine had now attained a very high speed, and it was obvious that any attempt at jumping must prove fatal. The train had passed through St Albans station when there was a sudden whistle, and the police officers immediately felt the brake being put on. In an instant they put their heads out of the windows, but could see nothing on either side. The train came to a standstill about a quarter of a mile north of St Albans, and the detectives at once got out and went to the compartment in which Koravitch was travelling.

"To their consternation it was empty, although both doors were still locked. When the guard came along to discover who had pulled the communication cord (for it was owing to this that the train had stopped), he found that the cord in question was undoubtedly pulled by Koravitch himself, for it was hanging slack outside the window of his compartment. A hasty search was made throughout the train, under the carriages, and along the line, but no trace of the man could be discovered. Of course it was broad daylight, and the line is fairly straight at the point, so that it is impossible to conceive how Koravitch could have escaped.

"The detectives declare that the man could not have jumped from the train, for their heads were out of the windows directly the whistle sounded, and they were careful to look in front and behind until the train stopped, and state that the line was perfectly clear when they alighted. One of them went on with the train to Kettering, where another equally fruitless search was made, while the other remained behind and carefully investigated the spot where the train drew up and the permanent-way, but to no purpose.

"It must be mentioned that the passengers all declare that they saw nothing; the guard and driver are positive that the brakes were put on immediately the communication cord was pulled; and same officials of the line, who have been interviewed on the subject, state that the affair is an inexplicable mystery.

"All agree that Koravitch must have got away from the train, but up to the time of

"'Stand away yourself!' said the man."

> The engine had now attained a very high speed, and any attempt at jumping must prove fatal

going to press not a vestige of him was to be seen anywhere."

I heard nothing more of Koravitch. After this, and for some time the affair remained a perfect mystery to me as well as to others. I often tried to work out his escape, but invariably came to a full stop; while some times I fancied that either he had been killed by jumping from the train and that the affair had been hushed up, or that, after all, he had been taken captive and some artful ruse had been employed by the detectives to throw the 'brothers' off the scent. At the same time I found it expedient to sink into obscurity for a time myself, as I had been rather implicated in the proceedings; so I left London, and, after some wanderings in South America, finally found myself, about a year or so after the events described above, in the United States. I was travelling one day in the famous 'Pennsylvania Limited', from New York to Cincinnati, and had strolled on to the observation car at the rear of the train. A man, whose build seemed to be familiar to me, was leaning over the rails admiring the passing scenery and puffing away at a cigar. Presently he turned round slowly and faced me, and, in spite of his Yankee 'goatee' beard, I recognised him at once.

"Koravitch!" I exclaimed.

He gave a start.

"Hush! my friend. I am Godfrey P Jackson, a citizen of the United States."

"How on earth..."

"Wait a moment! Let's make sure were alone. All right! Now come right on to the end of the car and we'll have a chat."

We went to the end, and I began to ply him with questions.

"Oh," said he, "you want to know how I escaped that day, do you? My dear fellow, I'm really surprised that such a ludicrously simple thing should have baffled not only the police but the railway officials. It only goes to show one on what a slender chance the great events of one's life often turns. Why, you'll laugh when I tell you how simple the whole thing was. It was my last chance, I admit, and I played the game boldly; but I assure you I never thought at the time that it could prove successful. First of all, it was broad daylight; that was against me; and then the obvious method of escape stood out so boldly – and stands to this day, I suppose. And yet none of them ever noticed it."

"Explain yourself," I said.

"Well, of course, when the detectives rushed down on the platform I thought the game was up, but I determined to try some dash for freedom first, and puzzled my brains to know what to do. I peeped out of the window once or twice, and saw that they were watching. At first I thought of jumping in a tunnel, but the risk was too great, and I knew I should be crippled and easily taken. When

we got beyond Hendon I noticed that the men who were after me had drawn in their heads, probably confident that escape was impossible.

"My next idea was to pull the communication cord and jump from the train when it drew up; but then came the thought that others would be on the alert as well as myself. Next I tried to think of any details along the line which might help me, and suddenly a wild idea suggested itself to my mind, and I at once prepared to put it into execution. There were several things against it, chiefly the being noticed by signalmen in their boxes; but I was a desperate man, and this is what I did: a little way before we came to St Albans I opened the door after a careful survey, got out on the footboard, locked the door again, and slipped round the end of the coach, in between it and the preceding carriage. It reminded me of that night when we tried to kidnap Sklavotski; but my plan was a different one this time. Directly we, were through St Albans station I climbed, by the steps at the end, to the roof of the coach, laid myself flat on the top with my head towards the engine, reached over the right-

My next idea was to pull the communication cord and jump from the train

hand side and, when I judged the proper moment had arrived, grasped the communication cord and pulled it with all my might, throwing the 'slack' over the carriage side immediately afterwards.

"Directly I had done so the whistle sounded and the train began to slow up. Lifting my head slightly, and looking in front, I saw what I wanted – what, of course, I knew, from my knowledge of the line, was there."

"What was that?" I asked.

"Why, a light footbridge over the line, only a few feet above the tops of the. carriages, and easily within my reach if I stood up as the train passed beneath. Do you comprehend now? Yes, very simple, wasn't it? I had calculated for the train to stop, or at least slow up, as it passed under the bridge. As a matter of fact, I had not pulled the cord quite soon enough, and I began to fear that the train would pass under the bridge too quickly for men to get off; but I screwed up my courage, remembered my old gymnastic exercises and my muscular power, rose to an upright position facing the bridge, and as we passed beneath, slowing down as we did so, I gave a spring, clutched the iron framework, getting frightfully banged about as I did so, quickly climbed the rail, and was actually making my way, stooping down, off the bridge

before the train had quite stopped beyond it. I had calculated that the train itself would receive all the attention of officials and detectives, and I suppose I was correct. My only wonder was that no one saw me get off the train on to the bridge, and that no one afterwards seemed to have guessed how my very simple escape was accomplished."

"And what did you do then?"

"Perhaps rather a foolish thing, but it turned out all right in the end. I at once made for the town of St Albans and crossed it, arriving at the L & NW station in plenty of time to take the 3.13 train to Willesden Junction via Watford, arriving at 3.56, just in time to catch the Manchester express at 4.12, and finally found myself at London Road station, Manchester, a little after eight.

"At once I hurried to the canal docks, and found to my great joy that my worthy friend the captain had waited for me, determining to sail the next morning. So the following day saw me on the Irish Sea, and, after lying low for a couple of months in the Emerald Isle, I came out here... Yes, I'm a law-abiding citizen now, though I still hanker after the 'cause', and time will show, I suppose, how long I shall remain so. But now come on the dining-car and have a feed; this fresh air makes one pretty hungry, doesn't it?"

"Yes," I replied; "better than Siberia eh?"

"You bet! But it was a risky chance between that Eastern clime and Westward Ho! wasn't it?"

And I think all will agree that it was. ■

The British railways at war

By JOHN R HIND

AFTER three and a half years of war there is still much about the activities of the railways which must wait until the curtains of censorship can be brushed aside, but some interesting facts can be told. When the time comes, the full story of the railways' locomotives, for instance, will show how British-built locomotives have set up new records despite bombs and machine-gunning. Remarkable mileages have been covered between repairs, extra heavy loads have been handled, and the splendid work of the enginemen and behind-the-scenes staffs in no small measure has been responsible for the high standards of locomotive performances which have been maintained through the most difficult conditions.

Many changes have taken place at the locomotive depots. Apart from the building of air-raid protection works, wartime schemes have been carried out to rearrange many locomotive workings as a result of the changed flows of traffic. Extensive efforts have been made to achieve an even greater utilisation of motive power. Locomotives have been extensively exchanged between the railways. For example, 'King Arthur' locomotives from the Southern Railway are working on the LNER, LNER 2-8-0 heavy freight locomotives are running on the GWR, many locomotives have been released to the War Department, and scores of locomotives have been loaned for use by the service departments. Enginemen have been temporarily transferred between the railways; firemen belonging to one railway are working with engine drivers of another, spare parts and repair staffs for engines are also exchanged to speed up overhauls and repairs.

The loss of 143 locomotives withdrawn for service with the Forces overseas may be contrasted with the safe return of the LMSR *Coronation* locomotive from a pre-war tour of the USA. The LMSR provided 51 standard class 2-8-0 freight tender type engines which, with the assistance of the GWR and Southern Railway, were equipped with apparatus for using oil fuel, Westinghouse pumps and brake valves before shipment and 92 Class O4 (formerly a Great Central design by Mr J G Robinson) were supplied by the LNER; of these 61 served in the last war. Reports state that these locomotives have given a good account of themselves.

In addition to locomotives, the railways undertook the construction of 1,000 steel-framed open 12-ton wagons, which were built in the record time of 10 weeks in a Southern Railway works. The LNER helped by cutting wagon timbers from logs and supplying ironwork details for the wagons, and the LMSR assisted by providing timber and stampings. Each wagon had 1,792 parts, and every piece was numbered, to assist assembly at destination. Rubber springs were also provided to save wear and tear. In all, 130 men, 19 boys, and 22 women workers, each

Soldiers arriving from overseas.

Locomotives in service with the Forces at a WD locomotive shed in Persia.

averaging 67 hours a week, assembled the wagons at the rate of one every 37 minutes. A report received from a South African unit which assembled the wagons abroad recorded that it was possible to erect them at a rate of 45 minutes each. The 20 working weeks from the date of the commencement of the manufacture of the first wagon to the time the last wagon was actually in service 12,000 route miles away, is thought to constitute a world record.

New types of locomotives introduced since war broke out include the LNER Class Q1, heavy freight shunting 0-8-0 tank locomotives rebuilt from obsolete 0-8-0 tender engines, thereby saving 900 tons of steel, 'Antelope' 4-6-0 mixed traffic locomotives, the first of which, No. 8301, is named *Springbok*, the Southern Railway 'Merchant Navy' class streamline locomotives named after shipping organisations using Southampton docks in peacetime, and a Southern Railway Q class six-coupled goods locomotive suitable for all lines on the Southern Railway system.

Heavy duty 'Austerity' locomotives based upon the LMSR standard 2-8-0 type of Sir William Stanier are also being built to Government orders for service on any standard-gauge railway in the world. The LMSR has rebuilt with larger boilers some of its 5XP 4-6-0 locomotives, and two locomotives of the LMSR 2-8-0 standard type have been built for the LMSR at Southern Railway workshops in the short time of two months. A number of 2-8-0 American 'Austerity' locomotives built in the USA have also been received and are in service.

Electric locomotives of new types have been introduced by the LNER and Southern Railways, and air raids on electrified lines have proved that electrification by the third and fourth rail systems has stood up remarkably well. Bomb damage on electrified routes has been repaired as rapidly as on steam-operated lines and alternative power supplies have proved their worth.

▶ **Farm machinery for the food front.**

One of many heavy loads in transit on the GWR.

Air-raid damage to carriage sheds on the LMSR.

Loading TNT: Great quantities of high explosive have been moved without incident.

On the operating side, the central control of wagons has been very successful, and railway operation by means of telephone control systems has been greatly extended and developed to meet wartime conditions. In addition to the normal daily operating conferences which take place on each of the railways a daily central operating conference takes place every morning, including Sundays, by means of special telephones which link up the chief operating officer of each of the four main-line railways at his desk. Immediate decisions are reached involving individual or collective working, and movements are allocated to the routes giving the best operating conditions irrespective of all other interests. The control systems of the British railways are similar to a military organisation with facilities in the form of private telephones and wireless. Close contacts are also maintained between the chief operating officers of the railways and the movement and transport officers of the service departments to dovetail railway transport into the schemes of the fighting forces. The ceaseless nature of this work can be appreciated by the fact that 150,000 special trains have already been scheduled and run for the conveyance of troops and their equipment.

The railway fleets of special wagons evolved for awkward and extra heavy loads have proved invaluable. Vehicles originally designed to carry large sheets of plate glass, theatrical scenery, private cars, circuses, and girders for buildings are now conveying parts of aircraft, guns, tanks, and all kinds of military vehicles and war equipment. Through the protective measures taken by the railways vast tonnages of high explosives

Trainloads of tanks have been made up and despatched.

and munitions have been moved without incident.

Despite official requests not to travel unnecessarily and the withdrawal of a variety of cheap tickets which became effective from September 5 last, heavy passenger traffics have been handled. By Government direction many restaurant and buffet cars have been withdrawn, some for more than a year. Sleeping cars are occupied by priority passengers, and goods have taken the places of pleasure travellers, apart from additional services for war workers.

Approaching a million loaded wagons a week have been despatched by the railways for several months, and amongst the hundreds of wartime improvement jobs to increase the capacity of the railways to transport much heavier war traffics, are the doubling, trebling, and quadrupling of tracks, and provision of new sidings, loop lines, and marshalling yards; extra signalboxes and extensive signalling installations, as well as additional telephones, radio equipment, and snow ploughs for abnormal conditions have been introduced.

Carriages have been converted into ambulance trains; railway workshops have made guns, tanks, aeroplanes and other war

Snowplough patrols have kept exposed but vital lines open during severe weather.

equipment, and railway steamships have done their full share of war work on Admiralty service.

Some 100,000 railwaymen have been released to join the fighting forces, 90,000 are training as Home Guards in addition to their railway work, 170,000 members of the railway staffs have been fully trained in ARP duties, and 100,000 railwaywomen are now employed.

No account of British railways at war should omit reference to the services rendered by the railways of London Transport, both surface lines and tube lines. All through the air raids, train services vital to the morale and war effort of the congested area served by London Transport were regularly maintained, except when damage from enemy action caused temporary interruptions. ■

BR Standard Class 7 'Britannia' No. 70039 *Sir Christopher Wren* storms Hoghton Bank near Blackburn with the LCGB 'Thames-Tyne' tour from London Euston to Carlisle and Newcastle on June 3, 1967. Note the wooden panel where the numberplate should be! PAUL GERALD

Enthusiast Specials

Right: Johnson Midland Railway 0-6-0 No. 58148 emerges from the narrow bore of the 1,796 yard Glenfield Tunnel with the SLS/MLS 'Leicestershire Railtour' returning from West Bridge (Leicester) to Coalville on September 8, 1962. G D KING

Left: BR Standard 2MT 2-6-2T No. 84008 pauses at Duffield with the SLS 'Derbyshire Railtour' about to take the branch to Wirksworth on April 21, 1956. The tour also visited Butterley, Stanton Gate and Derby Friargate. T G HEPBURN

Eastbound goods train, hauled by 0-6-0 locomotive No. 71, passing Melton Constable West signalbox, at the junction with the Cromer branch, MGNJR, in the mid-1930s. PHOTO: W VAUGHAN-JENKINS

Closing of the Midland & Great Northern Line

THE Eastern Area Board of the British Transport Commission has announced with regret that it has decided in principle that almost the whole of the railways formerly known as the Midland & Great Northern Joint line must be closed down. The railway extends from the London-Nottingham main line of the London Midland Region at Saxby, and from the East Coast main line at Peterborough, to Sutton Bridge, and thence to Melton Constable, through South Lynn. From Melton Constable, branches radiate to Cromer, Norwich, and Great Yarmouth. The total length of the line, including the 15 miles from Saxby to Little Bytham, built and originally owned by the Midland Railway, is about 192 miles. Of this total, it is intended that only the 15-mile branch from Melton Constable to Cromer shall remain open.

The board points out that during the last few years no effort has been spared to maintain the widest practicable network of railway services in the Eastern Region. In pursuit of this policy, considerable experiments have been made in cheaper methods of operation, combined in many cases with improved facilities. The losses incurred on non-paying sectors of the network have in consequence

been appreciably reduced. However, on certain services there are still big losses; and the extent to which these can be financed out of the proceeds of the profitable services has been much limited by recent trends. A new point of balance, it is stated, must be found between the obligations of public service on the one hand, and the requirements of the railway budget on the other.

An important and special consideration in this particular case is that the Midland & Great Northern line is largely duplicated by alternative facilities. No place served by it is more than a few miles distant from the Great Eastern line which parallels it across the north of East Anglia, and throughout most of the route there are bus services. It is this duplication of facilities which is mainly responsible for the poor loadings experienced on the Midland & Great Northern line, apart, of course, from the general sparsity of traffic in North Norfolk, and the fenlands around the Wash. The only towns in this area with a population of more than 10,000 are Norwich, Yarmouth, King's Lynn, and Wisbech, all of which are also served by the Great Eastern line.

Such traffics as are now carried by M & GN

services can be transferred elsewhere with advantage to both the economics and the frequency of the alternative services. In other words, the present proposal would not only remove the element of duplication, but should also make it possible to improve the remainder of the services. The strengthening of these other services is already under consideration.

It is estimated that net savings of the order of at least £500,000 a year will result from the changes contemplated. In addition, certain very heavy expenditure on engineering works, such as the rebuilding of the Clenchwarton Bridge, near King's Lynn, will be avoided. In all these circumstances, the board has had no alternative but to adjust its policy, and to instruct the management to prepare detailed plans for the closing of the line.

This will mean, on the passenger side, the withdrawal of stopping passenger train services, most of which are at present steam operated and carry a small number of passengers. Conversion of services to diesel operation has been tried over comparable sections of line where conditions are favourable, with admittedly beneficial results. However, the reduction in operating costs and the improvement in receipts have not been ▶

sufficient to bring the services into financial equilibrium and the field remaining on the M & GN offers a still less favourable ground for experiment.

There is now sufficient experience of diesel operation to establish that, to make this type of stopping passenger service profitable, there must be a very substantial increase in the carryings. Such increases of local traffic in the area served by the M & GN line are simply not available. In many cases the stations are a long way from the villages they serve, and the bus, rather than a railway, offers the best and most economical means of carrying the bulk of these local and short distance passengers.

On the freight side, the volume of traffic is not sufficient to justify maintenance of this line as a separate through route, particularly as the alternative Great Eastern line facilities are available for it in most cases and every effort will be made to continue a satisfactory transport service to the traders and other interests in the area.

About 1,500 men will be affected. The trade unions have been informed, and the arrangements necessary and proper in such circumstances will be discussed with them and settled so that, in accordance with normal practice, serious hardship or dislocation is avoided.

The average number of passenger trains affected by the closure will be about 140 on weekdays, and about 12 on Sundays, each carrying an average of 40-50 passengers. There is also an appreciable amount of holiday traffic during a few weekends in the peak summer season between the Midlands and the Norfolk coast, mainly to Yarmouth. An average of about 80 goods trains run on weekdays only.

It is intended that the closure shall take place in the following six stages: Yarmouth

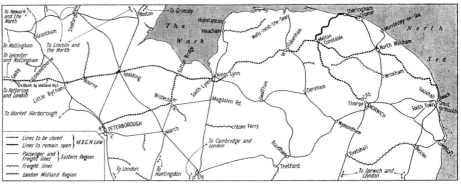

The Midland & Great Northern line, showing section to be closed and adjacent routes.

Beach to Melton Constable; Norwich City to Melton Constable; Melton Constable to South Lynn; South Lynn to Sutton Bridge; Sutton Bridge to Peterborough; and Sutton Bridge to Saxby. The closures will not necessarily be in this order, and special arrangements may be made to retain facilities at certain centres. The detailed plans are now being worked out for submission to the Transport Users Consultative Committees, together with the essential facts and figures.

This statement by the board is intended only to give notice of the proposal in general terms, and at the earliest possible moment, to all those who may be affected. As the plans for closure develop, and dates for the various stages are made known, the management will notify all persons or bodies known to be interested. The plans may be varied in detail, but it is intended that the first stages of the closure should take effect by the end of 1958, and the remainder follow as soon as possible thereafter.

Railway communication in the district served by the Midland & Great Northern line originally was provided by a number of small independent companies. The oldest of the

lines is that from Spalding to Holbeach, which was built by the Norwich & Spalding Railway (incorporated on August 4, 1853) and opened to passengers on November 15, 1858, and earlier for goods traffic. It was extended from Holbeach to Sutton Bridge on July 1, 1862. Two other railways – the Lynn & Sutton Bridge (incorporated on August 6, 1861) and the Spalding & Bourn* (incorporated on July 29, 1862) – continued the line eastward to Lynn and westward to Bourne, and were opened on November 1, 1864, and August 1, 1866, respectively. The Peterborough, Wisbech & Sutton Railway (incorporated on July 28, 1863) linked Peterborough with Sutton Bridge on August 1, 1866. By Act of July 23, 1866, the Midland & Eastern Railway was formed to take over the Bourne to King's Lynn line and to exercise running powers to Peterborough. The Midland Railway had already secured the working of the Peterborough, Wisbech & Sutton at 50% of the gross receipts, and the Midland and the Great Northern jointly worked the lines between Bourne and King's Lynn; the amalgamation left these arrangements unaffected.

A similar process of construction took place in the northern parts of Norfolk, east of King's Lynn. At Yarmouth, the Great Yarmouth & Statham Light Railway (incorporated on June 27, 1876) began building towards the north-west on January 15, 1877. The first section, from Yarmouth to Ormesby was opened on August 7, 1877, and extended to Hemsby on May 16, 1878. The name of the company was then changed (by Act of May 27, 1878) to the Yarmouth & North Norfolk, and powers were secured for an extension from Stalham to North Walsham. Martham was reached on July 15, 1878; Catfield on January 17, 1880; Stalham on July 3, 1880; and North Walsham on June 13, 1881.

During the same decade, the Lynn & Fakenham Railway (incorporated on July 13, 1876) was building eastward from King's Lynn. Its line was opened from Gaywood Junction (on the Lynn-Hunstanton branch of the GER) to Massingham on August 16, 1879; and to Fakenham on August 16, 1880. By Act of August 12, 1880, the company was authorised to extend its line to Norwich Holt and

MGNJR 4-4-0 locomotive No. 32, built by Beyer, Peacock & Co Ltd in 1888 and later fitted with a Midland boiler, at Lowestoft North station in 1936. PHOTO: J C THORNE

From *The Railway Magazine*, August 1958

Blakeney. From Fakenham to Guestwick was opened on January 19, 1882; thence to Lenwade on July 1, 1882; and through to Norwich (City) on December 2, 1882.

This was the position when, by Act of August 18, 1882, the Eastern & Midlands Railway was formed as an amalgamation as from the end of that year of the small companies that had remained outside the Great Northern and Great Eastern Railways, comprising the Lynn & Fakenharn, the Yarmouth & North Norfolk, and the Yarmouth Union. By the same Act the Midland & Eastern and the Peterborough, Wisbech & Sutton were merged into the Eastern & Midlands system as from July 1, 1883. It may be added that the Yarmouth Union Railway, incorporated on August 26, 1880, opened a connecting link between the YNNR and the GER on May 15, 1882.

An extension from Melton Constable to North Walsham having been opened on April 5, 1883, the newly formed Eastern & Midlands group had an unbroken system from Bourne and Peterborough to Norwich and Yarmouth. It then undertook a branch to Cromer, which was opened between Melton Constable and Holt on October 1, 1884, and extended to Cromer on June 16, 1887. An important connecting loop between South Lynn and Bawsey via Gayton Road, was opened on January 1, 1886, permitting through working between the eastern and western sections of the system without touching King's Lynn. The old section between Gaywood Junction and Bawsey was thereupon abandoned and still lies derelict. South Lynn was officially opened for goods traffic on November 2, 1863, but more than 22 years elapsed before it became available for passenger traffic with the opening of the Lynn loop.

Construction then remained in abeyance until the Midland & Great Northern Railways Joint Committee was incorporated by special Act of June 9, 1893, and took over from July 1, 1893, ownership of the Eastern & Midlands undertaking. The finishing touches to the

Yarmouth train near Corpusty in 1937, headed by Johnson 4-4-0 No. 01, built by Sharp, Stewart & Co Ltd in 1894. A zero prefix was added by the LNER to avoid number duplication with its own locos. PHOTO: W VAUGHAN-JENKINS

railway west of King's Lynn were made in 1893, when a short line avoiding Spalding station was brought into service. At the same time a continuation was opened (for goods in 1893 and passengers on May 1, 1894) from Bourne to an end-on junction at Little Bytham with the Midland Railway's line from Saxby. This gave a shorter route between the Midland system and the Norfolk coast. Until January 1, 1895, the western section (the former Peterborough, Wisbech & Sutton Railway and the Midland & Eastern Railway) was under a manager at Spalding, and the eastern section was managed from headquarters at King's Lynn. On that date the two sections were combined under a traffic manager with offices at King's Lynn.

In order to round off the Norfolk coast lines, a new joint undertaking – the Norfolk & Suffolk Joint Railways Committee – was established by the Midland & Great Northern

Joint Committee jointly with the Great Eastern Railway; this was incorporated by Act of 1898. A branch from North Walsham to Mundesley was opened on July 1, 1898; a line between Yarmouth and Lowestoft on July 13, 1903; and an extension from Mundesley to Cromer on August 3, 1906. The section from Mundesley to Roughton Road Junction, Cromer, was closed completely on April 17, 1953.

The standing of the MGNJR was unchanged by the Grouping of 1923, except that the owning companies, the Great Northern and the Midland Railways, became merged into the LNER and LMSR respectively. Passenger and goods traffic continued to be controlled from King's Lynn until October 1, 1936, when working responsibilities of the line were taken over by the LNER, and subsequently by the Eastern Region, on the Nationalisation of the railways in 1948.

The yellow livery which for so long characterised the locomotives of the MGNJR was depicted in the colour plate published in the July 1958 issue, and editorial reference was made to the change to brown which occurred in 1929. A further change, to LNER livery, took place after 1936. The tender engines (4-4-0s and 0-6-0s) were designed by S W Johnson, and displayed marked Midland features; with few exceptions, they remained in service until comparatively recent years. Passenger coaches were finished in varnished teak. The chief features of the system and its traffic were described and illustrated in *The Railway Magazine* for September, 1936, and a separate article on the locomotives appeared in the October issue of that year.

* In the Act of Incorporation, Bourne was spelt without the final 'e'. ∎

Up Midland & Great Northern parcels train at Wisbech North in 1953, with Ivatt class 4 2-6-0 locomotive No. 43093. PHOTO: R E VINCENT

The Hayling Island branch

By MICHAEL J C KENNETT

KNOWN affectionately to residents, and also to many thousands of holidaymakers, as the "Hayling Billy", the train service from Havant to Hayling Island is one of those recently to be threatened by British Railways' economy axe. During the summer months the railway carries many thousands of holidaymakers to the popular seaside resort of Hayling Island – tucked away off the south-eastern corner of Hampshire, and well-known for its sandy beaches and equable climate – regularly taking 5,000 passengers a day at peak periods and, indeed, on one summer Sunday in 1961, carrying almost 7,000 visitors to the island.

Alternative modes of travel are by road from Havant and by ferry from Portsmouth. The former, in spite of a newly built bridge, often entails a journey of anything up to two hours during summer weekends when, at times, traffic is brought completely to a standstill on the narrow and congested road leading from the mainland. The ferry, recently acquired by the Corporation of Portsmouth, carries foot passengers only, having no facilities for motor vehicles or any but the lightest of goods, and thus cannot be regarded as a serious competitor to rail and road transport. When one considers the tedious road journey, it compares very unfavourably with the ten minutes – or thirteen if stops are made at the two intermediate stations – taken by the train.

Nearly all branch lines are rich in history and that from Havant to Hayling Island is

certainly no exception. The island has for nearly two centuries enjoyed a reputation as a watering place, and its natural surroundings and amenities make it the ideal place for a family holiday without placing too much emphasis on commercial attractions. There are, however, no less than three holiday camps on Hayling which alone cater for many thousands of visitors during the season.

For many years before the advent of the railway the only means of access to the island was by way of a road bridge on the north side, some 860 feet in length, built during 1823 and 1824 by the Lord of the Manor – the then Duke of Norfolk – and a ferry at the western extremity, the forerunner of the present service, privately owned and providing a link with Portsmouth. Subsequently, the bridge, together with the 'manorial rights of the island', were sold to a Mr Padwick. Parliamentary powers had been granted to the Duke in 1823 to build a bridge to join Hayling with the mainland and these rights were later entrusted to a private company, the Hayling Bridge & Causeway Company. In the meantime, the Portsmouth branch of the old London, Brighton & South Coast Railway was opened on March 15, 1847, the line running from Chichester via Havant, as far as Portsmouth. By an Act of July 3, 1851, the Causeway Company was incorporated under the same title and authorised to conduct a horse-worked railway

from Havant to operate as far as Langston, the extremity of the mainland opposite Hayling Island. However, lack of finance precluded this line being constructed and the powers which had been granted under the Act were thus allowed to lapse.

The next move was made by the London & South Western Railway, which extended its line to Havant in 1859, rail communication with the metropolis being opened on January 24 of that year. Thus the situation arose that two separate railways were established within a short distance of the island and determined efforts were made by local residents and tradesmen to have the line extended to Hayling itself. As a result of these endeavours a company was formed locally and incorporated by an Act of 1860 as the Hayling Railway Company, being empowered to build a line from Havant to South Hayling – a distance

'Terrier' A1X No. 32640 waits at Havant with the 1.35pm to Hayling Island on September 6, 1960. PHOTO: R L PICTON

From *The Railway Magazine*, January 1963

A1X class 0-6-0T No. 32670 crossing Langston Bridge with the 4.35pm Havant-Hayling Island service, on July 27, 1963. RAILPHOTOPRINTS/DAVE COBBE.

of some five miles.

After leaving the mainland at Langston, it was intended that the line should be built on an embankment in the harbour, roughly parallel with the western shore of the island. One of the most active men behind this project was Robert Hume and the Act authorised that capital of £50,000 in £10 shares would be raised, with £16,000 on mortgage, for construction of the line.

It was anticipated that the embankment would be designed in such a way that it would be possible to reclaim more than 1,000 acres of mudflats off the western shore of the island – a very ambitious scheme in those far-off days. In 1864 further plans were approved for a short extension to South Hayling and also for the construction of docks and a harbour. It was planned that the channel from Langston to Hayling Island would be crossed by a bridge or

viaduct, constructed of open pile-work, some 320 yards in length and with a swivel-opening bridge having two openings of no less than 40ft space, to allow for the passage of the many large vessels using the harbour at that time.

Three years were allowed by the Act for the purchase of the land and the commencement

Nearly all branch lines are rich in history

of this far-reaching and ambitious project, and four years for the completion of all the works. Operations were shortly commenced, but by the autumn of 1869 it became very obvious that additional capital would be required and the time for completion extended. This was arranged the following year, when a further Act

(the Hayling Railway & Dock Act) was passed, this allowing for the completion of the docks and pier within five years.

However, it was not until January 1865, that the first mile of the railway from Havant to Langston was opened for public use, and there followed a very considerable goods traffic in coal, gravel and timber – many trading ships from all parts berthing at Langston Quay around this time. So far things had been comparatively easy for the designers and builders, but troubles were ahead. One of the difficulties which had not been envisaged was the constant washing away of the embankment by the sea, thus frustrating the completion of the project and eventually causing the company to abandon its plans for the southern portion of the line. This may well have been the death knell of the scheme but for the timely intervention of a London businessman – ▶

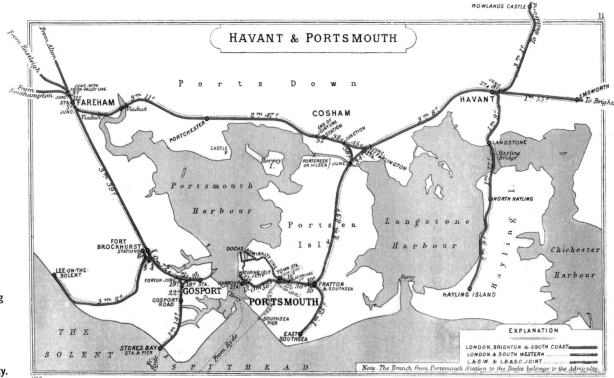

A Railway Clearing House map showing the Hayling Island branch and other lines in the vicinity.

EXPLANATION

LONDON, BRIGHTON & SOUTH COAST
LONDON & SOUTH WESTERN
L.&S.W. & L.B.&S.C. JOINT

Note. The Branch from Portsmouth Station to the Docks belongs to the Admiralty.

Francis Fuller – who, visiting the island on holiday, was immediately struck by its beauty and natural charm. Fuller realised the potentialities of Hayling as a seaside resort and at once commenced to play a very important part in the completion of the project.

An Act of August 12, 1867, granted new powers to relinquish the former plans for the embankment line and to allow the building of a new course overland direct to the south beach, where Fuller, the shrewd man of business, had already purchased building land and had laid out a racecourse as an additional attraction for potential visitors. However, things were far

from easy. With the works suspended and exposed to the worst of the weather, an almost completely empty exchequer, and the local councils divided among themselves on the project, the situation was difficult in the extreme. Thus it was only after long and patient negotiation that Fuller was eventually able to infuse new life into the scheme. He had quickly realised that an overland route, skirting, instead of crossing, the harbour would be constructed more easily and economically than that which had originally been .intended, and in the event his theory was fully justified. Having become a director of the company,

Fuller caused yet another Bill to be introduced into Parliament in 1867 to authorise the diversion of the line from that at first planned, and, in anticipation of subsequent events, he purchased all the land required, even before the Bill was finally approved, at the same time arranging for plans to be prepared and contracts sought for immediate construction.

Thus the scheme, which had been dogged with ill-fortune since its inception, at last reached maturity and, having seen the works completed, electric telegraph supplied for the line and the whole railway approved by a Board of Trade inspector, Fuller had the immense satisfaction of travelling in the first experimental train from Havant to South Hayling on June 28, 1867. The Hayling Railway was at long last a reality and was opened to the public on July 8 that year. Apart from a few months during the ensuing winter when services were temporarily suspended because of extremely bad weather, trains have been operated continuously until the present day, when, once again, the future of the line is threatened.

On January 1, 1872, a lease to the London Brighton & South Coast Railway came into effect, wherein that company took control of the Hayling line at a guaranteed net rental of £2,000 per annum. The line, however, remained independent until absorbed by the Southern Railway in 1923, and subsequently by British Railways on Nationalisation.

As originally constructed the line measured 4 miles 52 chains, with a 31ch branch to Langston Quay, the intermediate stations being at Langston and North Hayling. Renamed in June 1892, the terminus at South Hayling has remained as Hayling Island station until the present day. For nearly 70 years the line has

No. 32661 calls at Hayling North with a down train. PHOTO: C T GIFFORD

Plenty of activity at Hayling Island terminus after arrival of No. 32661 with the train from Havant. PHOTO: S CREER

been worked by 0-6-0 tank engines of the "Terrier" class A1X, the first of which appeared in October 1872, being originally designed for use on the East London Railway, which had bad gradients and very light rails, and also for the South London line plying between Victoria and London Bridge. Considering their diminutive size, these beautiful little engines have done remarkable work over the years. About 10 of the original 50 engines still exist, five of which – probably the oldest in operational service in this country – are used to operate the Hayling line.

Having no passing places or lay-by, the single-track Hayling branch is still worked on the old-fashioned 'staff-and-ticket system'; that is, any number of trains may travel in one direction, the first carrying the stationmaster's ticket and the last the staff; there being thus no danger of collision on the line. The rolling stock used today is usually S or BCK, depending on traffic requirements, and together with the "Terrier" engine, the "Hayling Billy" is limited to four coaches for the non-stop run to Hayling Island or to three when stops are made at Langston and North Hayling.

Some traffic statistics (kindly supplied by British Railways), showing specimen examples of tickets issued and of luggage carried during winter and summer seasons of 1961, make interesting comparisons: tickets collected during March – 2,077; tickets collected during August – 32,176; tickets issued during March – 1,705; tickets issued during August – 7,019; items of paid luggage in advance during August – 854 collected and 1,496 delivered.

Many are the stories told by old residents about the line. One of the most popular personalities among the railway staff was Sam Waldron, a guard, who knew all the passengers by name and would delay the last train until all

The single-track Hayling branch is still worked on the old-fashioned staff and ticket system

his regulars were aboard, even going so far as to meet and urge on the latecomers outside the station. He was responsible, apart from normal duties, for the issue and collection of tickets and the lighting and extinguishing of the old oil lamps at the intermediate stations, and it may well be that history will repeat itself if the proposals at present under discussion for some country stations are implemented!

During World War One, when the blackout was in force, the drivers worked out a system to stop at North Hayling station when the lights were not visible – "after crossing the bridge, watch for a clump of trees, then a

white gate, count six telegraph poles and apply the brakes". Remarkably enough, it worked very efficiently. Some of the busiest periods occurred when the farmers of North Hayling, a part which was very good agricultural land in those days, sent their milk to a Portsmouth dairy. Every day, at 8.15am and 4.25pm, the farmers would send a two-wheeled low cart, drawn by a trotting pony, to the station and a miniature chariot race would invariably ensue as each driver did his best to be nearest the wicket gate, all being required to roll several 12- and 17-gallon churns up the slope of the platform to the approximate spot where the guard's van would stop. At this time the return fare from North Hayling to Havant was fivepence, while a single from there to South Hayling (Hayling Island) was a penny!

It will be a very sad day, not only for the residents of Hayling Island, but for the thousands of holidaymakers who visit the resort every year, if the line should be closed and there is no doubt that hardship would result. With the matter still to he finally resolved, it is sincerely hoped that British Railways will think very carefully before reaching a decision which could adversely affect one of the most picturesque and historic branch railway lines in the country and, at the same time, one which performs a real service to the community. Who knows, perhaps a modern Francis Fuller will again come to the aid of the Hayling line. ∎

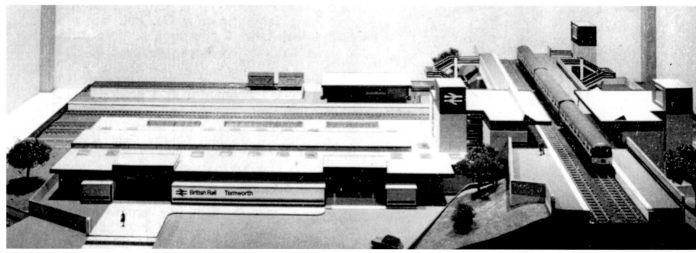

British Rail

Model of Tamworth station exhibited at the Design Centre.

Facelift for British Rail

New arrow symbol, standard 'house' colours, different livery, shorter name, and distinctive letter form for 'corporate identity' programme launched at an exhibition in London

By D S BARRIE

The new face of British Railways

Behind the many forms in which British Railways appears to the travelling or trading customer stands one national undertaking. So wide is the visible range of activity – transport by rail, sea and road, engineering, architecture, catering – that this essential unity tends to become obscured. The new house style, now being introduced, by stages, throughout the system, is an expression in modern terms of this unity. Everything seen and used frequently by the public, every station, sign, and piece of printed matter, will be given a recognisable family likeness.

AN exhibition entitled The New Face of British Railways was held at the Design Centre, London, from January 4-23. Its purpose was to launch British Railways 'corporate identity' programme. This programme, which covers the design of everything from tableware and uniforms to train liveries and the whole range of printed material, is intended to both project the forward-looking character of the railways to the public and highlight the improvements which have been made since the industry's modernisation plan was launched in 1955.

The three basic visual elements of the corporate identity programme are the 'house' colours, selected to replace regional colours, the symbol, replacing the 'double-sausage' device, and the logotype. Monastral blue and pearl grey, set off by flame red, have been chosen as the house-style colours: the blue and grey will be used extensively, probably including all locomotives and passenger rolling stock, while the red will be reserved for smaller areas and for emphasising the symbol. One of

the first applications of the new livery has been on BR ships. The hull is blue with a grey superstructure; the black-topped funnel is red with the symbol in white.

The symbol itself is in the form of a double arrow, representing two-way rail service, and is simple enough to retain its impact when used in a wide range of sizes and materials. The symbol will be seen on advertising materials, on station façades, on the funnels and flags of ships, and on cutlery, carpets and curtains, but has not yet been approved for use on rolling stock. The new logo-type has been drawn to suit modern typography and uses the abbreviation British Rail. This is considered more vigorous than the fuller phrase and fits more easily into a variety of settings.

Station exterior nameboards will feature the new symbol and the logotype British Rail, but there will be no uniform colours for stations as a whole; they will be repainted to harmonise with unpainted surfaces of the buildings and with the character of their surroundings. A new letter form of modern design will be used for station nameboards and signs, also posters, timetables, publicity

The elements of the family likeness, or corporate identity, which can be used and combined in a variety of ways, are:

1. A new, more purposeful symbol. This replaces the obsolete 'double-sausage' introduced nearly twenty years ago
2. Standard House Colours intended to replace the Regional Colours
3. A shorter name - British Rail - for publicity use and station signs
4. A distinctive new letter form of thoroughly modern design, for station name-boards, signs, and all printed matter
5. A new livery for rolling-stock.

The two-way track symbol lends itself to applications in all kinds of railway settings.

Shown here are: catering, with a table setting in a restaurant car; and the symbol in repetition on a carpet for use in trains and ships. A manual is being prepared to guide everyone in the correct application of the House Style.

Uniforms of more modern cut and style, to be introduced generally, are all part of the new Corporate Identity for British Railways which is now emerging

material and all printed matter. Identification of stations is in a medium-weight letter in white on blue. Direction signs are in a weighted letter in black, with the indication in blue. Colours are used functionally, black for a requirement, blue where it is to be found, red for prohibition and green for information.

Containers for the liner trains will be in grey, with a red band bearing the symbol and the word Freightliner in white. Otherwise, freight rolling stock will not be affected by the new scheme. Existing containers also remain unchanged, and the yellow livery of the road freight transport, together with the recently introduced freight symbol, are being retained for the time being.

The dominant feature at the London exhibition was a centrepiece illustrating how the symbol, the British Rail logotype, and the house colours will be used in practice. On display were examples of posters, timetables, advertisements and other printed material; cutlery, tableware and furnishings bearing the emblem; scale models of electric trains; and station signboards and lettering.

Passenger stock design studies

Other parts of the exhibition illustrated the breadth of British Railways' activities and showed progress that has been made since 1955. A section on passenger transport included models of ships in the new livery and also a full-scale mock-up of a proposed 10-seat luxury lounge car compartment. This has been designed to give first-class business passengers a standard of comfort in seating and space above that possible in a private car or in an aircraft. It is twice the size of a normal compartment and contains six fixed and four swivel seats. There would be two or three lounges in each carriage with the extra space used for food preparation, luggage, and, possibly, for such amenities as a telephone.

The lounge car is the result of one of a series of design studies now being carried out and will only be put into service if market research and trials prove it to be a commercial proposition. A club car (also based on this design), a high-density suburban coach, a luxury sleeping car, with individual WC and

Posters on all British Rail Stations will use the new symbol against a background of approved colours. Eye-catching and incisive, it will compel attention from a distance.

The time-table is the most important of all railway publications, the most frequently seen and consulted. It will therefore feature the new symbol boldly on the cover. The symbol instantly identifies the time-table as a British Rail publication, the colour distinguishes one from another

shower for each compartment, and a convertible day/night coach are other vehicles that are being studied.

A section on 'freight techniques in prospect' illustrated a prototype car-carrier, a tanker for road-rail operation, and the liner trains. Architecture, civil engineering, and research for the railways were also ▶

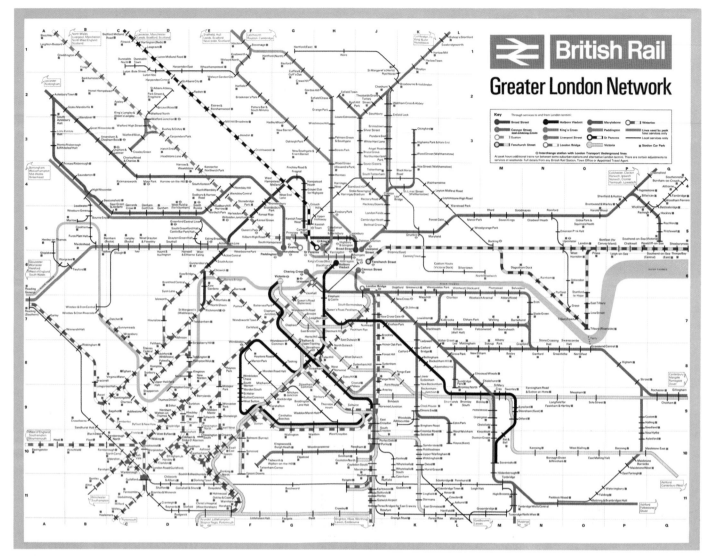

Poster diagrammatic map of the Greater London network of British Railways, indicating by colour the relevant termini. London Transport lines are marked only by interchange stations.

represented. The new uniforms for locomotive drivers, inspectors and women enquiry staff were worn by attendants at the exhibition.

The corporate identity programme will take some time to be fully implemented. The new liveries will be introduced as part of the normal servicing and repainting procedure, although priorities have been worked out for stations, rolling stock and ships. Already some 20 of the railways' fleet of more than 100 ships have been repainted in the new livery. Printed matter is the easiest and cheapest item to change, and literature in the new house style is now available. The new uniforms will be in general use throughout the country by spring 1966. The livery for trains will be introduced only after extensive trials, although 200 carriages of suburban electric multiple-unit stock at present being built for the London Midland Region will be painted in the new colours. ∎

Full-scale mock-up of lounge car compartment, one of several design studies being undertaken. There are three fixed seats at each end and four swivel chairs in the centre.

B1 class 4-6-0 No. 61192 heads south from Rugby with the 10.35am Manchester (London Road) to London Marylebone on August 23, 1959. JOHN BECKETT

Reduced Great Central Line Services

THE sweeping changes on the Great Central line, to which reference was made in the editorial columns of the December issue, came into force on Monday, January 4, when all through trains between Marylebone and Sheffield, Manchester and Bradford were withdrawn. As from that day, the following semi-fast services were introduced between Marylebone and Nottingham: 8.40am, 12.25pm (Saturdays only), 12.40pm (Saturdays excepted), and 4.30pm. The up trains leave Nottingham at 8.40am, 12.25pm, and 5.15pm.

All the above trains, at present still steam-operated, call intermediately at Aylesbury, Brackley Central, Woodford Halse, Rugby Central, Lutterworth, Leicester Central, and Loughborough Central. The 8.40am from Marylebone and the 5.15pm from Nottingham call additionally at Harrow-on-the-Hill. The 'South Yorkshireman' has been replaced by a train leaving Halifax at 8.30am and Huddersfield at 9.3 for Sheffield Midland, where through coaches are attached to the 8.52am from Bradford Forster Square to St Pancras. The return service leaves St Pancras at 5.5pm.

Cross-country services via Woodford Halse and Banbury will not be affected. The next stage in securing economies on the Great Central line will be the closing of some wayside stations between Aylesbury and Nottingham.

From February 1960 issue

Locomotive Firing with Turf

SOME of the trials of firing a locomotive with turf are referred to in a letter from Capt E N Cooke, who recently rode on the footplate of one of the 4-6-0 tank engines built by Barclay in 1902 for the Londonderry & Lough Swilly Railway. Of this system the Letterkenny & Burtonport extension is still open between Letterkenny and Gweedore for the conveyance of turf, which is handed over to the Great Northern Railway at Londonderry or Strabane for carriage to Dundalk and Drogheda; trains are run twice daily over the L&BER in each direction, and engines Nos. 2 and 4 are stationed at Letterkenny and Gweedore for this purpose. The bunker and cab have to be piled high with turf at the start, and replenished intermediately at Creeslough, where there is a loop for trains to cross. The fireman has to divide his time between getting up into the bunker to throw more turfs into the cab, and getting down on to his hands and knees to get it into the firebox. Even then a reserve supply of turf must be carried on a truck behind the engine, and stops must be made on each steep ascent to raise more steam. By contrast, a footplate journey on the Donegal Railways, where coal-firing is still possible, seemed a model of efficiency; 4-6-4 tank No. 9 *Eske*, though 40 years old, with three coaches and seven wagons, was able to maintain the schedule normally operated by a diesel railcar. Traffic on this line is heavy, and it has about it a general air of prosperity.

From Jan/Feb 1945 issue

Casey Jones Stamp

CENTREPIECE of a new US stamp is Casey Jones, America's most famous engine driver. He was killed in the wreck of the 'Cannonball Express' near Vaughan, Mississippi, on April 30, 50 years ago. The express ran into a goods train. The fireman jumped, but Casey Jones stayed to blow the whistle to give the goods train crew time to escape. His sacrifice is commemorated in a popular American folksong.   *From June 1950 issue*

0-4-4 tank Hauls Coronation

AN odd sequence of locomotive failures, on a day early in January 1939, caused the down 'Coronation' of the LNER to be hauled over two successive portions of its journey by No. 10000, the famous 4-6-4 of Class W1 and an ex-North Eastern 0-4-4 tank, No. 1837 of class G5 – about as great a contrast in locomotive power as could well be imagined.

The trouble began with A4 Pacific No. 4482 *Golden Eagle*, which ran hot and had to come off at Grantham. No. 10000 then took charge, and was doing well when J W Armstrong, who sends these notes, saw the express pass Darlington only 25 minutes late; but No. 10000 failed for the same reason and had to come off at Durham, after which No. 1837 had her turn.

Last of all, A1 4-6-2 No. 2575 worked the 'Coronation' forward from Newcastle to Edinburgh. Another unusual happening to 'Coronation' recently was a departure from King's Cross with three of the four blue twin sets of cars and two ordinary corridor coaches on the rear, the rear twin having run hot at a time when the reserve set of cars was in the shops for overhaul.

From April 1939 issue

Scottish Industrial Scenes

Top: NCB 0-6-0 No. 15 heads a coal train at Methil Weymss Private Railway (WPR) colliery branch on September 20, 1963. DEREK CROSS

Middle: Barclay 0-4-0ST No. 2017 of 1935 heads a rake of loaded coal wagons at Methil September 20, 1963. DEREK CROSS

Bottom: Barclay No. 1 *Dailuaine* (2073 of 1939) shunts in the distillery caskyard at Dailuaine on Speyside on June 23, 1967. JOHN M BOYES

Top: Barclay 0-4-0ST No. 885 pilots Hunslet Austerity 0-6-0ST No. 2880 from 1943 taking loaded wagons to the BR exchange sidings at Polkemmet Colliery on September 1, 1969. J G GLOVER

Middle: NCB Barclay 0-4-0ST No. 19 from the West Ayr area blows off furiously at Waterside spoil dump with a train from Waterside Colliery on April 17, 1969. DEREK CROSS

Bottom: NCB Barclay 0-6-0T No. 22 & 0-4-0ST No. 19 shunt near the washery at Waterside Colliery, adjacent to the Dalmellington branch on August 24, 1962. DEREK CROSS

The movable section of platform at Waterloo, LSWR, before the rebuilding of the station in 1922.

Moveable platforms

ONE of the characteristics of British railway operation from very early years has been the provision of platforms, now normally 3ft 1½in above rail level but in past times often lower, in order to enable passengers to board the carriages at footboard level. In contrast, many other countries have relied, and still do rely, on steps at the ends of corridor coaches and a series of footboards on vehicles with isolated compartments, so that passengers board from rail level. This simplifies station arrangements, as passengers can easily cross the line, but considerations of safety have recently caused some of the large Continental countries to adopt British type platforms at important stations,

Normally the British platform has always been a fixed structure, but, on a number of occasions, considerations of space have resulted in the adoption of a movable section, and various examples may still be found. An outstanding instance was that at Paddington terminus, GWR, where the station built by Brunel and opened on January 16, 1854, had one main departure platform, and an arrival platform (brought into use on May 29, 1854), separated by five storage roads. In addition there were two subsidiary departure lines, served by an island platform having no permanent connection with the 'mainland', as the present concourse space was occupied by small turntables to transfer rolling stock from one line to another. This island platform could

be approached only by the movable platform shown in the accompanying drawings. The following account is extracted from a book called Railway Appliances by John Wolfe Barry, which was published in 1878.

"At the Great Western station at Paddington, the booking offices are placed by the side of the main departure platform. A piece of cross platform (marked 'A' in one figure and shown in detail in the other), supported on a dwarf truck, is provided, which when required is drawn out by hydraulic machinery from beneath the main

A single line ran across what is now the circulating area of the main Waterloo station

departure platform, and rises to the same level as the main platforms, becoming a bridge across the rails, and giving access to the second departure platform. The upper position in the sketch represents the platform drawn out on its truck from the recess by means of a chain connected to an hydraulic apparatus, and the lower position shows it raised to the level of the platforms on each side. The raising is effected by continuing to haul on the chain after the truck has come out of the recess, which causes the two

rollers (shaded in the sketches) to travel along the lower surfaces of the inclined planes fixed below the platform. Small rollers at the end of the platform relieve the friction between the movable platform, and the side of the central platform. By the use of this movable platform three long trains can be loaded at once, if the two trains nearest the booking offices be temporarily cut in halves. When it is necessary to despatch these trains, the movable cross platform is run back to its position beneath the main platform, the first half of the train is backed and coupled up to the second half. Trains of shorter length can be loaded and despatched, when the movable platform is raised. The position of the booking offices, near the centre of the departure platform, is no doubt convenient, as passengers approach the train near its centre; and though there is some inconvenience in the use of a movable platform, the arrangement answers well for a terminal station like Paddington, where trains are not very frequent, while the central position of the booking offices is certainly advantageous where the amount of passengers' luggage is large." This movable platform remained in use until comparatively recent years.

Another London terminus which, for many years, had a section of movable platform was Waterloo, LSWR. When the London Bridge-Waterloo Junction extension of the South Eastern Railway was opened, on January

From *The Railway Magazine*, October 1940

11, 1864, a connection was made with the LSWR by a single line which crossed Waterloo Road on a bridge, ran across what is now the circulating area of the main Waterloo station, and joined the middle road which lay between Nos. 4 and 5 platform roads. Except for some LNWR trains which ran between Euston and London Bridge, via Camden, Kilburn, Addison Road, Battersea, and Waterloo, for a few months from July 1865, no regular train service used this connecting line, which was used for the exchange of vehicles and special trains. When the line was out of use, a section of movable platform was placed in position, as shown in the accompanying picture, to allow passengers and luggage to cross the connecting line at platform level, although they could also cross it at rail level by means of the ramps shown in the picture. The connecting line, and with it the movable platform, was abolished in the course of the Waterloo station rebuilding which was completed in 1922, in accordance with the Parliamentary powers obtained in 1899 and 1900, which provided for its closure. The LSWR began this rebuilding some years before the last war, and the impending removal of the physical junction with the SER station was announced by the South Eastern & Chatham Railway in February 1911.

Before the rebuilding of Baker Street station, Metropolitan Railway, which was in progress for several years until its completion in 1914, there was a piece of movable platform, giving access from platform 1 to platforms 2 and 3, across the single line which provided physical connection between the Circle and the St John's Wood lines. This movable platform took the form of a four-wheel truck and was run into a short siding in the connecting tunnel when the line was required for a train to pass. It was replaced

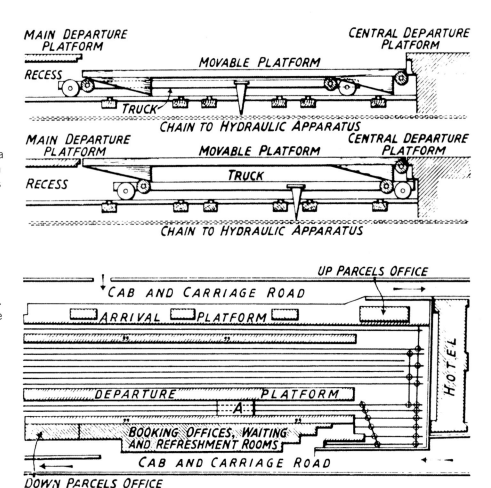

Arrangement of movable connection between two departure platforms at Paddington, GWR, in 1878.

in 1911, when the connecting line was doubled, by a form of drawbridge which was abolished in 1913 on the completion of new overhead access between the platforms.

Three stations on the Great Eastern main line of the LNER to Yarmouth are possessed of sections of movable platform, two of them, Saxmundham and Halesworth,

having been necessitated by road level crossings intersecting the platforms, and the third, Beccles, having a swing-bridge type of moving platform to facilitate getting milk churns and parcels from the down and branch-line platform to the up platform. At all three stations these movable platforms, which are worked by hand, are interlocked with the signals.

Movable section of platform over level crossing at Saxmundham. PHOTO: DR R O BROOKS

Movable platform sections at Halesworth, LNER, swung across the line, leaving the road level crossing open. PHOTO: DR R O BROOKS

Another type of movable platform is found at Wood Lane station on the Central Line of the London Passenger Transport Board. It is on the loop platform which is used by trains terminating at Wood Lane. Some of these proceed to the depot but others, as many as 50 a day, continue round the loop to return to the other end of the line at Liverpool Street. With the introduction of longer trains in March 1928, it was necessary to lengthen the loop platform but this lengthening occurred just where the depot line joins the running line. A section of movable platform was therefore constructed on rollers so that it can be pushed out to a maximum distance of 3ft over the nearside rail of the depot line to provide the necessary platform face for the extreme car of the train. It is pneumatically operated from the signalbox and is, of course, interlocked with the signals. ■

Above: Part of the Halesworth movable platforms closed across the road prior to the reception of a train.
PHOTO: REV DAVID T SCOTLAND

Movable platform at Beccles, to facilitate the transfer of milk churns across the line. The view was taken in October 1931. PHOTO: ASSOCIATED PRESS

From *The Railway Magazine*, October 1940

Talbot Road station, Blackpool, in the late 1920s, with nine special trains awaiting departure from the excursion platforms. Note the 'Big Wheel' being dismantled (left background). PHOTO: BRITISH RAILWAYS

Sixty thousand trippers a day

Summer traffic of holidaymakers to and from Blackpool was the equivalent of evacuating and repopulating the town daily

RECENT pruning by British Railways of Blackpool's rail facilities prompts a look at a former source of substantial revenue which regrettably would appear to have been lost for ever. Blackpool's first rail connection dates from 1846, when the Preston & Wyre Railway Company built a 3¼ mile long spur from Poulton, terminating at Talbot Road (now Blackpool North) station. In 1863, a second line was opened, diverging nearer Preston, at Kirkham station: by way of Lytham and St Annes-on-Sea, this terminated at Blackpool Central.

By the end of the last century the fast-developing seaside resort already had a three mile long three-piered promenade which extended from the South Shore Pleasure Beach to Gynn Square at the north end. Throughout its length it was served by electric trams, which made connections at the north with those of the Blackpool & Fleetwood Tramroad Company, and at the south end with the Lytham Company's gas-engined tramway

By G W PARKIN, M Eng, C Eng, FIEE

system, to be replaced in June 1903, by a conventional electric tramway.

With 17 miles of coastal tramways, Blackpool by the turn of the century was well-established as the holiday resort for the

It mattered not if inclement weather ruled out the golden sands or a cruise on a paddleboat

workers of Lancashire and Yorkshire. It mattered not if inclement weather ruled out its golden sands or a cruise on one of the paddleboats of the Blackpool Steamship Company; the Tower, Winter Gardens, Palace, Big Wheel, and the piers could provide a

variety of undercover entertainment to suit its visitors of all ages. Workers in the nearby industrial towns took their annual holidays during their 'Wakes Week', these weeks extending throughout the summer season, each district having its own particular 'wakes' date when every factory, colliery and shop in that district closed down.

The Preston-Blackpool road was then a winding macadam-surfaced lane, and apart from the more energetic who journeyed to Blackpool by cycle and tandem the Lancashire & Yorkshire Railway* enjoyed a monopoly of the holiday traffic. Saturdays were the days which introduced a rail traffic problem for this company, as, apart from having to transport anything up to 60,000 people to the coast in one day, a similar number might have to be returned home.

The solution to this problem was the quadrupling of the line between Preston and Kirkham by adding an up and down fast, and the building of a third pair of metals from ▶

Kirkham heading almost direct to Blackpool Central, joining the coast line some 300 yards north of South Shore station. This 6¾ mile long line was opened on April 21, 1903, bringing Kirkham distant from Blackpool, according to the three routes now branching from this point, to: 9¾ miles to Talbot Road (since renamed North); 13 miles to Central via the coast; and 7¾ miles to Central via the direct line. Kirkham Station still retained only its one island platform serving the slow lines. Waterloo Road was the only station built on the latter line, being located immediately short of where it joined the coast line. On July 14, 1916, this station was logically converted into a junction station by the provision of an island platform serving the coast line, South Shore station then being closed. On March 17, 1932, Waterloo Road was renamed Blackpool South. The only civil engineering work of note on the direct line was a flying junction carrying the up road over the Kirkham-Poulton lines, whence it then made connection with the up fast. Built with brick walls and piers and with steel girder work, it was numbered 27 in the Preston & Wyre section of the LYR bridge register.

To we Blackpudlians, the direct line was always known as the 'new line', and to those of us who can recall its building, its closure on February 12, 1967, following close on the heels of the closing down of Central, when South became the terminal station, brings back memories of the enormous rail holiday traffic formerly dealt with over the Preston-Blackpool lines. Apart from excursion traffic, freight and empty train movement, the 'new line' was used with rare exceptions by never more than two up and two down trains a day. The fastest throughout journey times between Blackpool and Manchester were afforded by this line, which timings have as yet been unequalled even under diesel haulage over the surviving longer routes.

LYR poster announcing regulation arrangements for the 1920 season.

Terminal passenger working arrangements at Blackpool were catered for by 16 platforms at Talbot Road and 14 at Central, affording an aggregate platform length of 18,790ft, or more than 3½ miles. Necessary for the working of Central station and its associated engine sheds and carriage sidings were three signal cabins. Central cabin had 132 levers and Spen Dyke 120, both installed in 1901,

Including both specials and ordinary trains, no less than 225 arrived and 242 departed, a total of 467 trains on that day!

the former cabin at that date being declared the largest on the Lancashire & Yorkshire system.

The heyday of Blackpool's rail excursion traffic was between the wars, and fostering it was the late Ashton Davies OBE, latterly a vice-president of the LMSR, with special responsibilities on the operating and commercial side. An old LYR man, his last appointment with that company had been that of superintendent of the line, but although he soon followed his old chief, (Sir) Arthur Watson, to Euston, he remained faithful to the county of his upbringing and early labours for he never moved his residence from St Annes-on-Sea.

As early as 1910 it is recorded that on an August Saturday 167 specials (arrivals and departures) were dealt with by Blackpool's two stations, Talbot Road handling 100 of these trains. The town's resident population was then 65,000 and on the basis of there being an equal number of arrivals and departures and with an average train loading of say 700 passengers, this movement was

practically equivalent to evacuating and repopulating Blackpool all in one day by excursion trains alone.

Following World War One, this growing traffic got out of hand at Blackpool and Manchester in connection with certain popular excursion trains. Large crowds would assemble on the platforms and as the train drew to rest the rougher elements, and not necessarily the first arrivals, would win in the general scramble for seats. The elderly and those heavily laden with luggage would be left behind to await their fortune on the following train. Order out of chaos was solved by 'regulated trains', being trains for which advance bookings were necessary. Such regulated passengers held supplementary tickets bearing the distinguishing number of their train and date on which valid, a facility provided without extra charge. Thus was ensured a seat for every passenger without having to fight for it, and also assurance that all such trains were loaded to capacity.

Regulated traffic in both directions was first introduced for the 1919 summer season commencing Saturday, July 5, and continuing for the following 11 weeks, the regulated days being Saturdays and Mondays. During this period 973,000 ticket-holding passengers arrived at Blackpool and the adjacent coastal towns, and of this number 413,000 who detrained at Blackpool had all travelled on a Saturday. The return traffic with respect to Saturday travellers totalled 453,600 during this same period. With seaside landladies averse to split weeks the LYR found itself saddled with the job of transporting almost half the season's holiday traffic on Saturdays alone. For the following year Fridays and Saturdays became the regulated days, as will be noted from the Regulations of Holiday Traffic poster herein reproduced.

These figures for the 1919 season traffic pale into insignificance compared with those for the summer of 1931, when it was not uncommon for 120 specials (arrivals and departures) having to be dealt with in one day

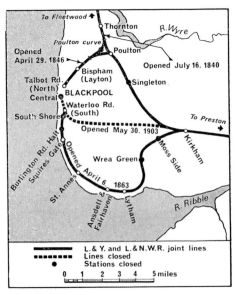

Railways in the Fylde district.

From *The Railway Magazine*, October 1967

at each Blackpool terminal. During the second week in August of this year, 190,000 tickets were collected, more than half representing passengers who had arrived on the Saturday of this week. By this date the borough's resident population had risen to 101,500 and again it will be noted that the Saturday arrivals approximated to this figure.

Peak figures for passenger train movements were probably reached during the years immediately preceding the Second World War. Taking one Saturday in August 1935 (not the one before the bank holiday), and including both specials and ordinary trains, no less than 225 arrived and 242 departed, a total of 467 trains into and out of Blackpool on that day!

In order to prolong its season Blackpool introduced the autumn illuminations. Much ingenuity was exercised in ringing the changes each year in the animated tableaux exhibited, this heavy financial outlay on Blackpool's part being largely offset by the increased earnings of the promenade trams. For the LMSR it resulted in mass movement by rail hitherto unapproached, particularly on Saturdays when the cheap half-day excursions from as distant as the Manchester area were in great demand.

On one such Saturday the train register at Kirkham North Junction showed that 90 trains had entered Blackpool within the period of three consecutive hours and that on this same day 115 specials left Blackpool after 8pm! This figure of 30 trains per hour into or out of Blackpool was exceeded on occasions.

Clearly much credit for such intensive line use is due to the art of the signal engineer, and C B Byles, signal engineer, Lancashire & Yorkshire Railway, 1897-1911, was responsible for much pioneer work on intermediate track circuit-controlled signals. By this arrangement a block section between two signalboxes, normally limited to only one train in section on each line, becomes two sections with consequent doubling of line capacity. By the provision of illuminated diagrams in the signalboxes associated with the track circuits, the signalman is not only visually informed of the positions of his trains, but by the same means his levers are electrically locked against premature movement. However, despite such aids, all signal and point levers had still to be manually worked and the Kirkham North Junction signalmen must have been fit men.

Equally remarkable was the handling of these close headway trains at the Blackpool termini. The platform roads were not provided with crossovers and engines drew right up to the buffer stops. Hence, as a train emptied, the carriages had to be pulled back to sidings whence the train engine then backed out to its own scheduled lay-over position. Such

Aerial view of the now closed lines between Blackpool South (bottom foreground) and Blackpool Central. PHOTO: *BLACKPOOL GAZETTE & HERALD*

special working arrangements involving certain trains being run in duplicate at short notice reflects credit on the excellent teamwork of those days. Contributing to this efficient working was a traffic control located at Blackpool Central which was in direct touch with Manchester Control, and via that office with the 300-odd Lancashire & Yorkshire stations coming within the scope of

The rougher elements would win in the general scramble for seats

the regulated traffic.

The fast morning and evening Blackpool-Manchester business expresses were diagrammed over all three routes between Blackpool and Kirkham, the fastest working being via the 'new line'. The timetable for July 1910, shows a train departing Waterloo Road (Blackpool South) at 08.04 (four minutes earlier from Central) and with stops at Preston and Salford, being scheduled to arrive at Manchester Victoria at 09.11.

This journey time of 67 minutes for an up journey from Blackpool South would appear to be a record for a regular daily working. This July timetable shows no evening down train via the 'new line'. However, the October timetable for that year introduced an additional evening down train departing Manchester Victoria at 17.10 for Blackpool Central via the coast line, but slipping the rear three coaches at Kirkham, which then travelled over the 'new line', arriving at Central ahead of the main portion of the train, which made its first stop at Lytham. This train, with its slip coaches, was still being diagrammed for the 1914 winter service.

Comparative timings of Blackpool South-Manchester Victoria trains via the alternative routes are given in the accompanying table. These express business trains in general avoided Bolton, branching off the Chorley-Bolton line at Red Moss Junction and by way of Atherton and Pendlebury picked up the Bolton-Manchester line about a mile north of Salford. The distances via these alternative routes were sensibly identical, but whereas the Bolton avoiding line had less p.w. slacks, ▶

it was, in the down direction, saddled with a 1 in 70 bank for 1½ miles after Dobbs Brow Junction and easing off to a further mile of 1 in 200 to Hilton House station. With a 300 ton trailing load of 10 bogie coaches the fast working over this route proved the capabilities of George Hughes 1400 class 4-6-0s.

It will be noted that the current coast line timings which still provide for all trains stopping between Lytham and, Blackpool South are the best ever, but unless British Railways elects to run an occasional train non-stop through the Fylde coast stations, the 'new line' timings are unlikely to be seen again. The term Blackpool South in the table is used to denote both that station's original name of Waterloo Road and also the subsequently closed station of South Shore. The distance from Blackpool South to Manchester Victoria via the 'new line' was 45½ miles and via the coast 50¾ miles.

Pride of place for fast timing was the 'Manchester Club' train which worked in and out of Talbot Road station. Inaugurated in 1895, this train included a palatial three-compartment saloon coach for the exclusive use of such first-class season ticket holders who were privileged members of the Travelling Club. A prominent notice, "Members Only", warned the non-eligibles to keep out, but a second line of defence was the attendant, an employee of the members, who barred entry to any unauthorised passenger who might be tempted to sample one of the inviting leather-upholstered armchairs. This attendant also served light refreshments and would function as valet when members, for instance, wished to change into evening clothes on the return journey.

For many years before and during the First World War, the morning up train was the 08.23, subsequently having another long run as the 08.20. At this period it was the general practice for a handbell to be rung by the ticket collector some 30 seconds before trains were due to depart, the barrier being closed immediately the guard signalled the train away. Special dispensation was provided for Travelling Club members: their train would draw out from the platform very slowly, the barrier meantime having been partially closed with the collector blocking the restricted opening. A last-second club member would be permitted to slip through, and sprinting down the platform would overtake his slowly departing tram. Today there is no longer a club train, nor, in fact, a business train scheduled to even approach the 65 minute start-to-stop timings of 50 years ago. The metamorphosis of the Talbot Road (North)-Manchester commuters train is depicted in the table.

The rundown of Blackpool's rail facilities

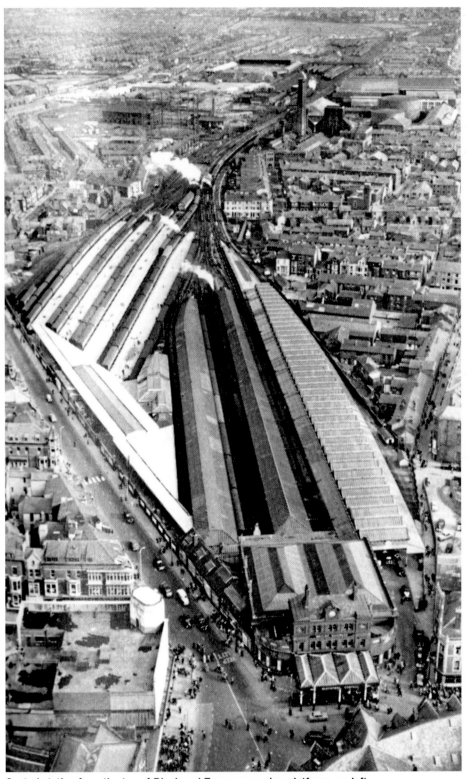

Central station from the top of Blackpool Tower; excursion platforms on left.
PHOTO: BRITISH RAILWAYS

dates from November 2, 1964, when the last train steamed out of Central. Subsequently the site was sold to Blackpool Corporation for £950,000. This area of roughly 24 acres embraced, in addition to the station, engine sheds, shops, houses and a large railwaymen's hostel. Lying parallel, and adjacent to Blackpool's 'Golden Mile', which extends from Central station to the Central Pier, the observation of the chairman of the corporation's negotiating committee that the deal "was a bargain" must rank as one of the understatements of the year.

Pending finalising of plans for development of this valuable site, the old station concourse has been converted into a huge bingo hall and all platform roads have been filled in to platform level to form a car and bus park. From the shell of Central signalbox, now devoid of its 132 levers and

COMPARATIVE TIMINGS OF BLACKPOOL SOUTH - MANCHESTER BUSINESS EXPRESSES

	Via the New Line					Via the Coast Line		
	July 1910	Oct. 1910	Oct. 1914	Oct. 1935	Feb. 1949	Oct. 1914	Feb. 1949	June 1967
Blackpool South dep.	08.04	07.34	07.36	07.32	07.32	08.16	08.10	07.55
Manchester Victoria arr....	09.11	08.48	08.47	08.48	08.48	09.40	09.40	09.12
Journey time, min.	67	74	71	76	76	84	90	77
Stopping at	A	B	B	B	B	D	D	G
Manchester Vic. dep.	No down train	slipped 17.10	slipped 17.10	17.05	17.03	17.10	17.55	17.20
Blackpool South arr.		18.18	18.15	18.03	18.04	18.26	19.23	18.35
Journey time, min.		68	65	58	61	76	88	75
Stopping at		NSS	NSS	NS	NS	C	E	F

Key to stops ... ...

A: Preston and Salford; B: Preston, Chorley and Salford

NS: Non stop; NSS: Non-stop except for stopping of slipped coaches

Stops in addition to those between Lytham and South
C: None; D: Salford; E: Chorley; F: Preston and Kirkham; G: Preston, Chorley and Salford

---

instruments, the ghosts of generations of signalmen must look down on a sight undreamt of during their earthly existence. Already the third and fourth pairs of rails between Preston and Kirkham have been lifted, and presumably the rusting rails of the 'new line' will follow suit.

To conclude on a more cheery note, the railway holiday traffic atmosphere will remain unchanged at North. The traffic during 'wakes' weeks and the illuminations still necessitates regulation. With its 16 platforms having an aggregate length of nearly two miles, Blackpool is still capable of dealing with railway visitors well beyond the capacity of any other seaside resort. ∎

* Preston & Wyre Railway vested jointly in the LYR and LNWR in 1888

COMPARATIVE TIMINGS OF BLACKPOOL NORTH TO MANCHESTER BUSINESS TRAINS

	Oct. 1914	July 1926	Oct. 1949	June 1967
Talbot Rd. dep.	08.23	08.20	08.18	07.29
Manchester Vic. arr. ...	09.28	09.32	09.34	08.47
Journey time, min.... ...	65	72	76	78
Stopping at	A	B	C	D
Manchester Vic. dep. ...	16.55	16.55	16.55	16.45
Talbot Rd. arr.	18.00	18.06	18.09	18.00
Journey time, min.... ...	65	71	74	75
Stopping at	E	F	E	G

Key to stops ... ...

A: Poulton to pick up and Salford to set down
B: Salford to set down
C: Layton to pick up and Salford to set down
D: Poulton, Preston, Chorley and Salford
E: Poulton to set down
F: Kirkham and Poulton
G: Chorley, Preston, Kirkham, Poulton and Layton

Below: 'Black Five' No. 45425 gets away from Blackpool Central with the 4:17pm to Glasgow Central on September 28, 1964.
PHOTO: P F CLAXTON

Filming The Titfield Thunderbolt

The Liverpool & Manchester Railway 0-4-2 locomotive *Lion* near Monkton Combe, on the Limpley Stoke-Camerton branch, during filming of The Titfield Thunderbolt. Midford Station, on the Somerset & Dorset line, is in the background. PHOTO: PHILIP M ALEXANDER

By BAYNHAM HONRI, FBKS ARPS

FILM producers always have been enthusiastic about railways. From the days of the early 'flickers' of 1897, when Lumiére put on the screen the first motion picture of a train – Arrival of Train at Station (filmed in Paris) – audiences have endorsed this enthusiasm. Since then, a steady flow of railway dramas and comedies has not satiated the irresistible appeal of the locomotive flashing past the camera.

Older readers may recall the hair-raising series, Hazards of Helen (1912-14), a cowboy-and-Indian saga in which the pretty heroine (a telegraphist at a whistle-stop station) and her pony performed unbelievable feats of daring midst thundering freight trains. The episode in which her pony operated the signals during the temporary absence of her mistress (who was lashed to a telegraph pole by the wicked train robbers) was immortalised by Stephen Leacock in one of his short stories.

Buster Keaton drew on historic events of the American Civil War for the back-ground to a classic comedy, The General, which was the name of a locomotive which changed sides several times. In England, too, railways have received much attention from producers, and particularly from Sir Michael Balcon, whose productions with railway backgrounds include The Wrecker, Rome Express, The Ghost Train, It Always Rains on Sunday and Train of Events. In The Wrecker, filmed in 1928, a real train smash was staged at a level crossing on the Reading-Basingstoke line, filmed by no less than 22 cameras simultaneously. The same line was used by the Twickenham Studios in 1933 for The Last Journey, a hair-raising story of a mad engine driver – this old film has been televised recently by the BBC.

Once more Sir Michael Balcon and the Ealing Studios have turned to railways for their newest Technicolor production The Titfield Thunderbolt, in which the title role is played by that fine 115-year old Liverpool & Manchester Railway locomotive *Lion*. The story of the film concerns the reactions of a village community to the news that their little branch line is to be closed. The locals buy the line and run it themselves, in the face of road competition, but almost come to grief as a result of sabotage by the villians who run the rival road transport. Feverish efforts are made to keep the service running for the visit of the Ministry of Transport inspector, and the line's only locomotive being derailed, the ancient 'Thunderbolt' is brought from the museum to save the day.

Directed by Charles Crichton and produced by Michael Truman from a story by T E B Clarke (the team who made The Lavender Hill Mob), the comedy idea has been developed in the style for which Ealing is famous. George Relph plays the part of the

Above: Monkton Combe station renamed for the film, with Western Region 0-4-2 tank locomotive No. 1401 and a former Kelvedon & Tollesbury Light Railway coach at the platform. This train is wrecked by the proprietors of a bus competing for local traffic. PHOTO: P HARDEN

vicar of the parish, a railway enthusiast, who becomes amateur engine driver, with Sir Godfrey Tearle (the bishop) as his fireman, while Stanley Holloway is the genial toper who provides the cash to buy the line.

Producing a film is a slow and laborious process; and progress is even slower when a lot of complicated facilities or 'properties' are required in the action. Add to this the uncertainty of the English weather, and you have an undertaking which is likely to become a headache. The script requirements called for railway co-operation in a big way, involving several weeks' exclusive use of a single track line passing through pleasant countryside. In addition, a junction with a main line (preferably with branch and main line metals running side by side for a quarter of a mile or so), a level crossing, a pleasant country branch terminus, engine sheds with a turntable, and a busy junction station on a main line. The assistance of the Railway Executive was

▶ 'Thunderbolt' in steam and passing the dummy water crane at Titfield. PHOTO: EALING STUDIOS

sought, and various branches were surveyed, including the East Kent Railway, the Kelvedon & Tollesbury Light Railway, the Kent & East Sussex Railway, and various branch lines in Suffolk. Each one of these lines had possibilities, but did not fulfil completely the producer's requirements. Turning to the west of London, the Maidenhead-High Wycombe line, the Lambourne Valley branch and finally, the Limpley Stoke-Camerton branch (near Bath) were visited. The latter branch had been used in 1931 for scenes in The Ghost Train, when Camerton station was the main location.

The producer was particularly impressed with the scenic possibilities of the Camerton line, which not only fulfilled most of the requirements of the script, but also turned out to be an excellent centre for other exterior scenes, such as Titfield village, the church, the old inn, and picturesque farms. Colour tests, shot with a 16mm camera, confirmed that the pleasant Bath stone buildings, the growing corn and crops and the undulating skyline were ideal subjects for Technicolor.

The Camerton line had been out of regular use for about two years, but an occasional freight train had been run until the end of 1951. The stations at Monkton Combe and Dunkerton already were in a poor state, and the platforms and halts at Radford, Timsbury, and Combe Hay had almost disappeared. Nevertheless, a very complete survey by the Western Region revealed no serious

deterioration of the line, and it was even possible to bring into use one of the colliery siding tracks at Camerton, including a road through two or three sets of points operated from ground frames. These had been oiled periodically, though many of the sleepers and chairs on the sidings had rotted away.

Producing a film is a slow and laborious process

The film unit commenced operations by reconditioning the station at Monkton Combe, and putting up new name boards, Titfield, together with other appropriate signs, and hiding as far as possible a quantity of bridge material which had been dumped in the station yard. Sections of the main track were treated for weeds, and a dummy home signal and signalbox were erected at the north end of the platform. The level crossing gates south of the station were removed and a dummy (removable) buffer stop provided to simulate a terminus. Two hundred yards south of the station, a dummy water crane was erected. At Dunkerton Colliery sidings, a picturesque occupation crossing was built, with cottage adjoining, for the scenes in which the 'Titfield' train is engaged in a battle with a steamroller.

In the meantime, rolling stock was marshalled from various places: one old Great Eastern branch line coach, with longitudinal

seating, two brakevans (in one of which was fitted a diesel-electric 300amp generator for arc-lighting), two 1400 class 0-4-2 tanks (Nos. 1401 and 1456) from Westbury shed, a cattle truck, and various 'Conflats'. For the ancient locomotive, the Liverpool & Manchester Railway 0-4-2 Lion, (built by Todd, Kitson & Laird in 1838) was borrowed from the Liverpool Engineering Society, who gave permission for it to be repainted in bright green with red lining and fitted with a new nameplate: Thunderbolt. The Lion was in store at Crewe, painted its original dark maroon colour, and it was shipped on a low truck to Westbury, for overhaul and steaming tests, which proved satisfactory. The two original Salter steam pressure gauges were checked against a modern gauge, and were found to be operating quite well; one of them was correct to a pound. A pressure of 45lb was used.

Shooting the film proceeded smoothly, so far as the weather would allow. Monkton Combe station was the centre of activities, and here was established a production office, field kitchen, canteen marquees, and stores. A siding was used to store unwanted rolling stock, including 'Conflats' used for mounting cameras and sections of sets. Two production units, each with a Technicolor camera, operated simultaneously. One unit concentrated on long-shot train scenes with the 'Thunderbolt' at a safe distance along the line towards Camerton, while the other filmed

Filming in progress at Titfield Station. PHOTO: EALING STUDIOS

From *The Railway Magazine*, March 1953

'Thunderbolt' being removed from the local museum at Mallingford, the junction with the main line in the film, so that the branch service may be kept running after the wrecking of the regular train. PHOTO: EALING STUDIOS

scenes with principal actors round Monkton Combe station, using tank engine No. 1401. Later on, the first unit took over the 'Thunderbolt', and the second unit carried on with 'run-by' shots of the tank engine and train, without principals.

Shortly after production commenced, it was found that the *Lion* consumed much fuel and water, probably due to the fact that it originally was designed for burning coke. The engine was returned to Westbury to be fitted with a damper, and thereafter was able to simmer all day, awaiting sunny periods for actual shooting. The going was a little heavy for the *Lion* on the gradients of 1 in 100 between Limpley Stoke and Combe Hay when hauling the train of about 90 tons, and an additional tank engine (No. 1456) was provided for banking when scenes were not being shot.

Marshalling and turning the train, as required for different camera shots, presented several problems, which were handled by Inspector H Alford (of the Western Region, British Railways). Drivers S Mitchell and E Burbidge, both from Westbury shed, drove the *Lion* and No. 1401 respectively. The former, appropriately dressed, doubled for George Relph (the vicar) in long shots, and the latter played the original tank engine driver in the earlier

sequences, with F Greene as fireman. Tank engine No. 1456, used for general banking and marshalling work, was driven in shifts by drivers H S Harris, A J King, and W Copeland, also from Westbury. Driver Mitchell expressed great satisfaction with the performance of *Lion*, and admiration for the excellent craftsmanship of its makers.

The day's schedule of railway shots was worked out carefully to reduce to a minimum the turning of engines or rolling stock. Nevertheless, this was necessary occasionally, and the triangular junction at Bradford-on-Avon was used. Re-marshalling could be carried out at Limpley Stoke or Monkton Combe sidings, and also at the Dunkerton Colliery siding. With three engines in steam on the branch line, precautions were taken to avoid accidents, and all train movements were carried out under the supervision of Insp Alford. In addition, as the film company was the holder of a GPO commercial radio-telephone transmitting licence, r/t communication was used between trains and also with the production office. This was extremely useful for directing the starting or stopping of trains out of sight of the camera, apart from the many business and organisational messages it conveyed.

Every evening the film units returned to Limpley Stoke, where the *Lion* was stored in

a siding for the night. In a disused mill building of the Avon Leather Works, close to the station, a projection theatre was improvised for judging the Technicolor 'rushes'. Here were viewed every evening the prints of the previous day's work, which were returned from the developing laboratory in London on the 5.5pm train from Paddington, arriving at Bath at 7pm. In character with the Emett-like atmosphere of the production, electric current for the high-intensity arc-light of the projector was provided by a generator driven by an ancient water wheel! This accounted for the cryptic notice board over the doorway: 'Hydr-o-Deon'.

The final scenes in the film, depicting the arrival of the triumphant old 'Thunderbolt' at Mallingford Junction, were filmed on the platform known as the Fish Bay at Temple Meads station, Bristol. Here, special running facilities were provided by the Railway Executive, and it was a delightful sight to see the old engine come to rest at its destination, amid the joyous welcoming shrieks from 'Halls', 'Castles', and other stalwarts of the Western Region.

The film unit returned to London with the knowledge that the dignified official façade of the Railway Executive conceals a delightful unofficial sense of humour which makes such wonderful co-operation possible. ∎

Notes and NEWS

'London-Irish Car Carrier' at Fishguard during a trial operation. Cars are being driven on to the flat deck wagons before the two portions of the train are joined.

London-Fishguard car carrier service

WESTERN Region's new 'London-Irish Car Carrier' train offers British Railways' cheapest 'package-deal' for the family motorist. The new train, carrying both cars and their passengers, will run during the coming holiday season between London (Kensington Olympia) and Fishguard, linking with the drive-on-drive-off ferry to Rosslare, the gateway to Southern Ireland's car-touring centre. A small family saloon, plus the car-party, can travel to Fishguard and back – a distance of 522 miles – for an 'all-in' rate of £18 (£10 single journey). With a car-party of four this is equal to 2d a mile for each passenger, including the cost of carrying the car. Larger cars cost £22, and big limousines £30.

This is an experiment to cut costs and develop a new market from within the growing numbers of family motorists. With growing congestion on the roads this new-style economy service should prove extremely popular and there were already more than 2,000 bookings for the train, with seven weeks still to go before the service starts. There are many families who take the car with them on holidays who do not want to meet the cost of sleeping berths normally associated with car-carrier trains. At the same time, they are concerned to travel as a family group. The intensive use of fixed train formation and freight-car carrying vehicles offers speed and comfort and keeps the family together. Instead of sleeping berths, each car party will have the exclusive use of a reserved compartment, together with pillows and rugs. In addition, a club-type buffet car will be provided on the train to serve drinks and other refreshments.

The new service will begin on June 18, when the train will run each way at weekends – Friday night outward and Saturday return. A daily service (except Saturday nights) will run from July 11 to September 25. On its outward run the 'Carrier' will leave Kensington at five minutes to midnight and cars and passengers will be in Ireland by 10.15 next morning. The return train will link with the midday ferry from Rosslare and be back in London by 21.55. The 'Carrier' has a capacity of up to 28 cars carried on seven open flat-deck vehicles. With handbrakes on, cars are held in position by wedge-shaped chocks firmly fixed against each wheel; steel pins fasten the chocks to the decks of the rail vehicles.

From the May 1965 issue

Conveyance of Large Transformers

SIX 124-ton transformers, the largest ever conveyed over the Southern Region of British Railways, have been moved by stages to the new CEA power station at Marchwood, near Southampton, from the Ferranti works at Hollinwood, Manchester.

The transformers, each 18ft 6in long, were loaded on new British Railways transformer trolleys with special traversing arrangements enabling the load to pass bridges, signals, and other lineside structures where sufficient clearance would not otherwise exist. The consignment was routed via Derby, Stratford-upon-Avon, Oxford, Reading, Basingstoke, Southampton Central, and Totton, the station for Marchwood. A special train was used throughout, hauled by a diesel locomotive from Reading to Totton.

From the April 1956 issue

A New Steam Locomotive Depot

THE fact that much of the £1.25million spent on the new depot at Thornaby-on-Tees is in respect of equipment suitable for steam locomotives only, such as the mechanical coaling plant and boiler-washing facilities, emphasises the continuing and long-term reliance which will be made on steam for motive power. Covering an area of some 70 acres, the depot, which can deal with up to 220 large locomotives, replaces the two obsolete depots at Newport and Middlesbrough. Of the three sheds provided, one is octagonal, nearly 300ft in diameter with a turntable giving access to 22 stalls. Originally two roundhouses were planned, but a change was necessitated by the provision for conversion later to deal with diesel and electric locomotives which it is envisaged will be introduced in this area.

From the October 1958 issue

Premature end of Callander-Oban line

A LANDSLIP which blocked the Callander-Oban section near Balquhidder during September expedited the closure of the railway between Dunblane and Crianlarich, already agreed by the Minister of Transport. Although the debris on the line was not excessive, it was supporting several thousand tons of rock on the mountainside. Before the line could have been cleared, blasting would have had to take place and the earthwork would have had to be removed. This would have taken about a fortnight at a cost probably of more than £30,000. Glasgow-Oban trains were diverted via Dumbarton and the West Highland line and connecting bus services provided between Callander and Crianlarich until October 30, after which the whole of this former Caledonian Railway route between Dunblane and Crianlarich was closed. There were eight intermediate stations, including the Killin branch terminus.

From the November 1965 issue

Four hundred miles at 70 miles an hour

The trial train ascending Shap at 60mph.

Glasgow to Euston in 5 hours 44¼ minutes

By CECIL J ALLEN, M Inst T

IT is a remarkable age in which we are living. No sooner have we recovered our breath from the 113mph maximum of the LNER 'Silver Jubilee' in August last than the LMS puts up the astonishing locomotive performances of November 16 and 17. The nature of the LMS record consists in the continuous steaming of one locomotive at such speeds for a distance of over 400 miles non-stop; on the down journey the time over the 401.4 miles from Euston to Glasgow was 353minutes 38sec giving an average of 68.1mph, and on the return journey of the following day the time was 344min 15sec, 15¾ minutes under the six-hour schedule which had been laid down for the test, with an

average of precisely 70mph. These are easily the fastest non-stop runs of over 300 miles in length, let alone 400 miles, that have ever been made by a steam locomotive; and it is notable that the combined average of two consecutive days was one of 802.8 miles at 69mph by the one locomotive. This compares with the 2,323 miles covered in each of two successive weeks by the streamlined LNER Pacific *Silver Link* at an average of 70.4mph, in the first fortnight's working of the 'Silver Jubilee', but divided up into two 232.3-mile runs daily, with 3½ hour interval between each pair.

Only diesel propulsion has made higher continuous speeds on rails; in this connection it will be remembered that recently eight cars of the new 12-car Denver Zephyr unit of the Chicago, Burlington & Quincy RR, of the United States, were run without a stop over the 1,017 miles from Denver to Chicago in 12hr 12½ min, at an average of 83.3mph for the entire distance. But the diesel engine, with no limitations of heavy reciprocating parts and no locomotive firebox to be fed and maintained in good steaming order, has a considerable advantage over the orthodox steam locomotive in running over indefinitely long distances at such speeds as these.

It has further to be remembered that two ▶

L.M.S.R. Experimental Runs : Euston to Glasgow and Back

Engine : 4–6–2 No. 6201 *Princess Elizabeth*. Driver T. J. Clarke, Fireman C. Fleet (Crewe)

| DOWN JOURNEY : November 16, 1936. Load : 7 cars, 225 tons tare, 230 tons gross | | | | UP JOURNEY : November 17, 1936. Load : 8 cars, 255 tons tare, 260 tons gross | | | |

Distance	Schedule	Actual	Speeds	—	Distance	Schedule	Actual	Speeds
Miles	Min.	m. s.	m.p.h.		Miles	Min.	m. s.	m.p.h.
0·0	0	0 00	—	EUSTON	401·4	360	344 15	—
1·0	—	2 23	32	*Milepost 1*	400·4	—	—	—
5·4	8	7 24	66	WILLESDEN JUNCTION	396·0	352	335 45	—
		p.w.s. (2)	*35				p.w.s.	*42
8·1	—	10 38	—	Wembley	393·3	—	332 38	84
13·3	—	15 42	73½	Hatch End	388·1	—	328 45	78
17·4	18	18 55	80½	WATFORD JUNCTION	384·0	342	325 38	80
24·5	—	24 20	78½	Hemel Hempsted	376·9	—	320 38	91
31·7	30	29 55	77	Tring	369·7	331	315 30	77½
36·1	—	32 56	95½	Cheddington	365·3	—	312 10	81
40·2	—	35 49	*76	Leighton	361·2	—	309 14	85
46·7	41	40 32	85/*79	BLETCHLEY	354·7	318	304 27	81
52·4	—	44 53	85½/*70	Wolverton	349·0	—	299 50	90/*70
59·9	51	50 53	79/77½	Roade	341·5	308	294 33	78½
62·8	53½	53 02	87/*73	Blisworth	338·6	305½	292 24	82
69·7	—	58 19	82/*68	Weedon	331·7	—	287 08	88/*73
75·3	—	62 46	77½	Welton	326·1	—	283 02	—
80·3	—	66 25	86½	*Hillmorton*	321·1	—	278 58	†75
82·6	70	68 33	*35	RUGBY	318·8	289	276 05	*35
88·1	—	74 17	77½/*68	Brinklow	313·3	—	270 58	87
91·4	—	76 58	76	Shilton	310·0	—	268 45	80
97·1	82	81 08	90/*83	NUNEATON	304·3	277	264 33	87
102·3	—	84 56	86/*64	Atherstone	299·1	—	260 48	79
106·5	—	88 22	82/*30	Polesworth	294·9	—	257 00	*35
110·0	95	92 53	67	TAMWORTH	291·4	264	252 58	80
116·3	100	97 38	85/*74	LICHFIELD	285·1	259	248 37	‡91
124·3	106	103 36	90/*71	Rugeley	277·1	253	242 25	82/*70
127·2	—	105 58	75/*62	Colwick	274·2	—	240 03	—
129·5	—	107 58	78½	Milford	271·9	—	238 13	—
133·6	114	111 52	*30	STAFFORD	267·8	245	233 46	83/*30
138·9	—	116 50	75/*60	Norton Bridge	262·5	—	229 37	84/*67
147·6	127	123 47	82/*60	Whitmore	253·8	233	222 53	81/*70
153·3	—	128 15	93½	Betley Road	248·1	—	218 25	77½
158·1	136	132 52	*20	CREWE	243·3	223	213 17	*25
160·8	—	136 24	72	*Coppenhall Junction*	240·6	—	210 32	95
165·5	—	139 53	88	Winsford	235·9	—	207 26	87
169·9	—	142 44	93½	Hartford	231·5	—	204 26	—
174·3	149	146 00	90/*50	*Weaver Junction*	227·1	209	200 37	*50
179·3	—	150 30	82/*65	Moore	222·1	—	196 30	77
182·1	156	153 30	*45	WARRINGTON	219·3	202	193 34	66/*55
185·6	160	157 03	*55	*Winwick Junction*	215·8	198	190 14	68/*53
187·9	—	159 27	*51	*Golborne Junction*¶	212·3	—	187 03	77½/*50
191·3	—	162 33	75	Bamfurlong	210·1	—	—	—
193·9	168	164 55	*50	WIGAN	207·5	190	182 42	*50
196·1	—	167 23	56½/54	Boar's Head	205·3	—	180 48	82
197·2	171½	168 30	66	Standish Junction	204·2	186½	179 58	—
199·7	—	170 41	‖90	Coppull	201·7	—	178 00	71½
203·6	177	173 36	*60	*Euxton Junction*	197·8	—	174 42	*62
206·7	—	176 25	80/*61	Farington	194·7	—	171 55	69
209·0	183	179 15	*20	PRESTON	192·4	175	168 55	*25
210·3	185	181 34	50	*Oxheys*	191·1	173	166 47	—
213·8	—	184 29	75	Barton	187·7	—	164 18	83½
218·5	191½	188 05	88	Garstang	182·9	—	161 00	87
225·7	—	193 08	86½	Galgate	175·8	—	155 46	79
230·0	200	196 35	*57	LANCASTER	171·4	158	152 07	80/*66
236·3	205	201 28	83½	CARNFORTH	165·1	153	147 12	86½/*65
240·8	—	204 47	74	Burton	160·6	—	143 42	72½
243·6	—	206 45	.85½	Milnthorpe	157·8	—	141 45	88
245·5	—	208 18	*62	*Hincaster Junction*	155·9	—	140 15	84/*65
249·1	215	211 38	68/*60	OXENHOLME	152·3	143	137 18	*65
252·6	—	214 51	65½	*Hay Fell*	148·8	—	—	80
254·3	—	216 22	68	*Lambrigg Crossing*	147·1	—	—	brakes
256·2	—	218 04	66½	Grayrigg	145·2	—	131 22	69
257·9	—	219 34	*65	Low Gill	143·5	—	129 45	76/*65
262·2	227	223 05	78½	Tebay	139·2	132	126 15	*68
266·0	—	226 28	61	*Milepost 36*	135·4	—	—	82
267·7	233	228 12	57	*Shap Summit*	133·7	127	121 50	66
269·7	—	229 58	82	Shap	131·7	—	120 03	64/67
272·9	—	232 37	75	*Thrimby Grange*	128·5	—	117 05	63
277·0	—	236 12	*65	Clifton	124·4	—	113 00	*55
281·2	245	240 05	79/*53	PENRITH	120·2	114	109 15	85/*75
286·0	249	243 45	88	Plumpton	115·4	110	105 45	83½/80
288·3	—	245 25	*75	Calthwaite	113·1	—	103 57	78/74
291·7	—	247 58	85½	Southwaite	109·7	—	101 18	71½
294·2	—	250 00	*60	Wreay	107·2	—	99 12	65
297·7	—	253 05	§81	*Carlisle No.* 13	103·7	—	95 31	51
299·1	260	255 24	*20	CARLISLE	102·3	97	93 20	*20
301·1	—	258 15	63½	*Kingmoor*	100·3	—	90 55	86
305·2	—	261 35	85½	Floriston	96·2	—	87 58	85/79
307·7	268	263 27	*58	Gretna Junction	93·7	90	86 10	*75

Engine: 4–6–2 No. 6201 *Princess Elizabeth.* Driver T. J. Clarke, Fireman C. Fleet (Crewe)

DOWN JOURNEY : November 16, 1936. Load : 7 cars, 225 tons tare, 230 tons gross					UP JOURNEY : November 17, 1936. Load : 8 cars, 255 tons tare, 260 tons gross			
Distance	Schedule	Actual	Speeds	—	Distance	Schedule	Actual	Speeds
Miles	Min.	m. s.	m.p.h.		Miles	Min.	m. s.	m.p.h.
312·1	—	267 39	70½	Kirkpatrick	90·3	—	82 45	86½
315·8	—	270 38	82	Kirtlebridge	86·6	—	79 55	86½/*75
321·8	—	275 15	75	*Castlemilk*	79·6	—	75 13	72½
324·9	282	277 40	80	LOCKERBIE	76·5	77	72 49	77½
327·8	—	279 50	85½	Nethercleugh	73·6	—	70 33	*75
330·8	—	282 00	82	Dinwoodie	70·6	—	68 24	89
333·6	—	283 58	90	Wamphray	67·8	—	66 20	88/77½
338·8	293	287 35	80	Beattock	62·6	66	62 29	75
341·4	—	289 34	68	*Auchencastle*	60·0	—	60 28	brakes
344·5	—	292 30	57½	*Greskine* ..	56·9	—	58 00	down
346·9	—	294 59	57	*Harthope*	54·5	—	56 00	bank
348·8	306	297 06	56	*Summit* ..	52·6	57	54 20	66½
351·7	—	299 26	—	Elvanfoot	49·7	—	51 57	80
354·4	—	301 40	81	Crawford..	47·0	—	49 49	77½/72½
356·9	—	303 49	*65	Abington	44·5	—	47 49	74
362·3	—	309 25	83½/*20	Lamington	39·1	—	43 17	86½/*65
366·0	—	313 15	69	Symington	35·4	—	40 35	71½
369·1	—	316 05	77½/66	*Leggatfoot*	32·3	—	38 01	64/77½
372·6	328	319 30	*35	CARSTAIRS	28·8	33	34 30	*45
375·4	—	322 47	64	Cleghorn	26·0	—	32 03	83½
377·6	—	324 44	75	*Craigenhill*	23·8	—	30 16	62½
379·8	—	326 29	79	Braidwood	21·6	—	28 10	58½
383·1	338	329 38	*40	Law Junction	18·3	22	24 30	48
		p.w.s.	*30				p.w.s.	*40
385·5	—	332 22	many	Wishaw South ..	15·9	—	21 24	48½
388·5	344	336 34	slacks	MOTHERWELL	12·9	16	16 50	55
								*30
391·9	—	339 50	68	Fallside ..	9·5	—	12 58	55
		p.w.s.	*20				p.w.s.	*25
394·8	—	344 03	many	Newton ..	6·6	—	9 05	*50
397·4	—	347 08	slacks	*Rutherglen Junction*	4·0	—	6 21	62½
400·4	—	351 06	—	Eglinton Street ..	1·0	—	2 28	—
401·4	360	353 38	—	GLASGOW CENTRAL	0·0	0	0 00	—

* Speed reduced by braking.   † Speed on entering Kilsby Tunnel.   ‡ Maximum at Hademore.   § Maximum below Wreay. || At Balshaw Lane.   ¶ Time at Golborne Station on up journey.

summits of considerable altitude – Shap, 916ft, and Beattock, 1,014ft, with a descent intermediately to sea level at Floriston – are included in the LMS route. Not only so, but throughout the journey a number of special speed restrictions, based on the existing super-elevation of the curves, were imposed on the test train, in some cases lower than those that are quite commonly maintained over the curves concerned in ordinary running. A Hasler self-recording speed indicator of the Tel RT835 type was fitted to the locomotive, and proved very accurate in operation, so facilitating the proper observance of these restrictions. At the same time a continuous Hallade record was taken of the motion of the train, relatively to the track, and the result of the experience so gained was that in not a few cases the running of the train round the curves was sufficiently smooth to justify the abolition of a number of these restrictions in future, and the easing of others. In addition, the now general limit of 90mph on maximum speeds was imposed. The effect was that speed restrictions to a total of roughly fifty in each direction were imposed, and as the table of times and speeds shows, the brakes were constantly in use. If and when a 6 or 6¼ hour service is introduced between

Euston and Glasgow, it will doubtless be possible to regulate the running in such a way that this rapid succession of brake applications is not a regular feature of each journey.

In the lengthy table annexed, the passing times and speeds of both down and up runs are given, from figures recorded by D S Barrie, together with the schedules to which the train was nominally working. It will be noted that the down schedule was faster than the best existing Euston-Crewe schedule (the down Lancastrian) by 19 minutes, and that it bettered the best Carlisle-Glasgow time (the "Midday Scot") by 16 minutes. Coming up, 13 minutes were knocked off the Crewe-Willesden schedule of the 5.25pm from Liverpool, and 13 minutes, similarly, off the Stafford-Euston booking of the up 'Comet'. Where double figures are given in the speed column, for the most part they indicate the range through which speed was reduced for a specified restriction, and in other cases the range of speed in the vicinity of the particular timing point. As is customary in such tables, the speeds shown are not of necessity those at which the timing points on the same line were passed, but the maxima and minima at the principal neighbouring changes of gradient.

The engine was 4-6-2 No. 6201 *Princess Elizabeth*, and driver Clarke and fireman Fleet, of Crewe (with passed fireman Shaw as reserve engineman also travelling on the footplate) were selected in view of the fact that first link Crewe drivers know the road both northwards to Glasgow and southwards to London. On the down journey the train consisted of dynamometer car, kitchen car, and five coaches of standard stock taring 225 tons; on the return another coach was added, making the tare up to 255 tons. Favourable weather prevailed for the northbound run, but not on the return, which was showery in the early stages, squally with rain on the exposed mountain sections, and hampered by strong wind and heavy rain over the final length, which makes the southbound running the more remarkable. To discuss the performance in detail would be impossible within the limitations of available space, and attention must therefore be concentrated on the outstanding features.

On the down journey the first features of note were the acceleration from the two Willesden slacks (one to 35mph) up 1 in 335 to 73½mph at Hatch End, and then the sustained minimum of 77 up the corresponding grade at Tring. Immediately after came the ▶

95½mph at Sear's Crossing – the maximum of the down journey. At Roade the minimum was again 77½mph, and also on entering Kilsby tunnel. Maxima of 90mph were reached before Nuneaton and Rugeley, and 932 at Betley Road and Hartford; 90 at Balshaw Lane was another unusually high speed at this point.

But the chief interest naturally centred in the two great climbs, both of which are much harder in the northbound than in the southbound direction. After Carnforth, 2½ miles at 1 in 134 reduced the speed from 83½ to 74mph; the short level to Milnthorpe permitted an accelera tion to 85½. Slacks were necessary both at Hincaster Junction and Oxenholme (the latter from 68 to 60mph), after which the 7.1 miles to Grayrigg were mounted in 6min 26sec, with speed steadily rising from 60 to 68mph up the 1 in 124-131, and falling to only 66 on the final two miles at 1 in 106. A slow was necessary round Low Gill curve, but Tebay was passed at 78½mph, and as far as milepost 36, after 1⅝ miles at 1 in 146, and then 2⅞ miles at 1 in 75, the speed was still 61mph; the final 1¼ miles at 1 in 75 reduced it to 57, at which unprecedented figure Slap Summit was breasted. The 5.5 miles from Tebay had been run in 5min 7sec; the 18.6 miles from Oxenholme in 16min 34sec; and the 31.4 miles from Carnforth in 26min 44sec, at an average of 70.5mph! From Crewe to Carlisle the time of 122min 32sec for the 141 miles compared with the historic 126 minutes of the 1895 'Race', with a load of 230, as against 105 tons, and far more scrupulous attention to curves than was paid in those hectic days of 41 years ago.

Then, from Carlisle, there came the attack on Beattock. Having attained 85½mph at Floriston, the train was slowed to 58½ through Gretna, but accelerated to 70½ on the 1 in 200 up past Kirkpatrick, and after 82 through Kirtlebridge, maintained 75 minimum on the 1 in 200 through Ecclefechan. A hurricane flight from Lockerbie to Beattock, with a top speed of 90mph beyond Wamphray, took the train up 4¼ miles of 1 in 202 to Beattock station without the speed falling below 80mph. At Auchencastle, after 2½ miles mostly at 1 in 88, the rate was down to 68mph; at Greskine, after three miles steepening to 1 in 74, it had dropped to 57½, and the short strip at 1 in 69 beyond reduced it to 56; the remainder of the bank, entirely at 1 in 74-77, was accomplished with the speed hovering between 56 and 57mph, so giving the amazing time of 9min 31sec for the 10 miles from Beattock station to Summit. The schedule of the train had to this point been noteworthy for the accuracy with which probable and actual performance had been related; but here the optimism of its compilers was completely beaten by the realisation, for 3½ minutes were gained between Beattock and Summit alone.

For the 59.7 miles from Carlisle to Summit the time was 41min 42sec and the average speed 71.5mph! The remainder of the route is so slack-infested, especially from Law Junction onwards, that nothing further of note was done.

For the same reason the southbound journey of the following day contained little of remark until Law Junction had been passed. But then came an acceleration up a gradient largely at 1 in 99 from 48 to 58½mph, and up the easier 1 in 130 grade to 62½ before breasting Craigenhill summit; from Carstairs, again, a level mile and 2¼ miles at 1 in 150 up produced an acceleration to 64mph at Leggatfoot, while after the abrupt Thankerton dip, Symington was passed at 71½mph an hour. From the Lamington bridge slowing, up the gentle grades past Abington, mostly a little flatter than 1 in 300, speed rose to 77½mph; the steeper 2¾ miles past Crawford - 1 in 240-145 - reduced this to 72½, but 1½ level miles through Elvanfoot raised the rate again to 80; and the final two miles at 1 in 99 to Summit were breasted at 66½mph – another remarkable piece of uphill work. So, although the train was 2½min down on the experimental schedule at Law Junction, by reason of the permanent way slowings, it was through Carlisle in 93min 20sec from Glasgow, 3¾minutes early.

Now followed an astounding climb from Carlisle to Shap. From 20mph through Citadel

Much has been made of the fact that this run was accomplished, without streamlining of engine or coaches

station, the driver accelerated up four miles at 1 in 131 to 65mph at Wreay; 1¾ miles up at 1 in 184 raised this to 71½, and three miles at 1 in 228 produced a further acceleration to 78, followed by an easing, up 1½ miles at 1 in 172 and a mile at 1 in 114, to 74 above Calthwaite. On the two level miles past Plumpton the maximum was 83½mph, followed by 80 minimum up two miles at 1 in 186, and 85 on the level before Penrith, which was passed at the slightly reduced speed of 75mph. Speed was further reduced over Clifton Junction to 55mph. Up the unbroken seven miles of 1 in 125 past Clifton, speed rose to a steady 64mph; 1¼ miles at 1 in 142 raised this to 67, and on the final 1 in 106-130 to Shap Summit the minimum was 66mph. So the 31.4 miles from Carlisle to Summit were compassed in 28min 30sec, and it says something for the anticipations of the authorities that here they had allowed no more than 30 minutes. The distance of 90.1 miles from Carlisle to Preston was spanned in 75min 35sec, at an average of 71.5mph – over Shap!

The next feature of note was an average of 90mph for six miles from Winsford Junction to Coppenhall Junction, mostly level, but including 1¼ miles each of 1 in 300 and 1 in 413 up; on the dead level a maximum of 95mph was attained. The minimum of the three miles at 1 in 177 from Betley Road was 77½mph, and there was almost a touch of humour in having to slow from 81 to 70mph through Whitmore on a southbound journey. After that the principal 'high spots' were the acceleration to 79 through Atherstone after a 35mph slowing over Polesworth pitfall, a speed never below 80mph on the rising grades past Bulkington and rising to 87 through Nuneaton and Brinklow; an acceleration from 35mph through Rugby to 75 at Kilsby tunnel; and a time of 11min 3sec from Bletchley to Tring with a minimum of 77½ mph over Tring summit. And thus there closed at Euston, 344min 15sec after leaving Glasgow, 401.4 miles away, one of the most amazing feats of locomotive performance that this country has yet witnessed.

Full regulator was generally used on both journeys, and a cut-off of from 15 to 18%, except in starting and recovering from slacks, and on the steep climbs, where the engine was opened out considerably further. From Tebay to Shap Summit, going north, cut-offs ranged from 25 to a maximum of 32%; drawbar horsepower averaged 1,187 and reached a maximum of 1,251, and the maximum calculated horsepower of the locomotive was 2,413. From Beattock to Beattock Summit the figures were 30 to 37½% maximum cut-off, 1,241 average and 1,350 maximum dbhp, and 2,428 maximum calculated ihp. In the reverse direction the cut-off from Lamington bridge slowing to Beattock Summit ranged from 20 to 28%, dbhp averaged 1,117 and reached a maximum of 1,260, and calculated ihp a maximum of 2,448 – the biggest on all four climbs. Finally, from Clifton to Shap Summit cut-off was increased from 30 to 35%, dbhp averaged 1,180 and rose to 1,260, and the highest calculated ihp was 2,343.

At no point on either run did the boiler pressure fall below 220lb per sq in, and on the first three of the climbs mentioned it varied between 240 and 245lb. On the down journey the coal consumption averaged 46.8lb per mile, or 3.68lb per drawbar-horsepower-hour, and the water consumption 34.5 gal per mile; coming south, despite the better times and the worse weather, but doubtless with the help of the experience gained on the previous day, the fuel consumption had been brought down to 44.8lb per mile, or 3.48lb per dbhp-hr, and the water to 30.2 gal per mile. There was also a striking reduction from 7.36 to 6.70 in the evaporation (lb of water per lb of coal) as between the up journey and the down. It is of interest in this connection that

LMS 'Princess Royal' class No 6201 *Princess Elizabeth* heads the up 'Royal Scot' near Gretna in September 1934. Note the Caledonian route indicator. *RM* ARCHIVE

Princess Elizabeth, with her domed boiler, now has a 32-element superheater in place of the original 14-element superheater, affording 594sq ft of heating surface as against the original 370sq ft.

Much has been made of the fact that this run was accomplished, without streamlining of engine or coaches, as if to infer, by comparison with the 'Silver Jubilee', that streamlining is unnecessary in high-speed running of this description. But the LNER has never claimed that it is 'necessary'; on the contrary, the 'Silver Jubilee' timings were observed in the preliminary tests by the non-streamlined engine *Papyrus* with a seven-coach train of ordinary stock, and the 'Silver Jubilee' has since been worked to time by the non-streamlined engine *Firdaussi*. The point stressed by Sir Nigel Gresley in his presidential address to the Institution of Mechanical Engineers was not so much that of speed as of economy.

As mentioned in *The Railway Magazine* last month, careful experiment has shown that the saving of fuel on the 'Silver Jubilee' at these sustained high speeds due to streamlining has amounted to 4lb per mile, which is 10% of the total consumption, and has brought about a total saving of 200 tons of coal in the first year's working of the train – a

by no means negligible interest on the comparatively trivial cost of the actual streamlining itself. It is not without interest to compare the 'Silver Jubilee' average coal consumption of 39lb per mile for a whole year, in every possible condition of weather, with the two LMS figures quoted in the left-hand column; even allowing for Shap and Beattock, and the extra coach and the bad weather of the up LMS run, the difference in consumption appears to confirm to Sir Nigel's contention. It also tends to bear out the conclusions of a remarkable paper read to the Institution of Mechanical Engineers on November 27 by Mr F C Johansen, research officer of the LMSR, which was summarised in *The Railway Gazette* of December 4.

There is the further advantage of the wedge-shaped front end of the 'Silver Link' streamlined Pacifics that it is very effective in lifting the exhaust clear of the cab – a more vital necessity than ever at such speeds as these. And as to streamlining itself, would it be possible to dispute that a train differing entirely in appearance from all others, as does the 'Silver Jubilee', is in itself sufficiently propagandist to attract traffic? At any rate, the general trend of world opinion appears to be that for the ultra high-speed service, streamlining is desirable, both on the grounds

of economy and publicity.

The justification of such brilliant achievements as those of the LMSR on the London-Glasgow high speed journeys – on which the chief mechanical engineer of the LMS, Mr W A Stanier, the driver and fireman of the locomotive, and the operating authorities who kept the road so remarkably clear, are equally entitled to congratulation – is that they shall result in public service. The historic speed contest of 1895 – and how remarkably history seems to be repeating itself between 1932 and 1937! – resulted in no public benefit by improved travelling times, but rather the opposite. Now, however, after 41 years, the records of the 'Race to Aberdeen' are at length being broken, with permanent advantage to the traveller. For the LNER test runs of March 5, 1935, produced the 'Silver Jubilee'; the test runs of September 27, 1936, between Newcastle and Edinburgh resulted in the announcement of the six-hour King's Cross-Edinburgh 'Coronation' service of 1937; and it may now be confidently expected that the LMSR, with the experience of the successful tests of November 16-17, 1936, as a guide, will reply to the forthcoming East Coast six-hour London-Edinburgh service by instituting a flyer at comparable speed from Euston to Glasgow. ■

Gone... With regret – 2

Top: Class 503 Wirral & Mersey unit led by car No. M28387M stands in a siding at Birkenhead Park station on May 29, 1976, while a sister unit works past on a service train.

Right: The Manchester-Bury Class 504 electric service ceased in 1991 when the line was temporarily closed for conversion to tram operation. A two-car unit arrives at Whitefield on July 11, just weeks before closure of the Crumpsall-Bury section on August 16, 1991

Left: Class 31 No. 31418 passes Burbage Common, near Hinckley, with the 08.19 Birmingham New Street to Norwich service on May 9, 1987. It's hard to understand how a five-carriage loco-hauled train has been replaced by two- and three-car DMUs.

ALL PICTURES: TRACKS NORTH

Top: AM10 EMU No. 091 passes through Queen's Park station on May 12, 1968, working a shuttle service between selected DC lines stations between Euston and Watford Junction due to engineering work.

Left: Former London Transport Tube train No. 032, reclassified as 3-Tis, slips downhill from Ryde Esplanade with a Shanklin service on March 24, 1967. The 'new' electric trains had been introduced on the Isle of Wight four days earlier.

Right: A North Tyneside electric unit heads east from Newcastle station towards Heaton on May 7, 1966. The electric service ceased on June 17, 1967.

Locomotives rebuilt

Rebuilt 4-6-2 tank No. 2162, Class A8 LNER. This locomotive was originally a 4-4-4 tank belonging to Class D, NER.

One of Holden's GER 4-6-0 express locomotives as fitted by Gresley with ACFI feed water heater, now Class B12, LNER.

LNER B12 4-6-0, based on Holden's design. This was one of 10 locomotives built by Beyer Peacock, and fitted by Gresley with Lentz OC poppet valve gear which was removed in 1932.

From *The Railway Magazine*, November 1941

Ex-NER Atlantic No. 727 (LNER Class C7) as rebuilt by Gresley with booster equipment on bogie – forming articulation between engine and tender.

Ex-GCR Robinson 0-8-4 tank locomotive. One of the engines used for humping at Wath, and rebuilt with superheater and reversible booster; now Class S1, LNER.

Robinson 2-8-0 locomotive No. 6371, GCR. As rebuilt with Gresley boiler and modified cab with single window.

Freight train hauled by electric locomotive No. 3.

A notable freight traffic electrification: North Eastern Railway

Equipment of the Shildon-Newport section

THE North Eastern Railway was one of the first in Great Britain to adopt electric traction, having as far back as 1904, when Sir George Gibb was general manager, successfully applied electrical operation to the Newcastle and Tyneside suburban traffic, one of the earliest electric traction installations for other than underground lines and on a considerable scale. This railway now claims a pioneer reputation in respect of electric traction applied to heavy freight haulage, and on a system including many special electrical features.

In 1911 the general manager, Sir A Kaye Butterworth, instructed Messrs Merz and McLellan, consulting electrical engineers, to report on the question of electrification with

The track runs over a portion of the original Stockton and Darlington Railway

reference to the special conditions of the North Eastern system, and following the visit of the chief mechanical engineer, Mr Vincent Raven, to the United States of America, in 1911 the directors decided to proceed with a preliminary scheme, and electric working was started on July 1, 1915, on the Shildon-Newport line, a limited service being run, as the overhead track equipment was not completed.

The Shildon-Newport route was selected for trial, this being an important freight line dealing almost exclusively with heavy mineral traffic. Some historical interest attaches to this selection, since the track runs over a portion of the original Stockton and Darlington Railway, the first public railway on which steam locomotives were used for conveying passengers and goods.* The fact that the first trial of heavy freight haulage on a large scale in England should be carried out on this particular route is noteworthy.

Beyond the usual considerations affecting the decision to apply electric traction to such a line, there was a special factor which differentiated the North Eastern lines from others in the United Kingdom. As is well known, the production and distribution of electric power has been developed upon a larger scale along the north-east coast of England than in any other part of this country, and a large proportion of the power is derived from electric generating stations using as fuel the waste heat and gases derived from coke ovens and blast furnaces in the Durham and the Cleveland districts. An ample supply of cheap electrical energy was, therefore, available, and this fact, obviating as it does the necessity for a large capital expenditure by the railway on powerstation plant, had an important bearing on the scheme.

The electrified line under consideration has a route length of between 18 and 19 miles, and connects the mineral sidings at Shildon, which form one of the largest marshalling yards in Great Britain, with the Erimus Sidings at Newport, near Middlesbrough. Considerable portions of the sidings at both ends are also electrified, so that, including the sidings, about 50 miles of single track are equipped for electric working.

The general gradient is in favour of the laden traffic, the steepest being 1 in 103. This route carries the heavy mineral traffic from the south-west Durham coalfields to the Middlesbrough district, supplying the numerous blast furnaces and iron works concentrated there. In the opposite direction the load consists mainly of empty wagons returned to Shildon Sidings.

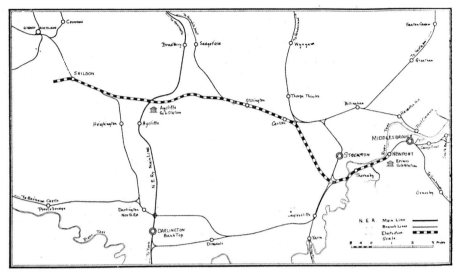

Map showing electrified lines and connections.

About 50 miles of single track are equipped for electric working

It was decided to adopt the high-tension direct-current system, current being supplied to the locomotives through overhead contact wires at a pressure of 1,500 volts from the two rotary-converter sub-stations described later. Overhead track equipment was carried out under the supervision of the railway's then chief engineer, Mr C A Harrison, and completed under the direction of his successor, Mr C F Bengough.

The overhead contact wires on the main portions of the track consist of two hard drawn copper conductors, but on certain portions of the sidings, where the loads are not so heavy, a single contact wire only is used. The wires are supported by a solid steel auxiliary catenary wire, to which they are attached by sliding clips. This auxiliary catenary is in turn suspended from the main stranded steel catenary by means of steel wire droppers. The main steel catenary wire is supported from the steel structures by means of special insulators, double insulation being used throughout.

The normal span between the steel structures is 110 yards, but on curves and sidings they are placed at lesser intervals depending on the conditions existing. The normal height of the contact wire from rail level is 16ft 6in, but at level crossings this is increased to 18ft 6in, and under some of the low bridges, of which there are a large number on this route, the height from the rail level is reduced, the minimum height being about 13ft 8in.

Each steel structure carries a pair of insulated steadying arms. These steadying arms are pivoted in all directions, and are attached to the contact wires by means of clips, their purpose being to fix the position of the contact wire relatively to the track. The contact wires are staggered in the usual way to prevent undue wearing of the bow collectors.

The general type of steel structure carrying the wires consists of two steel masts and a cross girder, each of these being made up of two channels with flat steel bracing. On curves a centre strut, steadied by steel tie rods, is added. In some instances cantilever construction is adopted.

In order to limit as far as possible the sag of the contact wires due to temperature ▶

Overhead structure with section switches, showing also positioning arms for overhead wire.

One of the new electric locomotives.

variation, automatic tensioning is adopted. The tensioning points are about 1,100 yards apart. On some of the sidings where only shunting work is done and the loads on the locomotives are not heavy, a single contact wire is used over each track with ordinary tramway span wire construction. At marshalling and reception sidings, which are not equipped throughout and on which it is only necessary for the overhead construction to permit of the locomotives entering to pick up their load, the wires are terminated at a sufficient distance. Danger boards are fitted beyond which electric locomotives should not pass, but if by any chance they should overrun these, the terminal construction is such that no damage would be done to the bow collectors or to the overhead track.

When passing under low stone bridges, of which there are a large number on the route, it is in some cases possible to carry the main catenary wire through the bridge, but at most of them it is necessary to anchor it off to the bridge. In these cases, in order to obtain the

necessary clearance, the contact wires, together with the auxiliary catenary, are brought towards the centre of the bridge, so that contact is made towards the extreme edge of the bow collector. In order to prevent the other edge of the bow collector from striking the bridge a guard wire is fitted. This guard wire is anchored off to the structures on either side of the bridge, and is only alive while a locomotive is passing underneath.

Section switches are erected as necessary, and one illustration shows a series of five fitted on a girder.

As the train control system of working is in use on this route, the signal cabins are connected by telephone with a central control office situated at Newport, and the handling of these switches is directed from the same point.

There are two sub-stations, supplied with three-phase current from the interconnected mains system of the North East Coast Power Companies through the Cleveland and Durham Electric Power Company. Aycliffe is supplied

at a pressure of 20,000v between phases through two overhead lines. The Erimus sub-station is supplied at a pressure of 11,000v between phases through underground cables connected to the power company's system in the Middlesbrough district, the alternating current switchgear being of the same type as that of Aycliffe.

A special feature of the transmission scheme is the high voltage DC gear. Thin switchgear has been designed somewhat on the lines of that usually adopted for high-tension AC boards; that is to say, the apparatus is of the remote controlled type, and is mounted in cell structures built up of brick walls with moulded stone division slabs, each equipment being thus entirely separated from its neighbour.

The individual cells are built up on the cubicle system, that is to say, special compartments are provided for:

1) Busbars and isolating switches (top cubicle).

2) Circuit breakers (intermediate cubicle).

Gradient profile: Shildon-Newport section.

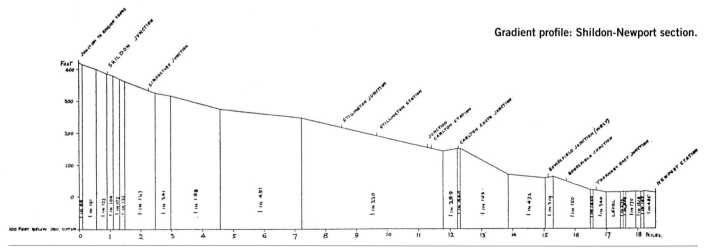

Aycliffe sub-station.

Interior of Aycliffe sub-station.

3) The bottom cubicle contains the operating mechanism for the isolating switches and circuit breakers, also the connecting cables passing up to the circuit breaker units.

The locomotives were designed and built at the North Eastern Railway works at Darlington, under the supervision of the chief mechanical engineer Mr Raven, the electrical equipment being supplied and fitted by electrical firms. They are designed to haul trains weighing 1,400 tons at a speed of not less than 25mph on the level.

The engine has two motor trucks. The trucks are connected by means of a buffer coupling and arranged for lateral movement with vertical rigidity. The sloping ends are partitioned off from the cab and contain the resistances, contactors, motor cut-out switches, multiple cut-out switches, and all high-tension electrical apparatus. Entrance to each sloping end can be obtained through doors which are normally locked.

The bow collectors on the roof of the cab are raised and maintained in connection with the contact wire by compressed air. A cock is fitted on the air system, the removable handle of which forms the key of the doors mentioned. This handle is so arranged that it can only be removed when the cock is in the exhaust position, so that it is impossible to open the doors of the sloping ends while the bows are in contact with the overhead wires.

In the cab two master controllers are fitted, one at each end. The cab also contains all auxiliary switches for controlling the air compressor and the two dynamotors described later, and for lighting and heating, together with the control valves for the Westinghouse brake and for air sanding. In the centre of the cab there is a vertical hand wheel for the hand brake. The dynamotors are securely fixed to the floor, the switches, etc, being fixed on the sides of the cab and weather boards.

The motor equipment of each locomotive consists of four totally enclosed motors, each driving an axle through single reduction twin gearing. The motors are suspended by means of a cross beam suspension bar with bearings and reaction springs. These, with the motor suspension bearings on the axle, provide the motors with four points of suspension.

The four main motors are fitted two in each bogie, and are each wound for 750v, the pair of motors in each bogie being connected permanently in series. The four main motors of each locomotive thus form two units which are controlled on the usual series parallel system. Each motor is capable of developing 275 brake horse power at a speed of 20 miles for one hour with forced ventilation. The motors and gearing are designed so as to run at a speed of 45mph without exceeding the limits of safety, but the normal speed on the level when hauling a train of 1,400 tons is 25mph.

Each locomotive is capable of performing four round trips in 12 hours, each consisting of

The locomotive also proved capable of hauling the 1,400 tons train on the level at 26mph

a trip from Shildon to Newport with a train of 1,400 tons, followed by a trip from Newport to Shildon with a train of 800 tons, the distance of each trip being about 18 miles. The locomotives are able to start a train of 800 tons from rest on a grade of 1 in 100 and accelerate to normal running speed.

A motor-driven air compressor is fitted in the cab of each locomotive for supplying air for the Westinghouse brake equipment, air sanding, raising the bow collectors, and for air whistles. An automatic governor is provided for the compressor, and is so arranged that the motor circuit is opened when the air pressure rises to 100lb per sq in, and closes again when the pressure falls to 80lb per sq in.

A hand pump is provided by means of which the bows are raised at the commencement of the day's working if no pressure is available in the reservoir. By means of the control cocks in the cab, either one or both of the bows can be raised or lowered. Each pantograph is raised and maintained in contact with the overhead wire by means of an air cylinder, so that in the event of a failure of the air pressure, the bows are automatically lowered. The air cylinders raise the pantographs through springs which maintain an even pressure against the contact wire notwithstanding variations in its height.

An existing engine shed at Shildon was adapted for the use of these locomotives, a sufficient portion being electrically equipped for the purpose. An automatic circuit breaker is provided controlling the whole of the shed equipment, and each engine stall is controlled by an independent isolating and earthing switch so that work can be safely carried out on the roof of any locomotive without interfering with the operation of locomotives in adjacent stalls.

Tests have been carried out recently with one of the electric locomotives. Several journeys were made between Shildon and Newport, a train of 1,400 tons of laden wagons being taken down from Shildon to Newport, and a train of 800 tons consisting of 92 empty wagons hauled from Newport up to Shildon with stops on certain of the heaviest grades. The 800-ton train was stopped and started on a grade of 1 in 103. The maximum drawbar pull during the tests reached 16 tons, the average speed on the run up from Newport to Shildon being 18.3mph, the maximum speed being 26mph. Up a grade of 1 in 230, which is four miles long, the 800 tons load of empty wagons was hauled at an average speed of 23mph. The locomotive also proved capable of hauling the 1,400 tons train on the level at 26mph. The general operation of the locomotive proved satisfactory in all respects throughout the test.

* This line was opened in 1825, and two of the original locomotives are now preserved in the Darlington station of the North Eastern Railway. ■

One of the loops in the 'double bow knot'.

The crookedest railway in the world

A N ordinary method of ascending by railway to high altitudes is to curve the line about in all directions, lengthening the mileage so as to keep the gradients within reason, though necessarily the length of such a line is quite disproportionate to the horizontal distance travelled. Lines of this character are very common in Alpine, Rocky Mountain, Himalayan, and other mountain districts. Thus, on the St Gothard Railway in Switzerland, before reaching the principal tunnel, a train travels in all directions, passing under the line that it has previously traversed in places, and traversing three spiral tunnels, two of which are nearly complete circles, while the other is a completed loop. And in some places in the Rocky Mountains the railway is visible at one time at three or four different levels, though there is actually only one continuous track. The loops of the Darjeeling Railway in India are other well-known examples of this type of railway construction.

Yet, interesting and curious as these excessively curved railways are, it is doubtful whether any of them more correctly merits the title of The Crookedest Railway in the World, at least in proportion to length, than the little pleasure railway now to be described, for we believe that its particular peculiarity in the way of curves – the 'double bow knot' – is unique.

One of the illustrations shows the

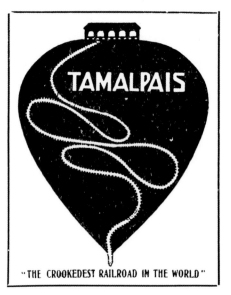

"THE CROOKEDEST RAILROAD IN THE WORLD"

The trademark of the Mount Tamalpais Scenic Railway.

trademark of the Mount Tamalpais Scenic Railway, from which it will be gathered that the officials of the line rather pride themselves on their curves, instead of considering them as unavoidable evils, as in the case of the other mountain railways referred to.

Mount Tamalpais is nothing very special as mountains go, even in this country, and in the United States, to which it belongs, it is really

very insignificant, for its summit is only about 2,500 feet above sea level; but its location, just north of the entrance to the world-famed Golden Gate of San Francisco, and its commanding position as regards the neighbouring country, cause the view which is obtained at the top to be one of the most wonderful in the world.

From the summit of the mountain a tremendous distance can be seen, and it is stated that on a clear day it is even possible to discern the Sierra Nevada mountains, about 155 miles distant.

The trip to the mountain is a favourite one among the inhabitants of San Francisco and the neighbouring towns; at any rate, when relieved from the disarranging effects of earthquake shocks and the like.

From the capital city the journey, which occupies about two hours altogether, is commenced by taking the ferry to Sausalito, a settlement on the opposite side of the bay. From there, train is taken on the North Shore line for a distance of six miles to Mill Valley, where the mountain railway is joined.

The 'scenic railway', as it is generally termed, was built in 1896, and is 8⅙ miles long. It is a standard gauge line operated by adhesion locomotives of special types, and although the gradients are severe they are never worse than 1 in 14, and as a rule 1 in

20 is about the stiffest. In its length there are no less than 281 curves, and it is calculated that, if continuous, there would be no less than 42 complete circles. The longest stretch of straight track is 413ft, and that occurs, curiously, on the 'crookedest' section of the line – the 'double bow knot'.

About half-way up the mountain occurs the special feature, the 'double bow knot', where the railway parallels itself five times in a distance of 300ft.

From the lower starting point the line passes through a fine forest of Redwood trees. Then it passes through a beautiful canyon, and past suburban residences, including a Japanese village with its quaint oriental houses. Crossing the head of the canyon the line swings back, gradually rising and passing through wooded districts until it rises beyond the trees and the distant panorama comes into view, each change of view being of wider range. It is not until the summit is nearly reached that the country to the north becomes visible, but from the hotel at the upper terminus of the line the view is said to be indescribably grand, embracing nearly 100 miles in all directions. Even on foggy days the summit is clear, and then observers are provided with most interesting effects of cloud and sunshine.

The Tavern of Tamalpais, a fine up-to-date hotel situated at the upper terminus of the line, is a favourite stopping place for holidaymakers. As shown in one of the photographs, the station is actually in the hotel premises. A usual practice is for travellers to stay overnight at the hotel in order to witness a 'Californian sunrise'.

Two locomotives are employed, one being of the 'Shay' geared type, and the other of the 'Heisler' geared type. In the former design a three-cylinder vertical engine is located at one side of the boiler, and drives a longitudinal shaft in universally jointed sections, all the wheels on that side being driven through bevel gearing. The boiler is located to one side of the centre line to balance. Locomotives of this type, it may be mentioned, are in use to the number of nearly 2,000 in various parts of America and Canada, so that it is hardly

A view of the Mount Tamalpais railway.

At the Tavern of Tamalpais.

correct to describe them as "freaks".

'Heisler' engines are not so largely employed. In this design there is a cylinder at either side of the boiler driving diagonally downwards to a central longitudinal shaft that is geared with the various axles. Both of these designs admit very great flexibility . anel great power, while the engines are comparatively small. The locomotives use oil fuel.

The usual load is one or two closed or open cars. The trains are shown in several of the illustrations.

A copy of a recent time table is given (below left).

The fares are very reasonable compared with those charged on many other mountain railways, though one cannot expect a 'penny-a-mile' rate. In this case the return fare is $1-50 (6s 3d), and the total cost, including ferry and ordinary train from San Francisco to the summit is only $1-90 (7s 11d)

A peculiar feature of the line and its methods is the "Gravity Car", which leaves the Tavern of Tamalpais every weekday morning. It is referred to in the time table.

This provides an eight mile coast by gravity down the mountain, controlled only by the brakes – a novel and exhilarating ride.

In conclusion, the writer acknowledges his indebtedness to the officials of the railway for particulars of this interesting and unique railway, and for the photographs reproduced herewith. ■

SPECIMEN TIMETABLE OF THE MOUNT TAMALPAIS SCENIC RAILWAY.

WEEK DAYS

FROM SAN FRANCISCO	TAVERN OF TAMALPAIS			TO SAN FRANCISCO	
Leave............	Arrive.............		Leave *9.10 a.m.	Arrive	10.45 a.m.
,, 9.50 a.m.	,, 11.40 a.m.		,, 1.05 p.m.	,,	2.55 p.m.
,, 1.45 p.m.	,, 3.37 p.m.		,, 4.30 p.m.	,,	6.22 p.m.
			* *Via* Gravity Car to Mill Valley.		

(EVENING TRIP)	SATURDAYS ONLY		(EVENING TRIP)	
Leave 4.35 p.m.	Arrive 6.29 p.m.	Leave 9.30 p.m.	Arrive 11.25 p.m.	

SUNDAYS AND LEGAL HOLIDAYS.

Leave	8.25 a.m.	Arrive	10.17 a.m.	Leave 10.40 a.m.	Arrive	1.30 p.m.	
,,	9.50 a.m.	,,	11.40 a.m.	,, 1.05 p.m.	,,	2.55 p.m.	
,,	11.00 a.m.	,,	12.50 p.m.	,, 2.30 p.m.	,,	4.23 p.m.	
,,	1.45 p.m.	,,	3.37 p.m.	,, 4.30 p.m.	,,	6.22 p.m.	

650, MARKET STREET - - TICKET OFFICES - - AND SAUSALITO FERRY

The West Highland section of the LNER

Afternoon Mallaig-Glasgow express near Bridge of Orchy. North British 'Glen' class 4-4-0 locomotive No. 9258 *Glen Roy*. PHOTO: D H CLARKE

By O S NOCK

THE construction of the West Highland Railway involved one of the boldest pieces of railway engineering that has ever been carried out in Britain. From the moment it leaves the shores of the Firth of Clyde and strikes off up the hillside from Craigendoran, the country traversed is exceedingly difficult; for fully one-third of the distance to Fort William it follows no main highway, and apart from walking there is no other way of seeing these wild regions. Even where there is a road running near, the railway invariably takes the higher ground "with the advantage of the eagle over the sparrow", as a Scottish writer expressed it; the result is a route that has been extolled from almost every angle by lovers of wild and majestic scenery.

But it is not the scenery alone that makes up the unique appeal of the West Highland. When studying the physical characteristics of any line of railway it is often interesting to speculate as to what changes in alignment and grading there might have been had the circumstances been different at the time of construction. The West of England line of the Great Western Railway would have been aligned very differently between Reading and Castle Cary had its present importance been foreseen, but while, in this case, it would have made things much easier from an operating point of view, it is doubtful whether the

ordinary traveller would be aware of any difference.

In the very unlikely event of the West Highland having been planned as an express route, its whole character would have been different. We should never have enjoyed those delightfully bewildering twists alongside Loch Lomond and up Glen Falloch, where there are frequent glimpses of the engine from the third or fourth coach in the train; changes in gradients so abrupt that they can be plainly felt in the train and sometimes cause ordinary travellers to remark upon them, would never have existed. Only the scenery would remain, and even then a fleeting glimpse of Beinn Dorain from a streamlined express bucketing up Glen Orchy at 70mph would be a very poor substitute for the ever-fascinating perambulation of the Horseshoe Bend.

I have dwelt rather on this aspect of the route because from previous articles on the subject, both railway and otherwise, one might have gathered that its peculiar characteristics are due solely to the nature of the country. Mr. J J Bell, writing of the Horseshoe, describes the site as "... a glen which no engineering could get across". This is not true. The glen beneath Beinn Dorain presents no more

formidable an engineering task than the gap bridged by the Midland main line at Ribblehead. The West Highland was built to open up the country; there were scant prospects of a remunerative traffic for many years, and the line was therefore built as cheaply as possible. No attempt was made to even out the grades, and it was a remarkable feat to plan such a line with only one tunnel, and that a bore of but 20 yards long on Loch Lomond side.

The degree to which earthworks have been reduced is remarkable; where the line climbs open hillsides it is often well-nigh impossible to detect the course of the railway when looking from the valleys below. The mountain sides are seared with clefts worn by small streams and as a consequence the track takes a very zigzag course. From Craigendoran to Tulloch is nearly 82 miles by railway, but only 61½ miles in a straight line; taken over the entire distance to Fort William the corresponding figures would show a still greater disparity, but give not altogether a true impression, for the line makes a wide detour round the 'massif' of Ben Nevis.

From Glasgow, the run down to Craigendoran forms an interesting prelude to a journey over the West Highland Railway proper, especially if, as in the case of the Sunday express, a start is made from the low level platforms at Queen Street. The Glasgow docks and shipyards, the products of which are household words, make a striking contrast to the lonely depopulated regions through which the train passes later in the journey. It is only, when Dumbarton is left behind, and the Clyde broadens out into a shining firth, that you get a vague hint of what is to follow in the way of scenery. From here onwards to Arrochar the left hand side of a north-bound train commands all the finest views.

The West Highland Railway begins at Craigendoran Junction, which is about a quarter of a mile east of the station. The line was originally constructed by an independent company, but from the very beginning was operated by the North British. The construction of the railway was carried out under contract by Formans & McCall, of Glasgow; it was authorised in 1890 and the line opened to traffic on August 7, 1894. Craigendoran station is in two parts. The low level, which consists of two through platforms and one terminal bay, serves the steamer pier and deals with the residential traffic from Glasgow; the high level is a single island platform on the West Highland line. With the exception of Tulloch, Roy Bridge and Spean Bridge, the stations throughout to Fort William are of exactly the same type; the buildings are neat and commodious and the floral displays delightfully attractive.

The line starts straight off with a climb at 1 in 58. Mounting high above the shore, and passing through Upper Helensburgh the Gare Loch comes into view, and once the railway has attained a fair altitude it winds along the hillside on a sharply undulating course. The Gare Loch is a placid beautiful inlet; the gentle slopes of the surrounding hills are charmingly wooded, the cottage gardens are a riot of flowers and in the season many handsome yachts may be seen at anchor. But just after leaving Rhu station, when the train swings round a right-hand curve, there comes a first sight of the mountains of Cowal, a range of wild rocky crags rising behind the smooth hills just across the water.

Abreast of Shandon numerous ships may usually be seen lying up. A few years ago the Gare Loch presented a sorry spectacle with scores of merchantmen lying idle, but when I travelled to Fort William last autumn there were a bare half-dozen vessels in this "Rotten Row", as a Cunard skipper once dubbed a similar assembly anchored off The Nore. Half-way between Shandon and Garelochhead, high above Faslane Bay, the railway makes a spectacular loop round the hill-side, where on a train like the Sunday express from Glasgow, which often loads up to 350 tons, the engines will one moment be travelling at right-angles to the rear coaches. So we come to Garelochhead; this station is the true gateway to the West Highlands, for in a single mile we pass from the sylvan scenery of the loch side into some of the wildest country imaginable.

There were scant prospects of a remunerative traffic for many years

Climbing begins in real earnest now and up such grades as 1 in 54 and 1 in 61, with only a few pitches as easy as 1 in 80, the engine pounds away up to Whistlefield, and then as we swing round the curve through the station the scene revealed below is of truly startling beauty. The railway has come out on to the edge of a steep hillside; 300ft below is Loch Long, winding sinuously among the mountains, and right opposite is the entrance to a still narrower fjord, Loch Goil. The very suddenness of its appearance makes this scene leave a most vivid impression, whether it be on a still summer day when the hills are mirrored in the loch, or in early spring when the highest peaks are still snow-clad and the water is the colour of steel. There is not a passing loop here and the station is only a single platform.

Very soon Loch Long is lost to view behind Creagan Hill while the railway climbs up a glen of lonely pasture land. At the summit is Glen Douglas crossing place; for a moment there is a vista eastwards towards Loch Lomond, but then the line swings round to the west. Framed in a 'V' of the hills are the terrific crags of Ben Arthur's summit, "The Cobbler", and remembering the nearness of Loch Long it seems as though this dive through a rock cutting must surely take us over the edge and into the loch. There is no more thrilling moment on the whole journey than this. The line emerges on a high ledge almost opposite to the entrance to Glen Croe; up this defile goes the main road from Glasgow to Inveraray, and at its head is the fine peak Beinn an Lochain. Readers who are familiar with the district will probably have come across variations in spelling of some of the mountains; throughout this article I have adopted that used in the Ordnance Survey maps. While the train is descending towards Arrochar there is ample time to study the magnificent mountain range across the water; from behind "The Cobbler", Ben Ime and Ben Vane come into view, and beyond the head of the loch is a shoulder of Ben Vorlich.

Approaching Arrochar, the line crosses the narrow strip of land that separates Loch Long from Loch Lomond, and just before reaching the station the latter comes into view, with the huge bulk of Ben Lomond across the water. To many travellers this aspect of the mountain is most unfamiliar and the long wedged-shaped summit, seen end-on, has the appearance of a slender cone. Just below the station is the village of Tarbet. One very noticeable point about train running over this route is the very smooth and even pace at which these long steep descents are negotiated. On similar gradients elsewhere you nearly always descend by fits and starts, the engine racing away one moment and then being severely braked the next, but the West Highland drivers have certainly perfected the art of steady downhill running. It is done almost entirely by putting the engines into full forward gear, giving the cylinders the merest breath of steam and relying on the compression created by a large volume of low-pressure steam.

Arrochar and Tarbet, to give the station its full name, is the northern terminus of the only local service worked over the West Highland line; between here and Craigendoran there is, during the summer, a service of three trains a day in addition to the through expresses to Fort William and Mallaig. Another train runs as far as Garelochhead, and on Saturdays there is an extra one to Arrochar. A single engine is all that is needed for working the whole of this shuttle service, and it is only in the busiest season that the train consists of more than two coaches. For ease of interchange with Glasgow-➤

9.54am train from Fort William near Arrochar. 'Loch' class 2-6-0 locomotive No. 4685 *Loch Treig.* O S NOCK

Helensburgh trains the Arrochar locals start from the low-level bay platform at Craigendoran, so that they have to back out to the junction before they can proceed up the West Highland line. An ex-North British 4-4-2 tank engine is usually employed on these trains, though lately some of the Gresley three-cylinder 2-6-2 tanks have been at work.

The through services are now mostly worked by the Class K2 Moguls, named after lochs, though a number of 'Glen' class 4-4-0s are still at work. At midweek, even in the height of the tourist season, these trains rarely load up to more than five or six coaches and come within the limit tonnage of 180 tons for a 'Glen', or 220 for a 'Loch', but at weekends a good deal of piloting is necessary. In bad weather conditions loads just within the limits often cause no little difficulty, and I have heard of 'Lochs' sticking on the 1 in 53 start out of Rannoch with 200-ton trains. It is an open secret that Sir Nigel Gresley is building a special type of locomotive for this line; remembering how the operating problem has been solved on other difficult routes, such as Edinburgh-Aberdeen, we may surely look forward to a remarkable machine for the West Highland.

At Arrochar the comparative nearness of Inveraray, the county town of Argyll, is a reminder that in 1898 a scheme was put

1.44pm up train at Fort William. 'Glen' class 4-4-0 locomotive No. 9100 *Glen Dochart*. O S NOCK

before the light railway commissioners for a branch line from Arrochar to St Catherine's, on Loch Fyne. There is a regular ferry service across the loch to Inveraray and the object of the branch was not only to serve the county town, but also to develop the Loch Fyne fisheries. If the line had ever been made it would presumably have been routed via Glen Croe; as such it would probably have been the most difficult section of the whole railway. But like the projected extension from Fort William southwards to Ballachulish, it was not

proceeded with, though the latter section was actually sanctioned by Parliament.

After leaving Arrochar and Tarbet, the railway follows an undulating, though on the average level course above the western shore of Loch Lomond. The hillside is thickly wooded and the loch is all the more beautiful from being seen through the trees. At the first glimpse of Loch Lomond a sightseer will naturally have moved over to the right hand side of the train, but about three miles beyond Tarbet a brief visit to the opposite window will

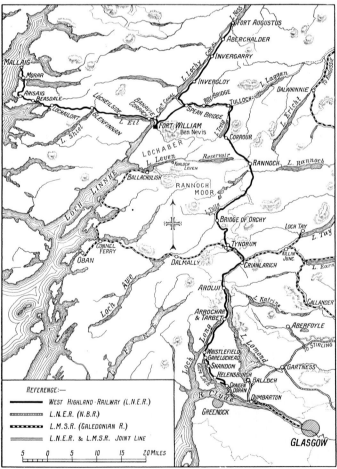

Map of the West Highland Section of the L.N.E.R.
Since December 1, 1933, the branch from Spean Bridge to Fort Augustus has been closed to all traffic except for one goods train weekly, on Saturdays

Scenes on the West Highland Section of the LNER. Trains about to cross one another on a passing loop.

be rewarded by a sight that will almost take their breath away. When Inversnaid Hotel and pier are nearly opposite across the water, the line swings away from the loch in order to cross the Water of Inveruglas; on taking the reverse curve, there, right on top of them it seems, is Ben Vorlich towering above the railway like a colossus. As the train crosses the glen two more grand peaks, Ben Ime and Ben Vane, are close at hand.

These two latter mountains were first seen while we were coasting down to Arrochar, but this is one of the tricks this route plays; a famous summit is pointed out, and then, three-quarters-of-an-hour later maybe, it is seen again from a different angle, and passes quite unrecognised unless one is following the route closely with a map. A westward swing of the track when nearing Ardlui reveals Ben Oss and Beinn Dubhchraig in a direct line with the head of Loch Lomond; 40 minutes later we shall be looking at them in precisely the opposite direction, from the other side of the carriage.

At Ardlui, the head of Loch Lomond is reached; as seen from the train the surrounding hills do not rise to any great height, and then comes the long grind up Glen Falloch. The country here is neither so wild nor so desolate as on other parts of the route, but in this waste of treeless grassland and heather-clad uplands there is nevertheless a solitude most profound. Not quite half-way up the track makes a big detour in crossing the Dubh Eas glen, which gives a brief respite to the engine; otherwise, it is continuous hard slogging at 1 in 60 or so all the way up. The viaduct over the Dubh Eas water is of the type used throughout the line; it consists of a number of lattice girder spans resting on granite towers. The spans themselves are of the deck type, with the main girders vertically beneath the rails. In the case of certain viaducts on sharp curves, not only are check rails fitted, but also an additional outer guard on either side of the running rails to act as a further safeguard in case of a derailment.

On reaching the head of Glen Falloch we are among the giants of the Perthshire highlands. The summit is almost exactly

Crianlarich station. O S NOCK

marked by milepost 35, the distance referring to Craigendoran junction, and a sharp downhill run of 1¼ miles brings us to Crianlarich, the most important intermediate station on the line. It is not merely the half-way house between Glasgow and Fort William, but also a junction point with the Caledonian route from Callander to Oban. At all other stations on the West Highland the stopping time is of the briefest, but at Crianlarich all trains spend at least five minutes, principally for the engine to take water. This halt is as nothing compared with the earliest days of the route, when Crianlarich occupied the same position, on this line as York in the case of the East Coast

This remarkable peak has, more than any other mountain seen on the route, the perfect volcano form

Anglo-Scottish expresses before the introduction of dining cars. At Crianlarich a huge notice board on the platform stills bears the legend "Refreshment Rooms. Luncheons, Teas and Dinners served. Time allowed by trains". Nowadays every through train between Glasgow and Fort William is composed entirely of the most modern stock, and carries a restaurant car in which *a la carte* meals can be obtained at any time of the day.

In the ordinary way, passengers transferring from the LNER to the LMSR line at Crianlarich have to change stations, but there is a

connecting spur that is regularly used by goods trains. Since the pooling arrangement between the two companies has been in force some interesting round excursion trips have been worked to Crianlarich, from Edinburgh outward by the LMS route and returning via the LNER; in these workings the connecting line has been used. The Callander and Oban line is single-tracked through Crianlarich station, and the crossing loop is located at the junction with the LNER. Although the connecting spur is also single-tracked, it joins the LMSR in a double line junction and the double-tracked portion is of sufficient length to accommodate a train on each road. This layout enables the LMSR to carry out regularly the unusual operation of crossing four trains at one place. In mid-morning, during the summer service, in each direction there is a passenger train scheduled to overhaul a freight. The two latter, arriving first, are stowed away one on each road of the LNER spur line, and then the two passenger trains cross each other on the ordinary running loop.

The engineers' department blue sleeping vans that are to be seen standing in sidings at some of the stations form a striking contrast to the gaily painted caravan coaches, but the former are invaluable for track maintenance and do away with the need for taking men to and from the site when work is in progress. At Crianlarich, too, we come into the sphere of operation of the Ro-Railer lorry that is used for the conveyance of men and permanent way material. When operating between Crianlarich and Fort William this very handy vehicle uses the railway between Bridge of Orchy and Tulloch, and for the remaining distance travels on the adjacent roads.

Leaving Crianlarich, the West Highland crosses the Oban line at right-angles, and then swings round parallel to it on reaching the opposite side of Strathfillan. Looking back, the magnificent group of mountains lying south-east of Crianlarich is seen to perfection; right behind the village Stob Coire Bhuide, Stob Garbh and Cruach Ardrain are clustered, a semi-circle of great beetling crags, and a little to the left is the vast gable of Ben More. In the meantime we are mounting steadily up the hillside; our old friends Ben Oss and Beinn Dubhchraigh are right opposite across the ►

Craigendoran, from the island platform on the West Highland line. O S NOCK

broad strath, and are now reinforced by a third giant, Beinn Laiogh. At Tyndrum the Oban line is still far below, but beyond it turns away through Glen Lochy towards Dalmally.

Still climbing at 1 in 60, or slightly easier grades, the line enters a very narrow defile. If the weather is fair, put your head out of the left-hand window for a first glimpse of Beinn Dorain; this remarkable peak has, more than any other mountain seen on the route, the perfect volcano form, and seen grey-blue on an afternoon of bright sunshine with some light cloud drifting over the summit, it looks for all the world like some northern Vesuvius. The head of the pass is also the Perth-Argyll county march; the summit level of the railway is 1,024ft and is almost exactly marked by milepost 43. From here the line descends steeply via the Horseshoe Bend to the head of Glen Orchy.

Expressions such as 'horseshoe', when applied to the alignment of a railway, are usually picturesque exaggerations, but the loop between Tyndrum and Bridge of Orchy is a true horseshoe-shaped bend which adds 1½ miles to the straight-line distance between the two stations. The approach to it, in either direction, is quite awe-inspiring. Going north the tremendous cone of Beinn Dorain is for several minutes directly ahead, with the continuation of the railway line just discernible round the base; then, suddenly, the line sweeps eastwards high on the slopes of Beinn Odhar and reveals the two viaducts at the head of the cul de sac, where Beinn a'Chaisteil rises almost sheer to 2,900ft. Once the train has negotiated the horseshoe and encircled the southern slopes of Beinn Dorain the line is fairly straight onwards to Bridge of Orchy, and on easy-falling grades speed often rises to 55mph before the stop.

Beyond this station the character of the country begins to change; Loch Tulla and the beautiful pinewoods of the Black Mount are left behind, and we are coming gradually into a more open landscape.

Still the engine pounds on uphill at a steady 27 to 30mph and then, silhouetted on the skyline of this rolling moorland, there

Ro-Railer used on the West Highland Section for permanent-way maintenance. O S NOCK

appears the distant signal for Gortan crossing; this box is one of the loneliest outposts on British railways. Here the King's Cross sleeping car express calls every morning in order to pick up the signalman's children and convey them to school, in Fort William, 42 miles farther on.

And now we enter upon Rannoch Moor. This wilderness of peat bogs and black reed-encircled pools is the great watershed of the Central Highlands; from it rivers, flow in all directions. There is a very vivid description of it in Hugh Quigley's book The Highlands of Scotland: "Rannoch Muir", he writes, "lies so close to the heavens that autumn clouds sweeping over from the west seem to crush it in their passage. No sign of life is here, except perhaps a herd of deer, their skins scarcely distinguishable from the fallow brown of the autumn moor".

The potentialities of the surrounding lochs have been exploited to the full for the generation of electricity. Loch Rannoch, the head of which is only five miles from the railway, and Loch Ericht, to the north, supply the two big generating stations of the Grampian Electricity Supply Company. In really clear weather the view eastwards from Rannoch Moor extends to the Atholl and Balmoral highlands; Ben-y-Gloe and Lochnagar can be clearly distinguished.

Approaching Rannoch station, which lies in the very heart of the moor, Loch Laidon comes into view on the left, and far away beyond it are the mountains of Glen Coe. The restart involves some very stiff pulling, at 1 in 53 for 1¾ miles, while the railway is working its way round the Black Corries; sharply curved, this can be a very nasty bit of line in bad weather. Nearing milepost 66 the rock cuttings are protected by very high snow fences, and just before the summit is reached is the only snow-shed to be found on a British railway. Here the cutting sides are extended upwards by means of concrete walls and the shed is partly roofed in with corrugated iron. Even on a day of cloudless sunshine the interior of the snow-shed is an eerie place. Just beyond this point the head of the Blackwater reservoir may be seen on the left; this supplies the Kinlochleven works of the British Aluminium Company. The factory was started as long ago as 1909, and was the first instance of the use of hydro-electric power in the Scottish Highlands.

Across this final length of Rannoch Moor speed usually rises to 50mph, or over, until there comes the final pull up to Corrour, the summit level of the whole route, 1,347ft above sea level. It is only recently that the crossing has appeared in the public timetables, for the station was originally a private one. There is not another human habitation in sight and the station takes its name from Corrour shooting lodge, at the western end of Loch Ossian; this lonely sheet of water can be seen just after leaving the station. From here, too, there comes the first view, away to the west, of the Ben Nevis group, and even from this high altitude their height can be fully appreciated.

By now the mountains are closing in on us once more, and running steeply downhill Loch Treig comes into view far below. This loch, together with Loch Laggan to the north-east, now forms the water supply for the vast works of the British Aluminium Company at Fort William. Considering the magnitude of the scheme, it has been carried out with very little

1.44pm train from Fort William crossing Rannoch Moor. 'Glen' class 4-4-0 No. 9035 Glen Roy, and 'Loch' class 2-6-0 No. 4700 Loch Lomond. O S NOCK

From The Railway Magazine, January 1937

disfigurement of the countryside, at any rate as far as Loch Treig is concerned. The loch was always a rather gloomy and solitary place; now that the water level has been raised some 40ft, it bears that still and lifeless look of most reservoirs, and in places there are trees growing out of the water; but it still mirrors the wild surrounding hills, and at the northern end Fersit dam is a model of graceful building. The raising of the water involved an alteration in the alignment of the railway at the outlet of the loch; here a higher ledge had to be cut in the hillside and a short tunnel bored to carry the line above the reservoir.

Loch Treig is now connected with Loch Laggan by a tunnel, and the combined waters of the two lochs are carried for 15 miles under Ben Nevis through a pressure-tunnel; the end of this tunnel can be seen when nearing Fort William. When nearing Tulloch the line swings round westwards into Glen Spean and away up the glen the dam at the foot of Loch Laggan can be seen. The countryside suffered a bigger change here, for the latter was lengthened by no less than four miles. There are many, I know, who deplore these developments, as a spoliation of the country, but it must be confessed that, fine though the hills are, this corner is not one of the choicest beauty spots in the Highlands, and one can have nothing but admiration for so magnificent a piece of engineering.

Beyond Tulloch the railway runs due west for a while, with the foothills of Ben Nevis always to the south. At first the Spean is a brawling stream, its bed strewn with boulders, but nearing Roy Bridge it flows through a spectacular gorge, the walls of which are carved into fantastic shapes by the swirls and eddies of the torrent. The line runs just above the river in the finest part of the gorge. Glen Roy now opens up to the northwards. On either side of the glen, if the light is favourable, may be seen what look like ledges on the hillside running absolutely level; they are known as the Parallel Roads of Glen Roy and are thought by archaeologists to indicate the water level of some former lake that existed when the mouth of Glen Roy was dammed up by a barrier of glacial ice. Three miles farther on is Spean Bridge, scene of the first clash in the Jacobite rebellion of 1745; here a detachment of the Royal Scots was ambushed and routed by Cameron of Locheil's men.

Spean Bridge station is the junction for the Invergarry and Fort Augustus branch. This line is now used by but one train a week, a Class D goods that leaves Spean Bridge at 10.30am, every Saturday and returns from Fort Augustus at 12.45pm the same day. From Spean Bridge the main line climbs over open moorland until the hills of Ardgour appear across Loch Linnhe; then comes a fast downhill run under the massive western escarpments of Ben Nevis, with a close-up view of the aluminium works,

Tyndrum station: Note caravan coach on left and snow fence on right. O S NOCK

Snow shed on Rannoch Moor, the only one to be found on a British railway. O S NOCK

and so past Mallaig Junction and along the shore of the loch into Fort William. The distance from Craigendoran is only 10 chains short of 100 miles and the journey time varies between 3¼ and 3¾ hours. We may just touch 60 on the final descent from Spean Bridge, but elsewhere 50mph is about the limit; going south the downhill stretches are aligned better and I have noted speeds up to 65mph.

During the winter there are only two passenger trains in the down direction, and three in the up; but from the point of view of locomotive power the workings are balanced by an early morning express freight and newspaper train; this leaves Glasgow (Sighthill) at 2.15am and reaches Fort William at 8am. There is no passenger train between the London 'sleeper', which leaves Glasgow at 5.45am, and the 3.48pm, though in the summer these are reinforced by a train at 11.23am. In the tourist season the London portion is usually detached at Cowlairs and worked on to Fort William ahead of the regular 5.45am from Queen Street. In the up direction trains leave Fort William at 9.54am, 1.44 and 4.10pm all the year round, though the actual minutes may vary a little in successive timetables; in the summer the King's Cross sleeping cars are run as a separate train, leaving Fort William at 5.15pm.

A great deal of the seasonal fish traffic from Mallaig is worked by passenger train and this produces some of the biggest loads worked over the route and the most awkward operating problems. A train of 15 to 20 fish vans, with four passenger coaches bringing up the rear, provides a delicate task for the driver in

drawing up. On account of station working at Fort William the passenger portion must always be marshalled at the rear of a southbound train.

One afternoon last autumn, when I was at Rannoch waiting for the evening train to Fort William, the only other passenger, an Englishman travelling over the route for the first time, waxed so enthusiastic about the scenery as to suggest that the company might charge extra fares for the privilege of travelling over such a route. A quizzical look spread over the stationmaster's face and he remarked: "Well, the company does offer a guinea for suggestions."

Instead of charging any extra fares however, the LNER have for some years now run on Sundays what is surely the most astonishing money's worth in the way of day excursions to be found anywhere. So justly popular has it proved that during the summer three portions are regularly scheduled, two from Glasgow and one from Edinburgh, and in the height of the season four, and sometimes even five trains are needed. With almost every section needing to be double-headed this rush taxes the resources of Eastfield shed to such a degree that engines other than the regular West Highland type are pressed into service, as, for example, the 6ft 6in 'Scott' class 4-4-0s. Such otherwise ideal engines as the K3 Moguls cannot be used owing to weight restrictions. These excursions are timed faster than any of the weekday trains, and to any railway enthusiast in Glasgow with a Sunday to spare this is an opportunity not to be missed. ∎

Nationalisation of railways

The inauguration of the railway system. Scene at the opening of the Stockton and Darlington Railway, September 27, 1825.

By C S DENNISS,
General Manager, Cambrian Railways

THE Nationalisation of railways is a subject of such enormous proportions, and its issues are so momentous to the entire community, that it is obviously impossible to more than indicate in, somewhat brief outline, rather than to discuss fully its manifold effects. Therefore, without any formal introductory remarks, I will at once endeavour as briefly as possible to set before you a statement of the case in some important particulars.

There are political economists who contend that railways, being the essential means of communication in a country, should be controlled by the people's government for the benefit of the population rather than as commercial undertakings, whose prime consideration is to make a dividend for shareholders.

This argument, no doubt, proves attractive to many, but I venture to question whether any Government officials, however expert they may be in discussing theoretical questions or in criticising reports of their subordinates, would be able either to effect any appreciable improvement in the general management of a railway system or to keep themselves in close touch with the trade requirements of the localities which the railways serve. The manager of a railway is usually selected because he has passed through a graduated process of training in subordinate offices – sometimes from the lowest grades. He has also spent many years in more or less intimate connection with the traffic to be worked, and he thus possesses a qualification which only such experience can afford. He has come into contact with all sorts and conditions of men, and he is as well able to deal with delicate and often complicated questions affecting the interests of the employees under his control as with the commercial requirements which have to be judiciously met. It is only in very rare instances that men thus qualified would be found in Government offices, the great majority of such having received only a theoretical training.

An efficient and alert railway manager, with a due appreciation of the necessity of applying strict and sound commercial principles to the management of his railway, will be found in frequent personal intercourse with the leading traders whose prosperity is intimately bound up with the progress and development of his line, and, as a result of their intimacy, the resources of the district served should be developed to the utmost extent. It is too often assumed by traders that an inevitable antagonism exists between themselves and the railway managers. This fallacy, however, is we believe, rapidly giving place to a sense of mutual confidence, the further development of which must without question have the most beneficent results. A railway manager can no more afford to indulge in arbitrary treatment of the traders, or to impose conditions of transit likely to hamper the development of industrial enterprise, than can a trader to quarrel with his customers or to unduly raise the price of his goods; and we contend that this most important consideration is more likely to be effectively regarded by carefully trained and thoroughly experienced commercial men, such as are usually appointed by railway directors, than could be the case if the appointments were made either by the heads of a Government department or the executive officers were required to submit their proposals to a Board of Government officials.

Advocates of the state ownership of railways frequently base their conclusions upon the efficiency with which the Post Office and Telegraph Departments are managed under Government authority; but it is to be feared that due regard is not paid to the wide difference beween the merely mechanical arrangements for despatching letters and telegrams and the requirements necessary for efficiently working the goods, mineral, and passenger traffic of large railway systems under ever-varying conditions.

I now invite you to consider the effect of the state control of railways in certain countries abroad?

In Belgium there are 2,043 miles of railway owned by the state, and 783 miles owned and worked by private enterprise. The Government lines are worked by a Department of the State under a Minister of Railways, whose appointment is political, and, with all the advantages which their excellent system affords, the patronage, which lies in the gift of the Minister, is well-known to be extensively exercised for party purposes. Promotion in the service is largely governed by consideration of the political tendencies of the individual concerned. The dual control in that country, however, also shows that there is a not altogether unhealthy rivalry between the two systems, and the private-owned lines are impelled as their *raison d'etre* to keep pace with the development of the state-owned lines. But in Belgium it cannot be stated that the Government control has been altogether free from abuses inimical to the fullest development of trade. Professor Hadley, in his able consideration of the question, states "that at one time the Government railroads themselves granted special rates to prevent people using the canals owned by the Government. They abandoned scheduled rates, and had recourse to personal discriminations, and to special contracts of every kind. And it has been charged against the Government that they have multiplied forms and offices of no use in actual business, and that there has been serious manipulation of accounts to make favourable showing for the Government".

In Germany there are under state ownership and control 25,415 miles of railway, and under private control 2,683 miles. It is claimed by the late Mr James Hole, in his excellent work on National Railways, that one of the best examples of state ownership must be looked for in the states comprising the German Empire. Prussia, particularly, has vigorously encouraged the development of state railways, and the practical result of the transfer to the state of those constructed by private capital was an economy in the cost of working the traffic, greater uniformity in the rates, and increased accommodation to the public; and, although Mr Hole declares that, by inquiry in numerous centres of trade manufactures and consumption, it is shown that these advantages were secured without any drawbacks, he admits that "one blot on the German system is that, in conformity with its protective system, the Government makes the railway rates a means of giving a bounty to exports and of protection against imports"; and, from a careful study of the general methods adopted by the iron hand of the state, it is abundantly evident that a similar

At the next stopping place the students were met by a guard of soldiers and marched off under arrest

autocratic policy characterises its administration throughout. As an instance, it is related that recently a party of American students travelling through Germany reached a railway station in one of the large cities just as their train was moving out. An official, observing that they ran after the moving train with the intention of travelling by it, called to them to stop, but as the train was only moving slowly they managed to get in. The result of this disregard of the official's command was that at the next stopping place the students were met by a guard of soldiers and marched off under arrest. The prisoners at first treated the whole affair as a joke, but speedily changed their tone upon being informed that they had already been tried, convicted, and sentenced to 30 days' imprisonment. Such 'Government control' as this would scarcely commend itself to either students or other members of the community in this country.

We are indebted to the Rt Hon Sir Bernard Samuelson for most valuable information, compiled with very great care, in a report which he made several years ago to the Associated Chambers of Commerce of the United Kingdom, on the railway systems of Germany, Belgium, and Holland. He states that the cost of the railway systems in Germany gives an average of £21,100 per statute mile. When compared with a similar cost in the United Kingdom per statute mile of £46,504, the lower tariff which the German railways can afford to offer to traders is easily accounted for. Nor is there any indication that in a matter of working expenses the German system offers any special advantage, the percentage being slightly over 56 of the receipts.

In Prussia the railways are managed by the Minister of Public Works, who is advised by a council consisting of a president and of three members nominated by the Minister of Agriculture, three members nominated by the Minister of Commerce and Manufactures, two nominated by the Minister of Finance, two by the Minister of Public Works, and 30 members elected by the various provinces and cities of the kingdom, all holding office for three years. Thus a railway is liable to have its entire policy interfered with, if not completely changed, at perilously frequent intervals.

In France the experience of the state ownership of railways is not particularly encouraging to those who advocate that principle; for, although the experiment has been tried for many years, based on an extensive scale, there are in that country many of the strongest expressions of ▶

The first passenger carriage – the 'Experiment' – on the Stockton and Darlington Railway.

disapproval of the system, and agitation is constantly being made for the absolute sale of the state railways to private companies on the ground that the existing system involves a heavy annual loss to the exchequer, and that whatever advantages might reasonably be expected to result from the present system are not gained by the public, but are chiefly applied to the furtherance of political objects. The Government has certainly given one advantage to the public, which will be appreciated, not only by the railway companies, but by the public at large in this country, by making a considerable reduction in the passenger tax, which was followed by a lowering of fares. But at the same time the through rates for merchandise to the Continent were raised. Thus, once again, the iron hand of the state is felt in France, arbitrarily stifling private enterprise, and restraining the due expansion of trade.

The experience which Italy has had in the different methods of railway management is perhaps greater than that of any other country. The railways have been worked by the state; by private owners; they have been allotted in districts to companies; and the Government has investigated the whole subject with the greatest minuteness. A Special Commission was appointed in 1878 for this purpose, and, after sitting for three years and taking evidence all over Europe, it deliberately decided against state management. The conclusion the Government arrived at may be summed up as follows: State management is more costly than private management. The state is more likely to tax industry than to foster it. Private management, therefore, must be accepted, and the only force powerful enough to at once restrain and stimulate private management is competition. Accordingly the Italian Government has divided out its railways between two great companies, on the east and west side, their lines meeting and competing at all the main points – at Florence and Milan, and at Rome and Naples; and the results have been altogether satisfactory.

In Russia there are 13,343 miles of state railways, and 6,635 miles of those under private ownership. The railways in that country are principally designed, as in many other Continental countries, for military purposes; the distribution of trade and intercourse of the population being quite a secondary consideration. Even on the lines owned by private companies the rates are fixed by the Government, and cannot be altered without its consent.

During the Russian famine a few years ago the lamentable inefficiency of railway management largely contributed to a disaster as serious as that of a terrible war. If the strategic railway happened to pass through

The Albion as rebuilt at the Cambrian Railways' Works, Oswestry, in January 1890.

grain-producing districts it was collected and very tardily distributed. The reports show that the famine was not so much owing to a failure in the harvest, as was represented, but to the complete breakdown of the railway system; and, whilst there was a super-abundance of food in the Caucasus, so that grain was actually rotting, in other parts of the country thousands of families were dying of starvation. The last instance we will cite of state managed railways is that of New South Wales, and, before doing so, on this occasion

State management is more costly than private management

I may be permitted to give expression to feelings of deep regret, which will be shared by the readers of *The Railway Magazine* and railway colleagues, at the apparently untimely decease of our distinguished and popular colleague, Mr E H G Eddy, the chief commissioner.

If the remarkable development and success of the New South Wales lines during the past few years furnishes, as it unquestionably does, one of the most conspicuous instances in the world of the ability of a Government to completely revolutionise methods of railway management under specific conditions, it is largely, if not entirely, due to the genius, statesmanship, and power of organisation displayed by Mr Eddy; and it is with, perhaps, pardonable pride that a railway manager in this country should ask you to bear in mind that Mr Eddy received his railway education and training upon one of the most splendid railway systems in this country – the London and North Western.

According to their last report, the total

outlay of railways in this colony is just over 37 millions. The mileage of railways open for traffic is 2,531, all owned and constructed by the Government, and there are 84 miles of private lines.

According to Mr Eddy's own statement, Australia is dependent to a much greater extent than other countries upon its railways, there being so few navigable rivers, and the necessity for the Government providing capital with which to open up the country is obvious, as private capitalists would not undertake works requiring probably many years to give a reasonable return for the outlay.

The history of railways in New South Wales, in many respects, is that of the other Australian colonies and, of New Zealand, and as it is the pre-eminent business and duty of the state to open up these countries with a view to the development of their resources by facilitating communication between the different points, the fact of their having done so can scarcely be claimed by other countries, and particularly the advocates of railway Nationalisation in England, as a substantial reason for a similar policy being adopted in this country.

In New South Wales various experiments have been tried, and have proved extremely costly; and it is only when the Government has wisely severed the management of its railways from all direct political influences, and put them into the hands of an expert trained according to the best English system, that the result has proved at all satisfactory,

The history of railways in the United Kingdom forms perhaps the most remarkable and interesting feature of scientific and commercial development the century has produced. It is hardly conceivable that only 76 years have passed since an Act of Parliament was obtained by the Stockton and Darlington Railway Company, in April 1821.

From *The Railway Magazine*, December 1897

We are indebted to George Graham, late assistant locomotive superintendent of the North Eastern Railway, for particulars of the opening of that line in September 1825, at which he was present. In a memorandum, which he kindly prepared, he states that the first train, containing carriages laden with coals and other goods, and some 450 passengers, and weighing 90 tons, left West Auckland for Darlington, and travelled thence to Stockton, after leaving six wagons loaded with coal at the former place, arriving at destination in 3hr 7min, including stoppages, the distance being nearly 12 miles; and a newspaper report of this interesting ceremony informs us that "this immense train of carriages travelled with such velocity that in some parts, the speed was frequently 12mph"!

Mr Graham states that about this time a race was run between No. 1 engine (which may now be seen on a pedestal in the principal station at Darlington) and one of the stage coaches plying between Darlington and Stockton on the ordinary road, and that, greatly to the amusement and edification of the public, No. 1 reached Stockton 120 yards ahead of its competitor. The comparison of this with the present performances of express trains running between, say, London and Scotland, at a speed in some portions of the journey of 70mph, with the enormous weight of from 270 to 300 tons, is but one indication of the remarkable development of our railway systems.

After the opening of the Stockton and Darlington line, others were authorised and constructed in quick succession. But that from London to Birmingham, which was sanctioned by Parliament in 1833, resulted in the tide of public opinion commencing to flow as strongly in favour of railways as it had previously moved against them. In the projection of this line a great struggle took place with landowners and other influential personages, and it is stated that the expenses of carrying the Bill, which was probably the most momentous Parliamentary campaign in the history of railways, were over £70,000.

An idea may be formed of the difficulties thrown in the way by greedy landowners and other interested opponents of the schemes by the fact that the Parliamentary costs of the Brighton Railway averaged £4,805 per mile; of the Manchester and Birmingham, £5,190 per mile; and the solicitors' bill for the South Eastern Railway, containing 10,000 folios, amounted to no less a sum than £240,000. There enormous additions to the cost of the construction of railways in this country have continued in a greater or less degree to the present time, and when there is added thereto the extravagant prices extorted by

property owners, amounting in many cases to hundreds per cent of their agricultural value, it is not surprising that the capital cost of our railways should have reached the enormous figure at which they stand, necessitating, in order to give the moderate average return of last year's working of 3.38% upon the capital outlay, the charging of higher rates than are in force upon many of the Continental lines.

The cost per mile of the Great Central (Manchester, Sheffield, and Lincolnshire) Railway was no less than £100,923, and of the Lancashire and Yorkshire, £102,504.

According to the Board of Trade returns recently issued, the mileage of lines opened for traffic in the United Kingdom to

The cost per mile of the Great Central Railway was no less than £100,923

December 31 last was 21,277, at a capital expenditure of £1,029,475,335. The number of passengers conveyed, exclusive of season ticket holders, was more than 980,000,000, representing an average of 25 journeys during the year for every one of the population. The tonnage of general merchandise was 101,796,825, and of minerals, 254,671,184; and the total revenue from all sources was £90,119,122. Of this, £50,192,424 was expended in working, or 55.69% of the total receipts; and in the working of this enormous traffic it is a remarkable fact that only five passengers were killed from causes beyond their own control, or one in about 196,000,000.

"Let the country make the railroads, and the railroads will make the country", was the well-known saying of George Stephenson; and, although railways have to a large extent ceased to compete in matters of rates and fares, the magnificent expansion of trade in this country is due in a very considerable

measure to the facilities afforded by the active competition of most of our large railway systems in regard to the conveyance of merchandise and passenger traffic.

It may be interesting to cite a few significant instances:

During the fruit season, train-loads of ripe fruit are daily sent from Kent via King's Cross and the Great Northern Company, and, although loaded and despatched late in the afternoon, are ready for delivery the following morning in Manchester at 3.55, Liverpool 4.55, Leeds 3.5, Newcastle 3.4, and even in Edinburgh at 6 and Glasgow at 7.18; and special trains of fish despatched from Tynemouth at 6.45pm, regularly arrive in London at 3.15 the following morning.

On the arrival in Liverpool of steamers containing live cattle from America, the animals are placed in lairages having accommodation for 6 or 7,000 head at a time, and, after they have been allowed to recover the condition lost in crossing the Atlantic, they are slaughtered, and the carcasses placed in a cooling chamber for 12 hours; they are then packed in canvas, loaded in specially built meat vans, and hung up by hooks fixed in the carriage roof, and despatched to London by express trains, which perform the journey of 229 miles in the astonishingly short time of 6hr 15min, so that the time occupied from the live beasts leaving the lairage to the carcasses being delivered in London is only a little more than 19 hours. This is by the express meat trains of the London and North Western Railway; and the Great Western Company from Birkenhead is able to perform an equally efficient service.

Cotton goods lying in London Dock warehouses may be sold one day by brokers, on the Liverpool Exchange, orders despatched to London by wire, the goods loaded up and forwarded the same night, and delivered to warehouses or mills in Lancashire by breakfast time the following morning.

It is scarcely necessary to refer to the ▶

Aberdeen joint station, the winning post of the 'Railway Race'.

splendid accommodation for passengers afforded by the corridor trains and corridor dining-car trains between London and Scotland, by the London and North Western, Midland, and East Coast companies; so that it is possible for a passenger to do his business in the metropolis, to leave in a train provided with first-class and third-class dining and sleeping accommodation, travel to Edinburgh or Glasgow (a distance of 400 miles) in eight hours; and to Aberdeen (a distance of 539 miles) in 11hr 15min.

The London and North Western Company has recently constructed the Riverside station at Liverpool, alongside the landing stage, at considerable cost, in order to provide for the excessive competition for the American lines of steamers as against the Southampton route. Their American specials are timed to leave Euston each Wednesday in connection with the sailing of the White Star steamers, and every Saturday in connection with the Cunard liners. The trains are vestibule from end to end, with accommodation for first-, second-, and third-class passengers, with lavatories in each carriage. Some of the first-class cars are fitted up as drawing rooms, and the trains are timed out of Euston only 4½ hours before the liner is due to leave The Mersey; 3¾ hours are occupied in running to Edge Hill (192 miles), 15 minutes, in changing engines at Edge Hill and running thence to the Riverside station, 30 minutes only being occupied there and at the landing stage for transfer from the train to the steamer.

The London and South Western Company also run express mail and passenger trains, for the American steamers between Southampton and London, the distance of 80 miles between Waterloo and the Empress Dock, Southampton, being covered in 1hr 40min.

Perhaps one of the most pertinent illustrations of the effect of competition is furnished by the service of hourly trains run between Liverpool and Manchester by the London and North Western, Cheshire lines, and the Lancashire and Yorkshire companies. The keenness of competition between these points has led to acceleration after acceleration, and the present service between the two cities is absolutely unrivalled. Several of the London and North Western and Cheshire lines trains perform the journey of 32 miles in 40 minutes, without making any intermediate stop.

I may be pardoned for alluding to an effort which has been made by the Cambrian company, which I have the honour to represent, during the last two years to develop the agricultural resources of the parts of Wales which it serves. We have invited some of the principal landowners and agriculturalists to meet us in conference to discuss the most effective means of increasing the dairy produce, cattle traffic, and other agricultural commodities, in order to successfully compete in English markets with the competition of Denmark, France, Scandinavia, etc, and, although we have not found anything like so much disposition on the part of the farmers as was hoped for to resort to new and up-to-date methods, some advantage is apparent. The general outcry is, as usual, for an indiscriminate reduction in the rates for

Cheshire lines trains perform the journey of 32 miles in 40 minutes

conveyance; but I venture to affirm that whatever concessions in this direction are made will have little effect unless it be accompanied by enterprise and active co-operation on the part of the farmers themselves and others concerned, and the adoption of carefully organised scientific methods, which to a great extent we have, unheeded, permitted our foreign competitors to develop.

It is thus inconceivable that anyone should deliberately assert that there is no effective competition from which the public derive benefit.

There is, however, no doubt that not a little advantage may in the future be given, both in regard to the further development of trade throughout the country and the still greater efficiency of means of inter-communication for passengers by a more intimate co-operation of the great railway corporations by means of the splendid system centred in the Railway Clearing House; and, in proportion as railway managers are freed from a great deal of the, in many cases, frivolous complaints to the Board of Trade which, during the past few years have occupied so much of their time (and it must

be admitted in not a few instances to very little purpose), railway managers will be able to devote more attention to the improvement of the facilities enjoyed by the travelling public.

The Light Railways Acts have not been sufficiently long in operation to enable a judgment to be formed as to their value, and it has yet to be determined whether the obvious advantage of financial assistance from the Government in the construction of light railways in sparsely populated and otherwise comparatively poor agricultural districts will be defeated by the imposition of excessive and costly restrictions by the Board of Trade.

So far, the effect of the operation of the Light Railways Acts of 1890 and 1891 in Ireland has been productive of great good; and, in regard to that country, it is a question whether the further development of the light railway system, and of further assistance being rendered by the Government, either in the development of the existing railway systems, or, as has been suggested many times during the past 60 years, their taking over their working altogether, would not lead to a partial, if not the entire, removal of the discontent which prevails in the Emerald Isle.

I will not weary you with further arguments in support of a continuation and further development of the present system of railways in this country, which has grown up somewhat indiscriminately during the past 70 years.

If it were possible, schoolboy-like, for us to make a clean slate and start afresh, it would not be difficult, with our past experience, to frame a system of railways which could at once be worked more economically, and more effectively meet the requirements of the community. But with the English system of railways as we find it today, we unhesitatingly claim that, with all its defects, it will bear favourable comparison in almost every respect with any system of state-owned railways in the world; and that conditions in other countries which render the ownership and working by the state essential for success are so conspicuously absent in this country that any attempt to apply them to our railway system would probably be attended with no appreciable benefits, and we might find ourselves precipitated 'out of the frying-pan into the fire'. ∎

The West Coast corridor dining-car train, at 60mph.

From *The Railway Magazine*, December 1897